Praise for *Negotiate Without Fear*

"My life's work has been to empower women by helping them tell their stories and giving them a voice on the Oprah Winfrey Show, the OWN Network and Apple TV+. The pattern I've seen is women not knowing their inherent worth and conducting negotiations—at home and at work—out of fear. From the first chapter to the last, Vicki will guide you step by step, with tangible tools, that will help anyone break their old patterns and start negotiating from a place of confidence and strength. Vicki is one of the smartest and most remarkable women I know, this book is like having this wise and brilliant advisor right on your shoulder."

—Tara Montgomery, Executive Producer, OWN / Apple TV+

"Vicki's strategies have helped me succeed in some of the most complex negotiations I have encountered across my career. Her focus on addressing the needs of the other side makes her strategies particularly powerful."

—Matthew Shattock, Former CEO of BeamSuntory,
Non-Executive Director of the Clorox company,
Non-Executive Director of the VF Corporation,
Chairman of Domino's Pizza Group p/c Board

"When I met Vicki, I thought I knew a lot about how to negotiate. As a leader at Microsoft and IBM, I negotiated all the time. Vicki taught me strategies I never even knew existed and highlighted the traps that expert negotiators encounter. I have consistently brought her into my organizations to raise the capabilities of my teams and increase our success."

—Gerri Elliott, Executive Vice President,
Chief Sales & Marketing Officer for Cisco

"I invited Vicki to teach negotiations to the leaders from my private equity firm and portfolio companies. Once I heard her, I asked her to join the board for one of our companies, recognizing immediately that her insights would add tremendous value in our many negotiations. She is a rockstar!"

—Justin Ishbia, CEO, Shore Capital Partners

"I wanted a world-class negotiator to teach the best techniques and create a cultural change in our sales team at Nextdoor. Healthy communities are built on trust and healthy client relationships are no different. I asked my former colleagues at Goldman Sachs and Vicki Medvec was the top choice and the results of the training underscored why. I have since recommended Vicki to other companies, such as Walmart. Nextdoor, and the neighborhoods we serve, thrive on the power of connections from trusted sources. Vicki Medvec is one of my trusted sources."

—*Sarah Friar, CEO, Nextdoor, Director, Walmart*

"I have worked with Vicki in many capacities and have personally observed the impact her work has had on large enterprises such as McDonald's, Google, and Discover. I am a big fan of her strategies, such as offering multiple simultaneous offers to communicate a powerful message."

—*Margo Georgiadis, Former CEO, Ancestry, Former CEO, Mattel,*
Director, McDonald's

"'WWVD?'—What Would Vicki Do?—is what I consistently ask myself every time I face a challenging negotiation in work or in life. I was very fortunate to meet Vicki twelve years ago when I was a Partner at Goldman Sachs. She conducted many programs for the Partners, Managing Directors and important clients, that people still talk about to this day. I'm excited that Vicki has gathered her actionable insights and terrific advice in Negotiate Without Fear. A must-read."

—*Lisa Shalett, Former Partner, Goldman Sachs, Founder,*
Extraordinary Women On Boards, Board member,
Accuweather, PennyMac Financial Services,
Bully Pulpit Interactive

"If I had read this book at the beginning of my career, instead of at the end, I would have been a more successful consultant, commanded higher fees and would have been a better professor and academic administrator, because the concepts in this book are so powerful and so very useful. The many war stores bring the concepts into clear focus and give the reader the competence and confidence to negotiate with great success. Every business-to-business seller and marketer should read this book. It provides the best, the most complete, and rigorous approach to managing complex account management of which I am aware.

It is an extraordinary book about negotiation, but it covers all aspects of relationship building, pricing and selling."

—Benson P. Shapiro, Malcom P. McNair Professor of Marketing,
Emeritus, Harvard Business School

"Vicki has advised me on many of my most difficult negotiations. Even as I have over 30 years of experience in high-stakes negotiations, having her voice in my mind always leads to a better outcome—for both sides. Go first . . . Offer multiple options . . . Make it about them, not you. Vicki's timeless touchstones have become the foundation of my negotiation approach."

—Michelle Seitz, Chairman and CEO, Russell Investments,
Director, Sana Biotechnology

"American Securities has come to rely upon Vicki for many years both to teach negotiation strategies and guide our portfolio companies through some of their most challenging negotiations. Our relationship started when she spoke to the CEOs of our portfolio companies at a CEO Retreat and due to her unique and differentiated approach, they insisted on having her instruct their teams. As a private equity firm, my partners and I have a great deal of experience negotiating, but Vicki makes us aware of the traps that snare experts and helps us to avoid these pitfalls. In her book, she shares the best ideas that expert negotiators employ and gives you confidence and examples to use these tools to your advantage. Even the most experienced negotiators will gain an edge from reading this book."

—Bill Fry, Managing Director, American Securities

"I wish I had had access to this book when I was running a company. The strategies Vicki presents would have helped me every day as I negotiated with customers, unions, government leaders, business partners, and community stakeholders. I would also have been able to use these ideas to guide the many highly successful women I have mentored across my career. Vicki includes an insightful section in each chapter on how to effectively negotiate for yourself. This book should be in the hands of every senior leader and, in fact, should be in everybody's hands."

—Georgia Nelson, Director, Cummins, Director,
Ball Corporation, Director, Simms, Ltd., Director,
Custom Truck One Source, Former President, Midwest Generation

"When you learn negotiation strategy from Vicki, you walk away with a full arsenal of tools that you can apply immediately and that will yield tangible results. I have been learning from Vicki for over a decade, and yet I still gain new skills every time I have a chance to participate in a seminar or a session. I have been a student, a customer, and a reference for the capabilities Vicki builds numerous times and she has exceeded expectations every single time. You will be challenged, you will grow your skills and your confidence, and you will be a better businessperson after spending some time with Vicki's words of wisdom."

—*Trish Lukasik, Operating partner, Atlantic Street Capital, Director, Sargento Food, Director, The Gorilla Glue Company*

"I have been negotiating for a living, both in government and the private sector, for almost 40 years and have studied with many experts. Vicki's thoughtful approach delivers the practicality and results beyond any other guidance. She provides actionable strategies that drive measurable success. Her ability to dissect the complexities in each negotiation and skillfully apply the strategies is an effective combination that truly sets her apart. The stories she shares in the book reveal the secrets to her techniques."

—*John Howard, Senior Vice President and General Counsel, W. W. Grainger, Inc.*

"I work with physicians every day and understand the power of unique knowledge. Vicki possesses unparalleled expertise in negotiations. She has trained my team on multiple occasions as our company has rapidly grown. Every single session has produced results for our business. In *Negotiate Without Fear*, she reveals the strategies she has taught to my team. Trust me when I say they work!"

—*Dr. John Di Capua, CEO, North American Partners in Anesthesia*

"Vicki Medvec has worked closely with my team at McDonald's. She has taught us how to differentiate ourselves and translate our differentiators into negotiable issues. She also encourages us to craft a message that conveys how our differentiators address the other side's pressing business needs. These strategies have completely changed our conversations and dramatically increased our success rate. And, we have been building stronger relationships at the same time. Her book will give you the skills to do this. Pay careful attention to the material on differentiating yourself. This is a critical capability both when you are negotiating for yourself and for your organization."

—*Morgan Flatley, Chief Marketing Officer and Digital Customer Experience Officer, McDonald's USA*

Negotiate

Without

Fear

Dr. Victoria H. Medvec

NEGOTIATE
WITHOUT
FEAR

Strategies and Tools to
Maximize Your Outcomes

WILEY

Published by John Wiley & Sons, Inc., Hoboken, New Jersey.

Published simultaneously in Canada.

For general information on our other products and services or for technical support, please contact our Customer Care Department within the United States at (800) 762-2974, outside the United States at (317) 572-3993 or fax (317) 572-4002.

Wiley publishes in a variety of print and electronic formats and by print-on-demand. Some material included with standard print versions of this book may not be included in e-books or in print-on-demand. If this book refers to media such as a CD or DVD that is not included in the version you purchased, you may download this material at http://booksupport.wiley.com. For more information about Wiley products, visit www.wiley.com.

Library of Congress Cataloging-in-Publication Data:

Names: Medvec, Victoria H., author.
Title: Negotiate without fear : strategies and tools to maximize your
  outcomes / Victoria H. Medvec.
Description: Hoboken, New Jersey : Wiley, [2021] | Includes index.
Identifiers: LCCN 2021008518 (print) | LCCN 2021008519 (ebook) | ISBN
  9781119719090 (hardback) | ISBN 9781119719137 (adobe pdf) | ISBN
  9781119719113 (epub)
Subjects: LCSH: Negotiation.
Classification: LCC BF637.N4 M433 2021 (print) | LCC BF637.N4 (ebook) |
  DDC 158/.5—dc23
LC record available at https://lccn.loc.gov/2021008518
LC ebook record available at https://lccn.loc.gov/2021008519

Cover image: Elephant and Mouse © urfinguss / iStock / Getty Images Plus
Cover design: C. Wallace

SKY10027943_070521

This book is dedicated to my mom, Margery Husted, who has always provided me with loving inspiration, and my sons, Barrett and Tyler, who have provided me with incredible motivation.

Contents

1

Take the Fear Out of Negotiation

Fear impedes people's ability to negotiate. Fear is not just a factor for amateurs who negotiate infrequently. Fear affects people who negotiate every day. For the past 20 years, I have advised clients on many high-stakes negotiations. I have consulted on mergers, acquisitions, large customer contracts, commercial real estate deals, partnership agreements, and supplier contracts. I have also taught negotiation strategies to thousands of executives around the world—from CEOs, to senior vice presidents of business development, to sales executives. I have taught those who negotiate every day, such as investment bankers, private equity partners, and commercial real estate investors, as well as those who are intimidated by the negotiation process. Google, McDonald's, IBM, McKesson, Cisco, and many other Fortune 500 companies are my clients, along with many smaller, growth-oriented businesses.

I frequently ask the senior executives that I am advising if they feel that fear impedes their own negotiations and the negotiations that their teams complete. They resoundingly agree that fear is a significant factor in these negotiations. Likewise, when I am teaching a negotiation course for a company, I often ask the participants if fear plays a role in their negotiations, and more than 80% of the attendees will raise their hands to say that fear limits their success.

What do people fear the most in negotiations? My extensive conversations with executives reveal that the biggest sources of apprehension are a fear of losing the deal and a fear of damaging the relationship. Other fears also include leaving money on the table, having a contentious discussion, experiencing conflict, allowing the other side to take advantage of you, and securing a poor outcome for yourself.

All of these concerns are reasonable, but the right strategies and tools can maximize your outcomes and take the fear out of negotiation.

This book is designed to teach you these strategies and provide explicit tools that will allow you to *Negotiate Without Fear* and maximize your success.

The timing for this book could not be better. The COVID-19 pandemic has created an environment where many companies are faced with challenging negotiations with customers, suppliers, partners, and sources of financial support. Likewise, many individuals need to negotiate to save their small businesses, protect their homes, and secure essential resources. Many individuals' jobs have been threatened by the economic crisis that has accompanied the pandemic and have an urgent need to negotiate for themselves. This book will help with all of these situations, whether you are a large industrial company negotiating to secure the equipment needed to operate your plants, a sales executive negotiating with new customers who need your technology services to help them excel in the new virtual world, a small business negotiating with your landlord for rent abatement, or an individual negotiating to secure a new role. The negotiation strategies presented in the book will also help you excel in the many negotiations you will encounter in the future, both at work and in your personal life. In addition, these strategies will enable you to effectively negotiate for yourself across the rest of your career.

People are often very afraid to negotiate for themselves. Research reveals that women are less likely than men to negotiate for themselves. In a famous study of graduating MBA students at Carnegie Mellon University, 93% of women did not attempt to negotiate higher salaries for themselves, while 43% of the men did not attempt to negotiate either (Babcock & Laschever, 2007). Even expert negotiators, who fiercely negotiate on behalf of their organizations, often fear negotiating for themselves. Because of this, in each chapter of the book, there is a special section included on applying the tactics to help you negotiate effectively for yourself and reduce your fear.

Each chapter will present specific strategies and proprietary tools to help you to take the fear out of every negotiation that you face. The book will include many real-world examples to highlight how to use the tactics being discussed. Some of the examples will relate to negotiating in the everyday world, such as buying a car or purchasing a house. Others will focus on high-stakes negotiations with customers, suppliers, and business partners. Still others will focus on negotiating for yourself. The strategies and tools we will discuss will give you an advantage in all these situations.

Chapter 2 will highlight how you can eliminate fear by putting the right issues on the table. Purposefully including issues in the negotiation that are important to the other side and easy for you to offer will allow you to focus the rationale on the other side and get more of what you want. Chapter 2 will also discuss common objectives that should drive the issues that you include in a negotiation; it also presents a unique Issue Matrix that can be used to assess the issues you are putting on the table before you open your mouth. Having the right issues on the table eliminates the fear of having an emotionally charged, contentious, single-issue discussion and ensures that you negotiate the right deal.

People are also afraid to negotiate because they fear that the other side will walk away and they will lose the deal. This is particularly concerning when a negotiator does not have strong outside options. Chapter 3 discusses the importance of building your options. This chapter highlights that your Best Alternative to Negotiated Agreement (BATNA) is your biggest source of power in any negotiation. Because increasing your power will reduce your fear, building your BATNA is essential.

Your BATNA is your biggest source of power, and it is also the most significant determinant of your bottom line; that is, your Reservation Point. Chapter 4 highlights the importance of knowing your Reservation Point and discusses building a Scoring Tool to assess your Reservation Point. A Scoring Tool helps to ensure that you do not become fixated on a single quantified issue and that you pay attention to the entire package of issues, establishing your Reservation Point across the bundle of issues. Knowing your bottom line provides clarity and reduces the fear that you will take a deal that is worse for you than walking away would be.

While you need to know your bottom line, you need to focus on your goal. Establishing an ambitious goal will help to reduce the fear that you will leave money on the table with a poor outcome for yourself. In Chapter 5, you will learn that your goal should be based on the weakness of the other side's options; that is, the weakness of their BATNA. The more you know about the fragility of the other party's BATNA, the more accurately you can estimate their reservation point. This chapter discusses a proprietary BATNA Analysis Tool to assess the weakness of the other side's BATNA and establish an appropriate goal. The BATNA Analysis Tool will also help you identify issues that you should add to the table to educate the other side on what is lacking in their alternatives. In addition, this tool will help you to uncover the best opportunities to reduce the other side's BATNA over time. Companies lose millions of dollars a year because their negotiators do not establish ambitious goals. The material in Chapter 5 will help to mitigate this risk and decrease your fear of leaving money on the table.

Once you have the right issues on the table and have completed an analysis of your goal, your BATNA, your Reservation Point and the other side's BATNA and Reservation Point, you are ready to begin the negotiation. Chapter 6 discusses the importance of making the first offer and connecting your offer to a compelling message that highlights how your differentiators address the other side's pressing needs and challenges. People are often afraid to lead in the negotiation and prefer to let the other side go first; however, this chapter presents extensive evidence that making the first offer allows you to anchor the starting point, frame the discussion, put the right issues on the table, and secure the relationship-enhancing position. Leading with the first offer provides you with advantages that set the stage for better outcomes, and it allows you to build a rationale that focuses on the other side to build the relationship at the same time. The strategies presented in Chapter 6 will take the fear out of making the first offer.

Chapter 7 highlights how your fear of making the first offer and your fear that the other side will walk away can be mitigated by making multiple offers simultaneously rather than providing a single offer. There are many advantages to delivering multiple equivalent simultaneous offers (MESOs) rather than single offers. MESOs pull the other side into a discussion and change the frame of the conversation from "whether we will work together" to "how we can work together." This reframing jettisons a sense of conflict and replaces this with a feeling of problem solving. MESOs also allow you to anchor an attractive starting point more effectively than a single offer does. In addition, a multiple offer makes your first offer seem more reasonable, decreasing the chances that an ambitious MESO will lead to an aggressive counteroffer or the other side walking away. Moreover, a MESO allows you to uncover more information from the other side and surface deeper levels of intelligence revealing not just what the other side wants but what it is worth to the other side to get what they say that they want. While you are securing anchoring and information advantages, a MESO makes you look more flexible and cooperative and allows you to persist longer on the issues that are important to you. Research reveals that harnessing a MESO will allow you to maximize your outcome and build your relationship with the other side so you can be more fearless when you put a MESO on the table. Chapter 7 not only discusses the advantages of using multiple offers, but it also highlights how to design the MESO to reinforce your message and make your offer a storyboard that emphasizes how your differentiators address the other side's pressing needs.

Chapter 8 highlights how fear can be further reduced by delivering your offer in the correct communication channel. This chapter stresses that you should "say it, don't send it," by delivering your offer in a synchronous communication channel. Although face-to-face in person is the best way to negotiate, the COVID-19 pandemic has made this difficult to do. When you cannot meet in person, you should use a virtual video platform such as Zoom, WebEx, Microsoft Teams, or Google Meet to deliver your offer face-to-face on screen. When you deliver your offer in a synchronous channel with visual cues, you can immediately see the other side's reaction, frame your message, modify your offer, and make appropriate concessions. When you negotiate in a synchronous channel, you are able to ask for more without the fear of losing the deal so I would encourage you to "say it, don't send it and see them when you say it." Chapter 8 also illustrates how to deliver your MESO effectively in order to communicate a compelling message to the other side.

You want your first offer to focus on how your differentiators address the other side's pressing needs and highlight the other side's interests. In addition, you want to ensure that you are leaving yourself room to concede. People often fear that the interaction in the negotiation will be emotionally charged and conflict laden; you can manage this by leaving yourself room to make concessions. When you concede, the other side feels like they are winning, and this increases the other side's satisfaction with the deal. You also want to concede because if the other side takes your first offer, it suggests you should have asked for more. Chapter 9 underscores that you want to approach the negotiation with an intent to concede and a plan for how you will do this. In this chapter, we also discuss other closing tactics such as using ratification and trigger strategies to close the deal.

Chapter 10 summarizes the critical strategies to make negotiators fearless. It stresses that, in order to take the fear out of negotiations, you need to prepare well and then you need to go first, focus on the other side, frame the offer correctly, be flexible, and make no feeble offers.

The chapters in this book reveal the negotiation strategies I have been sharing with my clients for the past two decades. Every strategy discussed is based on academic research but has also been tested in many real-world situations. These strategies have helped generate billions of dollars for my clients, and as I share them, I will include stories of times when these tactics have been successfully deployed. I am confident that these strategies will help you become a fearless negotiator and achieve great success in the many different negotiations that you will encounter. In short, you will learn to *Negotiate Without Fear*.

2 Put the Right Issues on the Table

Many people fear negotiation. They fear they will lose the deal, that the other side will walk away, or that the conversation will become contentious. These fears are rooted in the fact that many people have a narrow view of the negotiation. They may be focused on discussing a single issue with the other side, such as price, and recognize that on this single issue, the two sides will have completely opposing preferences; no wonder they worry the discussion will become contentious, conflict laden, and may result in an impasse. The key to eliminating these fears is to think about the negotiation more broadly and to become well prepared for the discussion. This chapter will provide you with the tools to prepare, help you put the right issues on the table, and reduce your fear of the interaction.

The better prepared negotiator always does better. You actually *add* power to your side when you prepare appropriately. Information is a significant source of power in any negotiation; the more you know about the other side's interests, objectives, and options, the more power you have. Likewise, the more information you have about your own interests, options, and priorities, the more power you have in the negotiation. Information is not the biggest source of power in a negotiation, but it is the source of power over which you have the most control. You decide how well prepared you will be and how much information you will secure, and when you do this, you control, to some extent, how powerful you will be in the negotiation.

It is easy to say you should be well prepared, but what does it really look like to prepare well for a negotiation? There are three key steps to get ready to negotiate:

1. Put the right issues on the table
2. Analyze your goal, best outside option, and bottom line
3. Have a plan for the discussion

This chapter will focus on putting the right issues on the table. Putting the right issues on the table is the first step in taking fear out of the negotiation.

Generating the Issues

I teach a course for expert negotiators on the traps that experts encounter in negotiations. The first trap I discuss is that many experts negotiate the entirely wrong deal. Many experts negotiate the standard or typical issues rather than ensuring they are discussing the right issues with the other side.

Experienced negotiators know they do not want to focus on solely one issue. Single-issue negotiations become very contentious, and they are particularly dangerous if you are interested in building or maintaining a relationship with the other side. If you are negotiating only one thing, it is very likely that you will either damage the relationship or secure a poor outcome for yourself.

Consider a situation where you are selling something and only negotiating on price. The buyer wants the price to be low, while the seller wants the price to be high; every dollar the seller claims is a dollar out of the buyer's pocket. Negotiating a single issue creates a hostile environment and a win-lose mentality.

When you care about your relationship with the other side, you want to maximize the outcome for yourself while simultaneously maintaining or building your relationship with the other side, so you want to negotiate multiple issues rather than a single issue. When there are multiple issues on the table, you can uncover differences in each side's preferences—one thing may be important to you, while something else is more important to the other side—and you can identify tradeoffs.

Although experts may recognize that they want to negotiate multiple issues, they unfortunately often negotiate the wrong ones. Because experts negotiate frequently, they may have a tendency to negotiate what is standard in this type of deal, or what is typically negotiated, rather than ensuring that they are putting the right issues on the table. How can you ensure that you are putting the right issues on the table?

> **TRAPS EXPERT NEGOTIATORS ENCOUNTER**
>
> Even expert negotiators get trapped.
>
> 1. **Negotiating the wrong deal—negotiating what is standard or typical rather than putting the right issues on the table.**

Objectives Drive Issues

In order to develop the list of the issues to include in any negotiation, you need to begin by thinking about your objectives. Your objectives reveal what you want to accomplish with the other party in the negotiation, in both the short and long term. Make a thorough list of these objectives. Once you have completed the list, you should develop one or more negotiable issues for every single objective that you have identified.

Negotiable issues are items that you will discuss and negotiate with the other side; you might or might not agree on these issues, but you will definitely discuss each of them with the other party.

I want to distinguish negotiable issues from another term that we frequently use in negotiation, which is rationale. *Rationale* is the storyline or explanation for your offer. Rationale is incredibly important, but it does not substitute for negotiable issues. Often, negotiators have a lot of rationale but only one or two negotiable issues. For example, negotiators often have a lot of rationale for the single issue of price. I want you to have a great rationale, but it is also critical to have many negotiable issues that you will actually negotiate with the other side. Your objectives should drive your negotiable issues in all types of negotiations.

In the following pages, I will show you how your objectives should drive your negotiable issues in a customer negotiation, then I will highlight the three objectives that should drive negotiable issues in every negotiation we conduct where we care about our relationship with the other side. Finally, I will end this section by applying all of this to a negotiation at the top of many of our minds, showing you how to put the right issues on the table when you are negotiating for yourself in an employment situation.

Developing Your Objectives and Negotiable Issues for a Customer Negotiation

Let's consider a typical negotiation with a customer. As you approach a negotiation with a customer, you probably have many different objectives. The first one that comes to mind may be to get the best price possible. However, you would not want to go into a customer negotiation and negotiate only price. If you focused only on price, you would create the type of win-lose, distributive negotiation environment (Raiffa, 1982; Harnett & Cummings, 1980) that I described earlier, where you are very likely to damage the relationship with your customer or secure a poor outcome for yourself. Instead, you want to add more issues to the table to unlock the integrative potential of identifying differences in the two parties' preferences (Raiffa, 1982). To do this, you need to begin by making a list of your objectives for your short- and long-term interactions with this customer and connecting at least one negotiable issue to each of these objectives.

Address the Customer's Pressing Business Needs

While one objective may be to maximize price, in every customer negotiation the first objective should be to address the customer's pressing business needs. It is shocking to me how many sales executives do not explicitly consider this to be one of their key objectives. A lot of sales executives are focused on what they want to accomplish in the negotiation—the product they want to sell or the growth they want to achieve—but are not focused on meeting the customer's needs. I always argue that you are more likely to get what you want in a negotiation if you focus on addressing the other side's pressing business needs.

In order to achieve this objective, you need to know what the customer's most pressing business needs are. When I ask sales executives how they can learn about such needs, they often suggest asking the customer. This is a reasonable idea, but the problem with doing only this is that you are likely to hear about the needs of the individual you are asking rather than the company's business needs. For example, if you speak to the head of procurement, you are likely to hear about procurement's needs, whereas if you talk to a plant manager, you are most likely going to hear about the needs at that one facility.

What you really want to know, though, is what are the company's most pressing business needs. What is keeping the CEO up at night?

To gather this information, you need to begin by doing some research. If your customer is a publicly traded company, I would start by reviewing three to four quarters of earnings calls with analysts. You generally can access these from the company's investor-relations pages on their website, or you can use a service such as *Seeking Alpha* (https://seekingalpha.com/). I like to scan three to four quarters of earnings calls at a time, paying particular attention to the Q&A section at the end of each call. The beginning of the call can help you learn about the company's initiatives, the metrics on which they are focused, and the language that the company tends to use. These pieces of knowledge will be valuable to you, but the questions and answers at the end of the call are a gold mine of information.

As you scan this section across the quarters, look for common questions the analysts are asking. When analysts are focused on particular questions quarter after quarter, or when two analysts ask a similar question around one subject area, this often reveals something that will impact share price. In my experience, the problems that impact share price are the concerns that keep a CEO up at night. You want to know what these topics are and think about how your product, service, or insight might help the company address these pressing business needs. Unless you are a strategy consulting firm, it is unlikely that you will solve all or even many of the customer's most pressing needs, but you want to find the one or two needs that you can address with a service you offer, a product you sell, or an insight that you possess.

Whenever I work with a client on a customer negotiation, an acquisition, a sale of a company, a commercial real estate deal, a partnership agreement, or a supplier contract, I encourage them to begin by reviewing analyst calls if the other side is a public company. If the other side is a start-up company that is not public, it is helpful to review presentations from investor conferences, paying attention to the questions that the potential investors are asking. (These presentations are often posted on a company's investor relations site under Events.) If the other side is a large private business, I will encourage negotiators to review the analyst calls of the company's competitors and news articles that relate to the organization. If the other side is a not-for-profit organization or a governmental body, news articles can also be a great source of information. It is critical for you to know the customer's most pressing business needs, and I encourage my clients to use all available sources to secure this information. In fact, I argue that failing to review this publicly available information is actually a sign of disrespect to your customer, because there was material available for you to learn about your customer and you chose not to do it.

This advice is not always appreciated by my clients. Often, they look at me as though I am crazy when I suggest this information collection as the starting point. However, my experience has revealed that this first step pays off with tremendous dividends. For example, I was once working with a client who sold tiny wire connection pieces. When I told the company's sales team that we needed to begin our preparation by reviewing the analyst calls for the customer's last four quarters, the team looked at me as though I was from Mars. They had never reviewed analyst calls before, had no idea where to get this information, and saw no need to begin with this activity. I am a stubborn adviser, though, and I persisted in my view that we needed to start with this information. This client's sales team now boldly endorses this approach, having seen for themselves that you sell a lot more tiny wire connectors when you go to the table focused on the customer's need to address the security of their supply chain (something the analysts had been focused on for months) rather than if you go to the table talking only about how your wire connectors compare to your competitor's connectors. You should always have the objective of meeting the customer's pressing business needs, and you have to know what those needs are.

Once you have listed the objective of meeting the customer's pressing business needs, you will want to develop negotiable issues that link to this objective. Remember that you should have at least one negotiable issue for every single objective on your list. You might find that there are components of the product or service that you provide that will meet the customer's pressing business needs. For instance, a customer may have a need for more brand recognition, and your advertising agency could negotiate to create an ad campaign that will improve their brand image.

Another example comes from a client of mine who was working with a large hotel chain under pressure from analysts because their sales were off trend, and the predictability of their sales cycle was becoming an issue. My client was rolling out a technology solution for the hotel's reservation system and was able to identify specific changes that would assist frontline staff in securing customer reservations. This obviously increased the scope of the project, and therefore the price point, but my client was addressing the hotel chain's key pain point by directly improving their customers' experience and driving sales. My client also negotiated a briefing with the hotel chain's CEO and CFO before the next four analyst calls to prepare for the sales questions that they were likely to be asked and prep sessions before the next four board meetings to get the CEO and CFO ready to address the board's questions as well.

As these examples reveal, beyond the product or service that you can offer, you can also provide insight sessions, updates to senior leaders, briefings before analyst calls, preparation for board meetings, and other services that can address the customer's pressing business needs. For example, you may have insight into the market or relevant changes that are occurring in their industry. These perspectives may be extremely valuable to your customer. So, as you think about negotiable issues to tie to the objective of addressing the customer's pressing business needs, consider items such as insight sessions for senior teams, updates on the industry for the company's leaders, and briefings to the CEO and other senior executives.

I was once working with a client that provided sustainability consulting services, and one of their clients had been getting a lot of pressure from analysts regarding their carbon footprint. Clearly, one issue they would negotiate with their client was the consulting service that they would provide. However, they also negotiated two insight sessions for the client's senior team; one would focus on the sustainability goals different companies in their industry were adopting, and the other would focus on anticipated changes in the regulatory environment. My client also negotiated to provide a 20-minute briefing with the CEO before the next four analyst calls to help him prepare for answering any questions that might arise around sustainability.

Another example comes from a large property management firm. The firm had a marquee, publicly listed tenant who was trying to renegotiate their lease. The tenant was considering building their own property outside of the city instead of renewing the lease. Over the past five earnings calls, the tenant had been facing increasing pressure from analysts regarding their costs and questioning the company's ability to

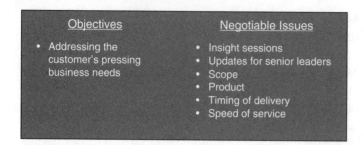

Figure 2.1: Typical Objectives and Issues in Customer Negotiations

attract and retain millennials to replace their aging workforce. I worked with my client to generate offers for their tenant with payment terms to reduce immediate cost pressure and assistance developing joint press releases highlighting how the tenant was addressing the analysts' specific concerns by saving money staying in their existing space. In the lease renewal discussions, my client also focused on how the downtown location would be advantageous to recruiting young talent. My client supported this rationale by including negotiable issues to highlight the attractiveness of the location to the tenant's targeted millennial workforce; to focus on the desirability of the location, some of the offers included passes for the subway since a convenient stop was next to the building, memberships for the gym in a neighboring building, food coupons for the many local restaurants, and a building-sponsored happy hour on evenings when there was a concert in a nearby park. Happily, the tenant stayed in the space with an increase in the rent.

As you can see from these numerous examples, there are many issues you can put on the table to address the customer's pressing business needs, so you do not have to limit yourself to thinking only about the product or service you provide. Many of these additional issues help you not only address the customer's challenges, but also build the relationship with the customer as well. (See Figure 2.1.)

Build the Relationship

Another common objective in a customer negotiation is to build your relationship with the customer. I would argue that this should be an objective in every customer negotiation, and I encourage sales executives to think specifically about with whom they would like to build the relationship and in what time frame. I suggest, for example, that they have a specific goal, such as building relationships with the CEO and the CFO over the next six months or building relationships with the vice president of Procurement and the vice president of Regulatory Affairs over the next three months. This more tangible and specific objective is much more actionable than the general objective of "building relationships."

I think too often people flippantly talk about building relationships but are not very focused on how they will do it. You need to have an action plan to end up with the relationships that you want to build, and you need to put the right negotiable issues on the table to accomplish this goal. When building a specific relationship is a concrete goal, such as a relationship with the CFO within six months or with the CEO or a board member within one year, you can examine your behavior every day and think about what you are doing, or could be doing, to establish and deepen that connection.

Sometimes, relationship building seems to be the excuse for a poorly negotiated outcome, for instance, saying to your boss, "I know the margin is terrible, but we are building the relationship." Rather than thinking about relationship building in this post hoc, defensive manner, I encourage my clients to be proactive in thinking about the relationships that they would like to build and in putting specific negotiable issues on the table that will allow them to achieve this goal.

I have a number of clients who are large strategy consulting firms. I was working with the partner at one of these firms on a proposal to win more work from an existing client. The economic buyer for the project was the CFO, who was new to the company and the industry. When my client was considering the objective of addressing the company's pressing business needs, I encouraged him also to think about the pressing needs of the new CFO to learn about the company quickly, establish himself in the industry, prepare for board interactions, and perform well on the company's quarterly calls with analysts. The partner included issues in the negotiation, such as insight sessions for the senior team on changes in the industry and briefings for the CEO and CFO before the next four analyst calls. This savvy partner also included a meeting with the CFO every month to help him navigate his first 100 days in addition to prep sessions before the next eight board meetings. It is clear that the partner was focused on addressing the pressing business needs of the company and the needs of his buyer.

Consider, though, how the insight sessions, industry updates, and briefings for the CEO and CFO before the analyst calls will help meet the customer's business needs and will also link to the objective of building relationships with the CEO and CFO over the next six months; likewise, the coaching sessions and prep before the board meetings will cement the partner's relationship with the CFO even further. Meeting with the CEO and CFO before analyst calls to brief them on issues that they might need to discuss will give the partner the opportunity to provide essential information when they need it the most, creating a dependency on the partner and cementing his relationship as a trusted adviser to the company's leadership team.

People are often focused on trying to get their customers to like them. I always advise my clients that it is nice if your customers like you, but essential that they need you. You want to include negotiable issues that position you to create this type of dependency.

Often, executives will try to build relationships with their customers' senior executives through the products or services that they provide. You might imagine in the previous example that the partner on the project would try to build senior-level relationships by doing good work and briefing the CEO on the project. However, the challenge is that if an employee lower in the organization is responsible for the project being completed, it is unlikely that the work itself will be a pathway to a strong CEO or CFO relationship. The people responsible for the project who "own" this work are not going to want to have the partner

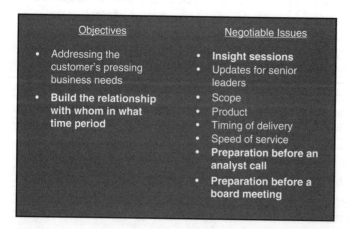

Objectives	Negotiable Issues
• Addressing the customer's pressing business needs	• **Insight sessions**
	• Updates for senior leaders
• **Build the relationship with whom in what time period**	• Scope
	• Product
	• Timing of delivery
	• Speed of service
	• **Preparation before an analyst call**
	• **Preparation before a board meeting**

Figure 2.2: Typical Objectives and Issues in Customer Negotiations

speak to their boss about the project, as this might make them look like they are not fulfilling their responsibilities. When you want to build senior-level relationships, you want to create *pathways to the C-suite* by including negotiable items such as insight sessions for senior teams on an industry trend, briefings for senior leaders on market issues, or prep before analyst calls or board meetings into your offer. These extra services create pathways to building senior-level relationships separate from the direct products or services provided. (See Figure 2.2.)

Differentiate Your Company, Product, or Service

Another objective you should include in every customer negotiation is to differentiate your company, product, or service from that of your competition. Whenever I teach a sales team, I always have them all stand up and only allow individuals to sit down after they have given me a specific objective not stated by another member of their team. Frequently, no one states the objective of differentiating the company, the product, or the service. If you are a CEO reading this book, I would encourage you to test this with your sales team. It is striking just how many sales executives fail to focus on differentiation. They will discuss the objectives of maximizing price, obtaining a long-term contract, and winning the work, but often they do not focus on the critical objective to achieve these goals; that is, to differentiate your product, service, or company. If you are not differentiating, you are commoditizing your offering, so the lack of focus on differentiation leads to the commoditization of products and services that CEOs fear and analysts attack. As a CEO, I want my team to be differentiating our services in every customer interaction.

When looking at your company's differentiators, you need to analyze what is unique about your product, service, or company. Keep in mind that a differentiator is only a differentiator if the other side cares about it. If you are a small, privately held company competing against many large, publicly traded companies, you may want to say that your differentiator is your size or ownership structure; the key question, though, is why do your customers care that you are small and privately held? What does this do for them? Does this mean that they will have quicker access to decision makers? Does this mean that you are nimbler because you are able to adapt to their changing needs? You can only differentiate yourself on something that the other side cares about.

Sales team members sometimes say that their differentiators are expertise and high quality. I doubt that competitors are walking around saying "we lack expertise" or "our product is low quality," though. Try to identify things that are truly unique about your product or service. A consulting firm that is a client of mine used to say that their differentiators were their people and their expertise, but this did not really distinguish them because their competitors would also say that they had great people and superb expertise. I pushed my client to identify more specifically what was distinctive about them and uncovered that my client has the unique ability to access third-party brokers that their competitors cannot, and that they maintain an executive in residence who is a former CEO from the industry that they serve. These are both unique differentiators, which are stronger and far more tangible than "people and expertise."

Once you have identified your differentiators, you need to turn them into negotiable issues. Even sales executives who differentiate their product or service often do it only through the rationale they provide. The challenge, though, is that differentiating only through your rationale does not work. Often your differentiators blend into your comments and get lost, especially because competitors will often provide a very similar rationale. In order to have your differentiators stand out and shape the decision-making process of the other side, you need to turn your differentiators into negotiable issues, and you need to have these issues on the table at the time the decision is being made.

For example, I have a client that sells monogrammed bags and other personalized items. They have an incredible in-house design team, and their quality is superb because they monitor their production plants in China on a regular basis. The sales team who works for this client is quite experienced, and they would always tell customers about these differentiators in their sales calls. Unfortunately, though, while the sales team would talk about their differentiators, they would often negotiate only price. This was a huge problem since their competitor had a lower price. I actually once asked the CEO if his sales team worked for the competition because they appeared to be negotiating on behalf of the competitor; they were only negotiating price, and on price the competitor would win. Their competitor did not say "we buy our designs off the Internet, so they are ordinary and ugly, and our bags rip and tear, but our price is really cheap." Rather, their competitor would say, "We have great quality and awesome designs, and our price is cheaper."

My client's sales team needed to learn to turn their differentiators into issues that could be discussed and negotiated with their customers at the same time price was being discussed. For instance, the differentiator of the in-house design team could be the basis for many negotiable issues such as:

1. How many times per year could a customer meet with the design team?
2. How many designs could be proposed for the customer to make their selections?
3. How quickly could a design be created?
4. How quickly could a design be modified?
5. Who owned the Intellectual Property for the design once it was created?

By negotiating each of these five issues, the sales team was able to draw attention to their in-house design team and how this distinguished them from their competitor, who did not have a design team. Moreover, the sales team was able to show the customer how this unique advantage affected the product that they would receive and what this differentiator meant to them.

When I am helping my clients think about how to turn their differentiators into negotiable issues, I ask them to think about their differentiators as thumbtacks on a corkboard. Hanging off each of these thumbtacks are tiny pieces of string, and every piece of string is attached to a negotiable issue that allows you to emphasize the differentiator on the thumbtack: Think about the strings as the words "because we," and you can see how these issues will allow the negotiator to highlight each differentiator. For example, my client could offer to deliver a customized design in one, two, or three weeks, "because we have an in-house design team." They could also offer to modify the design in an expedited way in 12, 24, or 36 hours, "because we have an in-house design team." As they negotiate each of these issues, they will bolster the differentiator of the in-house design team and set the company apart from its competitors who purchase designs from third-party sources. (See Figure 2.3.)

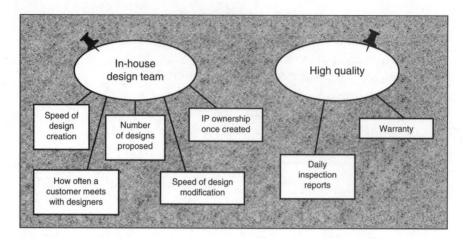

Figure 2.3: Promotional Sales Company Differentiators

The concept of turning differentiators into negotiable issues is often daunting, so I want to provide another example. One of my clients is a family-owned food manufacturer who controls their entire supply chain. The control of their supply chain is extremely unique in their specific industry; they are the only company in their industry who owns their entire supply chain, and they invested a great deal of capital to secure this differentiator. This is a key advantage because this control reduces the likelihood of any contamination in the products that might result in a product recall. This is particularly important to customers who purchase private label products from my client, because when the product bears the name of the customer, recalls are very painful. If a branded product has a recall, the brand takes the hit; but if a private label product has a recall, the retailer takes the hit; thus, quality is especially important in the private label space. It would be devastating if my client's unique control over their entire supply chain got lost in the sales discussion, but I think this is likely if the sales team does not turn this differentiator into negotiable issues. I doubt that my client's competitors would say, "I have no idea where the products are sourced." The competitor would stress that they have high-quality farms, excellent plants, and a secure supply chain, and it is likely that my client's control over the entire supply chain would fade away in the discussion. So, I encouraged my client to take this differentiator and turn it into issues that could be negotiated, not just discussed (see Figure 2.4).

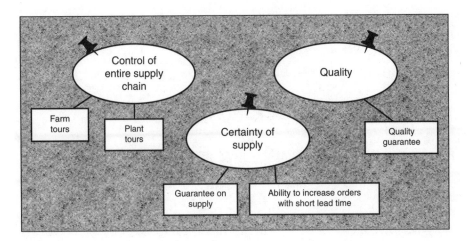

Figure 2.4: Food Supplier Differentiators

For example, the control over the supply chain could be stressed by negotiating issues such as farm tours and plant tours.

I proposed the issues of plant tours and farm tours to the vice president of Sales, and he said, "Vicki, no one wants to tour the farm or the plant." I stressed to him, though, that I did not care if anyone ever toured the farm or plant (although his customers actually loved the farm tours). Instead, I wanted him to use this issue to prompt a discussion about the company's complete control over the supply chain and how this would ensure a higher quality product and a lower likelihood of recalls that would damage the retailer's reputation. It is critical for your team to know your company's differentiators and then turn them into negotiable issues so that they do not get lost in the discussion.

My son Tyler was reading this section in the first draft of the book and asked me how I differentiate my company. He said it is great to hear stories about what you do for other companies, but how do you do this for your own business? As the CEO of Medvec & Associates, I am constantly speaking to my team about our need to differentiate our offerings from what other larger consulting firms or training companies provide. One of our differentiators (see Figure 2.5) is that we combine the expertise from decades of advising on high-stakes deals with the capability to train people on how to leverage the strategies we have developed. We do not deliver a canned training program but are able to customize our offerings uniquely to a specific business and

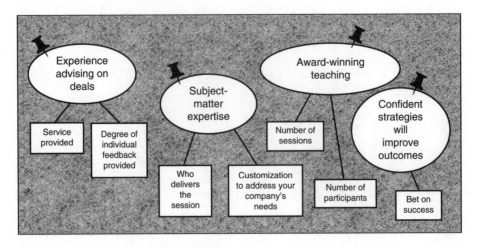

Figure 2.5: Medvec & Associates' Differentiators

provide recommendations for particular negotiation challenges. We provide award-winning training but also advise on deals. Another differentiator is that we are subject matter experts in negotiation so we can tailor solutions for any situation. In addition, we are revenue generators and are confident that the strategies we teach will improve negotiation outcomes.

It is one thing to talk about these differentiators, but as I have said, it is critical to translate these distinctive capabilities into negotiable issues. To highlight our advising and teaching capabilities, we vary whether we are providing consultation alone, only teaching sessions, or combining teaching and consultation. To further bolster our unique expertise to advise on deals, we also vary whether we provide individual feedback on participants' negotiation plans between our teaching sessions or not. To emphasize our subject matter expertise, we vary whether the sessions are led by me or by one of my senior associates, all of whom are award-winning faculty and negotiations researchers. Varying this allows us to stress the experience I have advising on deals and also demonstrates that we are unique because we do not offer any programs led by individuals who are not subject matter experts, as might be found in trainers from other companies. Finally, to underscore our confidence that we will improve negotiation outcomes, we offer a bet on the outcome we will help our clients to achieve. Clients can pay us a daily rate,

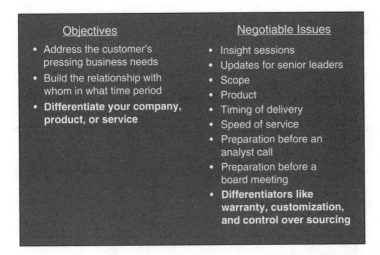

Objectives	Negotiable Issues
• Address the customer's pressing business needs • Build the relationship with whom in what time period • **Differentiate your company, product, or service**	• Insight sessions • Updates for senior leaders • Scope • Product • Timing of delivery • Speed of service • Preparation before an analyst call • Preparation before a board meeting • **Differentiators like warranty, customization, and control over sourcing**

Figure 2.6: Typical Objectives and Issues in Customer Negotiations

or a fee based on the results of the negotiation, or a combination of the two.

Notice how we are translating our differentiators into negotiable issues and then planning how we can vary these issues in our multiple offers. It is critical to vary these issues across your multiple options because people pay more attention to what is shifting and changing than to what is constant (Franconeri, Hollingworth, & Simons, 2005; Theeuwes, Kramer, Hahn, & Irwin, 1998). You want to draw the other side's attention to your differentiators so you want to convert these unique capabilities into negotiable issues (see Figure 2.6) that you can vary across your three options, as we will discuss in Chapter 7.

Highlight Your Company's Expertise

Another objective that you should have in a customer negotiation is to *highlight your company's expertise*. This is particularly important if you consider your company to be a category leader. Often, we assume that our customers know about the expertise we possess, but we do not emphasize this expertise through our negotiations. Whenever I speak about this topic, I immediately think about a client of mine that is one of the largest bottled water companies in the world. This client is definitely the category leader and knows all about bottled water.

Objectives	Negotiable Issues
• Address the customer's pressing business needs	• Insight sessions
• Build the relationship with whom in what time period	• Updates for senior leaders
• Differentiate your company, product, or service	• Scope
• Highlight your company's expertise	• Product
	• Timing of delivery
	• Speed of service
	• Preparation before an analyst call
	• Preparation before a board meeting
	• Differentiators like warranty, customization, and control over sourcing
	• Forecast data
	• Strategic updates
	• Sharing best practices from the industry

Figure 2.7: Typical Objectives and Issues in Customer Negotiations

One of the company's competitors is Nestlé. When you first hear the name Nestlé, I doubt that bottled water jumps into your head. Instead, you probably think about chocolate. Unfortunately, for my client, though, whenever Nestlé enters a market, they are very skilled in highlighting their expertise. They might send in dieticians to talk about the importance of water in the diet and forecasters to help retailers predict how much bottled water should be on the shelves based on the ambient air temperature outside. Note that in doing these things, Nestlé emphasizes their expertise in bottled water. You need to negotiate issues to showcase your expertise so that it is salient to your customers. (See Figure 2.7.)

Expand Your Footprint Within the Customer's Business

When you are negotiating with a customer, you should also have the objective of *expanding your footprint* within their organization; you want to expand your business with the customer to have more of their wallet come to you rather than going to your competitors. I often say that you want to become an octopus on every account—an octopus has an incredibly strong grip because it has many points of connection. Expanding your footprint allows you to leverage your current customer relationships in order to generate new business. Sometimes, companies fall into a trap of thinking only about business development with new customers without attempting to get every piece of business from existing customers. When you expand current customer relationships, business has a lower cost of sale, and it is often less competitive, more sustainable, and more profitable than new business. This makes footprint expansion critical to margin improvement.

When you want to expand your footprint with a client or customer, there are four issues that you should negotiate. These issues are in addition to the product or scope you will provide, the deliverable you will complete, the team you will use, and the timing you will achieve. They are also in addition to the insight sessions, updates, and briefings that you are providing to address the customer's pressing business needs and create pathways to the C-suite. Moreover, they are in addition to the issues that you include to differentiate your product, service, or company.

The four footprint expansion issues are added to the table specifically to allow you to expand your business within a customer's account, gain more points of connection, capture a bigger piece of their wallet, and increase the barriers to competition for your customer's business. These four footprint expansion issues are: (1) dedicated, on-site team; (2) volume incentives; (3) exclusivity discounts; and (4) up-front payment. Each of these footprint expansion issues is described in detail in the following sections.

Dedicated, On-site Team

The first key to expanding your footprint with a customer is to embed yourself with the customer. For example, if you are a partner in a consulting firm, you might achieve this embeddedness by negotiating a dedicated on-site team one day a week, or a dedicated on-site partner two days a month. If you are a manufacturing company, you might achieve this by negotiating to provide an on-site engineer building prototypes for the customer. A critical component of *embeddedness* is to be on site with the customer or closely connected to them. When you achieve this type of connection, you have the opportunity to learn more about the customer's needs, gather information in the hallway and cafeteria, and secure competitive intelligence. You also have the chance to build stronger relationships with the customer's management team. Research demonstrates that proximity leads to increased liking (Newcomb, 1960), so the customer will tend to think of you more favorably and more often when you are entrenched.

During negotiations, you should never say, "I want to be embedded," because that rationale is focused entirely on your company's needs. Rather, you should negotiate to "provide a dedicated service team on site each week," or "a dedicated engineer once a week," or something else that will allow you to be close to your client and create barriers to competition.

This type of embeddedness is key both to businesses that sell to other businesses and those that sell directly to consumers. People may perceive that embeddedness is an issue of the past, and that with the online, mobile environment, this type of connection no longer matters. I definitely would disagree with this assessment. In fact, I think some of the best online merchants have discovered techniques to embed themselves with their customers in very clever ways. For example, I was conducting an advanced negotiations session for a group of CEOs in Salt Lake City six years ago when I met the CEO of Olive & Cocoa, an online gift company that sells many specialty items, including crates filled with sweets and salty snacks that you can send to friends, relatives, and corporate clients. I was intrigued by this company, and I really liked the fact that I could have my company logo branded on the crate, so I ordered my corporate gifts from the company that holiday season. My clients loved the treats and commented on the great packaging in the wooden crates embossed with my logo.

The following August, I received a call from Chrissy, the sales consultant responsible for my corporate account. I could not believe that my small company would warrant a sales consultant, but I was very impressed by the initiative. She told me that she was sending me a package with some new items being added for the following holiday season. The next week, I received a crate with my logo on it filled with small sample bags of treats that I might want to consider for the next holiday order. I loved the treats, and the branding on the top of the crate reminded me of what I paid to have the brand custom designed the prior year. A month later, I received an envelope with a small piece of wood with my logo on it, a letter from Chrissy, a catalog with holiday gift ideas, and a list of the names of the clients to whom I sent gifts the prior holiday season. The letter explained that all I needed to do was to add any addresses for new clients and select what I wanted to send.

This online retailer successfully embedded themselves into my consulting firm's business. The money I paid to have the customized branding on each crate and the ease of ordering they created by tracking my data from year to year created barriers for me to switch to another holiday gift provider. Until I found Olive & Cocoa, I used a different supplier every year for my corporate gifts. In fact, my assistant and I took pride in finding a new company each year to source the gifts. Not surprisingly, since Olive & Cocoa effectively embedded themselves and created barriers to change, I have sent all my corporate gifts from them for the past six years.

Volume Incentives

The second footprint expansion issue is a *volume incentive*—you want to incent your customers to give you more of their business. You get the behavior that you reward, not what you desire (Kerr, 2008); if you want a customer to give you more of their business, you need to reward them for doing so. Many people think about a volume incentive as a pricing tool, but I consider it to be a tool to motivate the other side and to market your company's capabilities. A volume incentive could be structured as a volume discount, a rebate program, or a combination of both. Regardless of the incentive that you provide, it is critical to structure your incentive program appropriately.

Before you structure the incentive plan, it is crucial to think about your goals and what specific behaviors you are trying to drive. I encourage my clients to consider their goals for both the coming year and for a three-year period. Your goal may be to increase revenue on the account, but you may also have the goal of expanding to a new geography or a goal of selling a new service that will increase the stickiness of your relationship with the customer. Consider all of your goals and think carefully about what behaviors you want to incent.

It is also important to review the history on the account; you should never craft a volume incentive without examining the account's history, because there could be something idiosyncratic about the past year. I encourage my clients to look at a five-year history, or as far back as possible if the customer relationship is under five years.

For example, I had a client who was trying to grow a customer's business from $25M to $40M in one year. The first things we discussed were my client's goals. Clearly, they were trying to grow the account to $40M, but they were also trying to eliminate a nasty competitor who was constantly nibbling at their margin. The goal was to get the account to $40M in one year, but there was a strong sense that the total that could be achieved in three years was only $45M; they immediately wanted to get to $40M so that they could eliminate the competitor in the first year. When we looked at the history on the account, my client had $25M in revenue from the customer this year, $18M the year before, $15M the year before that, $22M the prior year, and $25M five years ago. So, it is clear that this account had some bumpiness between $15M and $25M.

Once you have reviewed the account history and have determined your goals, you are ready to establish the volume thresholds that you will use for your incentive plan. You want to base your incentive on the actual achievement of volume thresholds, not the promise of future purchases. In addition, you want to have many thresholds rather than a single one. People often create a single volume threshold that does not push customers enough, or a threshold that is so high that it is perceived to be unachievable and therefore not motivating. Try to create many thresholds with increasing rewards at each threshold.

Applying this to the example above, we decided to establish the first threshold between $15M and $25M. We put the next step between $25M+ and $35M, the next step from $35M+ to $45M, and the final step at $45M+ (see Figure 2.8).

Notice that my client's one-year goal is in the middle of the plan, with the three-year goal anchoring the final step, even though this is only a one-year plan. It is important to put the three-year goal as the final step with a significant incentive attached to it. You want to use this incentive to grab the customer's attention and spark a conversation so that you can educate your customer about what else you could be doing for them.

For example, one of my clients, a major strategy consulting firm, was generating $5M of revenue from a customer but learned that this customer was spending $500M on work my client could have been providing. My client was literally a rounding error in the customer's total spending. I encouraged my client to offer a volume incentive, and since the three-year goal was $100M, we set $100M+ as the final threshold. To be clear, we included many other thresholds that increased

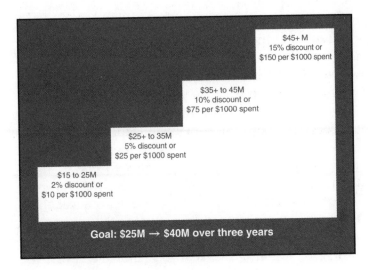

Figure 2.8: Multiple Volume Thresholds

from the current $5M to the $100M three-year goal, but the last step was at $100M+.

When my client presented this incentive plan, the customer was shocked, saying, "What do you mean $100M, we only spend $5M with you?" This presented the perfect opportunity for my client to say, "Yes, you spend $5M with us because we are only helping you with this one narrow problem. But we could be helping you with this other challenge, helping you to address this additional problem, and we could also be working with you to solve the problem you have in this other area." The customer was surprised and said, "We did not even know that you worked in those areas; we currently do not even consider you for work in those arenas."

On that day, my client was added into the consideration set for five new areas of work and quickly grew the account from $5M to $20M. This is the type of education that every company wants to provide to their customers, but you first need to get their attention. The incentive attached to the final threshold with the three-year goal can attract the other side's attention, allow the education to begin, and help you to market your products and services.

Once you define the thresholds, you need to determine what incentive will be tied to each threshold. You might decide to use a volume discount and offer different discount levels at each threshold. For example, a 2% discount for the first threshold with a 5% discount the next level, a 10% discount at the next threshold, and an 15% discount at the final step.

An alternative would be to structure a *rebate incentive plan.* When I use the word rebate, I do not mean that you would give a customer cash back. If you give a customer cash, they can spend it with your competitor. Instead of giving cash, think about allowing your customer to earn "(Insert Your Company Name) Dollars." For example, I often provide "Medvec & Associates Dollars" to my clients. Medvec & Associates Dollars are much better than awarding cash because they can only be applied to services that my company provides. Moreover, these Medvec & Associates Dollars are like magical money that disappears in a certain period of time if they are not used. This expiration period creates a sense of urgency for purchases that you cannot achieve if you rebate cash. If you are a company that has other businesses as clients, you might make the rebate dollars expire in one year or six months. If you are a company who sells directly to consumers, you will probably want the dollars to expire in a shorter period of time. You can also guide your customers' purchases toward specific products or services that you want them to try by designating what can be purchased with these dollars.

For example, one of my clients is a manufacturing company that was trying to expand their business by developing a service business to complement their manufactured goods. When I first began my work with this organization, the company was using a rebate program that gave cash back to their customers. I encouraged them to begin to provide "Company Name" Dollars to their customers rather than providing Uncle Sam Dollars. The CEO liked this idea and thought that they could make this change and provide "Company Name" Dollars that customers could use toward their purchase of the manufactured goods. I suggested that rather than having customers use this money to purchase goods that they were already planning to purchase, the company should instead have customers earn rebate dollars based on their purchases of the manufactured goods that could be applied toward the purchase of the company's new services. In this way, rebates can incent the customer to try a new service or product. You want to incent the customer to do what you want them to do (try the new service or product) rather than incenting them to do what they were already planning to do (buy the same things from you that they have always purchased).

In the past, I have been impressed by the way Neiman Marcus used volume incentives to capture my wallet. In my favorite version of their loyalty program, I earned points based on the amount I had spent and they then sent me a gift card with a value based on my earned points. They sent the card in early Spring, a period when consumers typically are not shopping as much. Of course, they did not send the card just before the holidays, as people would already be buying during this peak shopping season. They did not need to incent their customers to shop during a period when they would already be shopping; instead, they wanted to encourage them to purchase at time when they might not otherwise be shopping.

The card also had some limitations on the types of products I could purchase with it. For example, I could not use the card to buy couture or makeup. I think they presumed that if people needed an outfit for a very special occasion, they would head to Neiman's to buy couture anyway, and they probably knew that most of us would buy the makeup we needed without a discount. They were clearly incenting me to do what they wanted me to do, not what I would naturally do. They would incent me to purchase items from them that I might have bought somewhere else. Moreover, if I didn't use the value on the card within a specific two-week period, the money disappeared. This created a clear urgency for me to shop. Not surprisingly, if the card had $500 value on it, I generally spent far more than $500 when I used it. Neiman Marcus did not give me a rebate in cash for shopping with them, because I could have spent that cash at Bloomingdale's. Instead, they gave me money that I could spend only with them (and, as I always told my husband, I felt obligated to do so).

Notice that Neiman Marcus sent me a card that had the rebate on it; this became my money, and I did not want to lose it. When I work with companies to create programs like this for their customers, I stress that rebate dollars should not be called *credits*. If you refer to them as credits, they will not provoke the same perception of value in the mind of the recipient because they will be seen as the issuer's money rather than the recipient's money.

Daniel Kahneman, Jack Knetsch, and Richard Thaler once demonstrated that if you ask someone to assess the value of a mug on a shelf, they will provide a lower value than if assessing the value of the same exact mug that they own; ownership creates the endowment effect (Kahneman, Knetsch, & Thaler, 1990). So, when you are awarding rebate dollars, you want people to feel like they own them so that they value them more highly. You may not send a card to your customers like Neiman Marcus did, but you want to ensure that they feel that it is their money because they will value this more, not want to lose it, and feel compelled to spend it.

Creating a sense of urgency to purchase is achieved by having the rebate dollars disappear if they are not spent within a certain time period. You also have the ability to control when your customers will experience this urgency. I encourage my clients to look at their revenue cycle and identify if they have dips across the year. A strategy to try and "smooth" out those dips is to make the rebate dollars expire at the end of the slowest month. I once had the chance to speak to the CEO of a company who makes high-end customized closets for homes (think "closets for the stars"). People typically do not want to have closets installed if they are having family over for Thanksgiving, making November a slow month, and they want to avoid the mess over the holidays, making December installations very rare as well. Then, they often do not get things organized quickly enough for a January installation, leaving the closet installation company with three very slow months. I encouraged this CEO to give customers rebate dollars that expire at the end of December but that can be used for purchases made up to one month in advance. This allowed the company to narrow the dip down to a period of two weeks of slow activity at the end of December rather than three months of inactivity.

I encourage my clients to select whether they want to offer a volume discount or a rebate based on their goals. I suggest volume discounts for customers with decentralized buying units where you are trying to incent your current buyers to introduce you to potential buyers in other parts of the business. The volume discount rewards them for these introductions because the total spend may increase, providing an additional discount on their own purchases. On the other hand, I recommend rebates when you are trying to foster trial of a new product or service that the customer currently does not purchase from you. At times, you may want to layer both types of incentives into your customer agreement to drive both introductions and the trial of new goods or services.

When you want to expand your footprint with a customer, you want to include issues that allow you to be embedded (such as a dedicated, on-site team for one day a week) and a volume incentive. You should also consider the other two footprint expansion issues, which are an exclusivity discount and up-front payment.

Exclusivity Discounts

Exclusivity is a power changing issue; when your customer is exclusively using your services, or only purchasing products from your company, you gain power in the relationship. This is because the customer will become dependent on you and will lack alternative suppliers. Exclusivity does not change the competitive landscape (your competitors are still out there), but it changes the customer's perception of the competitive landscape because they are uncertain about competitors they have not used for a while. This uncertainty makes these competitors less attractive, weakening the customer's perception of their alternatives, and giving you more power. Because exclusivity is a power changing issue, procurement executives are often the "exclusivity police" and try to avoid single-source relationships.

If I were advising a buyer, I would tell them never to make any supplier an exclusive supplier. However, when I am assisting sellers, I tell them always to try to secure exclusivity. One way to achieve this is to include an exclusivity discount in your negotiation whenever you are negotiating with a customer. The customer does not need to make you exclusive; instead, you simply agree that if at any point they are solely using you to provide some good or service, you would provide the customer with a discount. While it is hard to get an exclusivity commitment past the procurement department, exclusivity discounts often make it past the scrutiny of procurement and encourage the economic buyer to purchase only from you, rather than splitting the purchase. Getting 100% of a customer's business is not just 10% better than getting 90% of their business; when your customer buys 10% from another supplier, they secure certainty with a readily available and convenient alternative whom they know. An exclusivity discount incents the customer only to use you, and creates a strong competitive barrier.

Up-front Payment

The fourth footprint expansion issue, asking for *up-front payment*, also creates tremendous competitive barriers. My clients are always skeptical when I discuss this idea with them. Remember the consulting firm client that I discussed earlier who was trying to increase a customer's spending from $25M to $40M in one year? The partner on this account was very interested in expanding his firm's footprint in this particular client account. I suggested that he use all four footprint expansion strategies. He was excited about the idea of negotiating a dedicated on-site team, a volume incentive, and an exclusivity discount. Then I told him that we should suggest that if the client paid the firm $10M a quarter in advance, the firm would provide a discount on the hourly rate and charge all of the services performed against this pre-payment. In response to this idea, he used the words "stupid" and "idiotic." I cannot remember if he thought I was stupid, and the idea was idiotic, or if he thought I was an idiot and the idea was stupid, but his views of both me and the idea were clearly negative. I explained to him that the idea came from my many years of working with procurement executives who told me that they were surprised that more suppliers did not ask for payment in advance because they would be willing to give it to them in exchange for a discount. Remember that many procurement executives are incentivized by the discount that they achieve, not by when they pay the money, so they may be indifferent about when exactly they pay the cash. On the other hand, a supplier would love to get paid in advance because up-front payment locks in the purchase and makes it very difficult for the customer to use another firm; once a company has paid a supplier, they would have to find more budget to use a competitor. Pre-payment creates a barrier that limits the customer's ability to use someone else.

For many years, I worked with one of the big four accounting firms and always encouraged them to negotiate up-front payment with their tax and consulting clients. Many of the partners in the firm resisted, saying that no one would pay up front. I pointed out to them that, in fact, their firm paid me up-front for the multiple sessions that I conducted for them each year, so it was clearly not the case that no one would pay in advance. However, their reluctance persisted. Then the firm encountered a client that they had been trying to break into for five years to sell tax services. They had exposed the client to some of their finest tax partners, discussed many potential projects with them, and even had the client saying, "Wow, what a talented tax group you have." Yet in five years, they had not generated any tax work.

Then they found out that one of their competitors had a two-year pre-pay on all tax services that re-upped every single year. The competitor had literally built a brick wall around the account, and all my client was doing was banging their head against the wall. Similar to the rebates we discussed earlier, pre-payment creates a strong barrier dissuading a customer from switching to a competitor.

I do not think that you will get prepayment 100% of the time, but I think you can successfully obtain this 25–35% of the time if you ask for it all of the time. When you ask, I would encourage you to make it a first concession issue rather than a first offer issue. I will offer a price that I know the other side will react to by saying it is "too high." In response, I concede to lower my price if they pay me in advance. This way, the prepayment request does not appear to be made because you do not trust the other side to pay; instead, it is framed as a concession made to address the other side's request for a price discount.

Once I was in Washington, DC, speaking to a group of 1,200 executives, so I wanted to get my hair blown out by a professional. I found a service that would send mobile stylists to you. The woman who arrived at 5:00 a.m. for my service, informed me that she was the owner of the company and explained that she personally covered all of the early morning calls to ensure that there was never a delay. I was impressed by her attitude and then became intrigued by her business model. She explained that in addition to the mobile hair care for transient hotel guests, she also ran a salon that operated as a "membership club." Salon club members would prepay for a year's worth of hair care services and, in return, they would get blowouts free of charge anywhere in the metro area. I was dazzled by the entrepreneurial know-how of this salon owner. She was masterfully using pre-payment to lock in her customers' hair care needs and create a reliable, consistent revenue stream.

The footprint expansion strategies of asking for payment up front and providing rebates have some psychological similarities. An earned rebate of "Company Name Dollars" that will disappear if not used creates a similar type of urgency to spend, as does the money that is paid in advance that will be forfeited if it is not used.

Some companies believe that they can expand their footprint within a customer by simply reducing price. I always stress that lowering price is not a footprint expansion strategy. Low price does not lock in a customer; low price does not make a customer less likely to buy from a

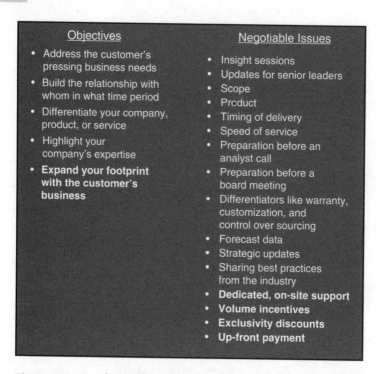

Figure 2.9: Typical Objectives and Issues in Customer Negotiations

competitor; low price does not create switching costs. If all you do is to reduce price, then all you do is not get paid a lot of money. As you think about expanding footprint in a customer's account, you want to consider how you can create barriers to switching from your company to someone else's (pre-payment, rebates, exclusivity, and embedded-ness), how you can know more about the customer's business than others (embeddedness and exclusivity), and how you can incent the customer to give you more work (volume incentives in the form of volume discounts and rebates). (See Figure 2.9.)

Maximizing Margin

Another objective in a customer negotiation would be to maximize margin. This objective relates to negotiable issues such as price, payment terms, customization of the product, level of service, and other typical issues that would impact the margin achieved. These are all critical issues that should certainly be included in the negotiation, but it is essential to ensure that these are not the only items discussed. (See

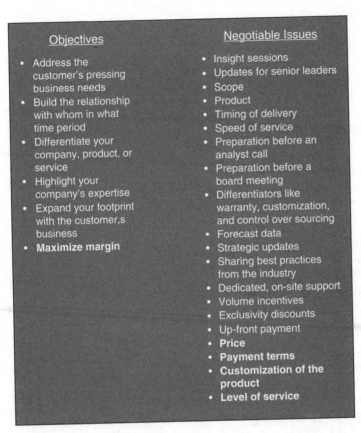

Objectives	Negotiable Issues
• Address the customer's pressing business needs • Build the relationship with whom in what time period • Differentiate your company, product, or service • Highlight your company's expertise • Expand your footprint with the customer,s business • **Maximize margin**	• Insight sessions • Updates for senior leaders • Scope • Product • Timing of delivery • Speed of service • Preparation before an analyst call • Preparation before a board meeting • Differentiators like warranty, customization, and control over sourcing • Forecast data • Strategic updates • Sharing best practices from the industry • Dedicated, on-site support • Volume incentives • Exclusivity discounts • Up-front payment • **Price** • **Payment terms** • **Customization of the product** • **Level of service**

Figure 2.10: Typical Objectives and Issues in Customer Negotiations

Figure 2.10). Too often, these more standard issues are the only ones included. This is a common but extremely costly mistake that makes you more likely to damage the relationship with the other side and less likely to get what you want. You are much more likely to maximize margin if you are addressing the customer's business needs, differentiating your product, and highlighting your company's expertise than if you are only negotiating price. It is vital to put the right issues on the table to achieve your goals.

Putting the Right Issues on the Table in All Negotiations

While the examples above described the objectives and related issues for a customer negotiation, the discipline of generating a list of objectives and related negotiable issues is essential in all negotiations. Four objectives that commonly exist in negotiations with ongoing relationships are the following:

1. Address the other side's pressing needs
2. Differentiate yourself, your product, or your service
3. Build the relationship with the other side
4. Maximize your own outcome

Whether you are negotiating with a supplier, a business partner, a potential acquirer, or negotiating for yourself in an employment situation, you want to keep these four objectives in mind. You may have additional intentions in specific negotiations, but these four objectives persist across all negotiations where you want to maximize your outcome and build the relationship at the same time. See the following box for more about how these four objectives apply when you are negotiating for yourself in employment situations.

NEGOTIATING FOR YOURSELF IN EMPLOYMENT SITUATIONS

People often ask me how to negotiate their salary, and I always tell them that they should never find themselves only negotiating salary. It is critical to put the right issues on the table when you are negotiating for yourself in employment situations—whether you are entertaining an offer with a potential new employer or discussing your role with your current company. You want to begin by listing your objectives for the negotiation and then, for every objective you have, you should put at least one or more negotiable issues on the table.

When you are negotiating for yourself in any type of employment situation, you want to focus on how you can address the employer's pressing business needs, differentiate yourself, build the relationship with the potential employer, and maximize your outcome. Begin your preparation by thinking hard about the company's goals and challenges:

1. What are the company's specific goals or your bosses' key objectives for the upcoming year?
2. How can you help your boss and team to achieve these objectives?

3. Do they need to develop new customers, grow revenue from existing customers, or establish a foothold in a new geography? Be specific about the company's objectives and the metrics your boss needs to achieve.

Put issues on the table to reflect how you can help the company and your boss to achieve these goals. For example, perhaps you can commit to expanding your days in the field, joining a professional organization to meet potential new customers, or increasing the time you spend at client locations. If the company's need is to establish a foothold in a new geography, perhaps you can offer to shift your hours to come in early three days a week to provide telephone coverage to support customers in this new location. Think about the company's needs and how you can help to address their challenges.

Also, consider how you are uniquely positioned to address these challenges. What are your differentiators and how can you translate these into negotiable issues? *It is essential to differentiate yourself in employment negotiations.* If you do not distinguish yourself, you cannot demonstrate how the company can do something for you that they do not need to do for everyone else at your level. Companies are often very concerned about establishing precedent when they negotiate with individual employees; they often are not constrained by what they can do for one employee, but they are very concerned about the precedent that their actions might establish. You must highlight how the company can do something for you without establishing a precedent. This is why it is so critical to highlight your unique differentiators and set yourself apart from others.

Imagine, for example, that one of the company's objectives is to expand business in South America, and you are fluent in Spanish and spent many years working in Chile and Argentina. You could offer to come into your office in Boston early several days a week to cover calls coming from South America ("because you are fluent in Spanish"). Remember too that you will want to vary the options around your differentiators perhaps by negotiating whether you would come into the office at 6:00 a.m., 6:30 a.m., or 7:00 a.m. to handle these calls. You could also negotiate whether you would do this two or three days a week, "because you are fluent in Spanish and can help the company to build this new market." You might also offer to conduct lunch and learns once a month or once a quarter for the sales team to focus on cultural differences between business in North and South America "because you have the unique experience of working in South America for many years." In order to achieve your objective of building your relationships with senior leaders in the company, you might offer to meet with some members of the leadership team to discuss the content that you would cover in these lunch and learn briefings.

Another key objective in an employment negotiation is to demonstrate that you are confident that your differentiators will help your company or your boss to achieve their objectives. The best issue you could add to the table to reflect this confidence would be a contingent, performance-based bonus that you will receive if you achieve the stated goals or deliver the agreed-upon metrics. In essence, you would be "betting" on your ability to achieve these goals and emphasizing your confidence. We will discuss this type of contingent agreement more fully in Chapter 6 and show you how to include it in your offer in Chapter 7, but for now, keep in mind that one of your objectives in an employment negotiation is often to stress your confidence in what you can achieve, and to do this, the issue you would put on the table is a specific performance-based bonus tied to these metrics.

Beginning with a list of your objectives and connecting each of these objectives to a negotiable issue is the first step in changing a salary negotiation into a broader discussion about your employment engagement.

Issue Matrix

Once you have considered your objectives and developed a list of negotiable items, you should lay out your issues on an Issue Matrix in order to ensure that you have the right issues on the table. The Issue Matrix considers the relative importance of each item to both parties. As you can see in Figure 2.11, the X-axis reveals what is important to you and the Y-axis focuses on what is important to the other side.

The figure shows four quadrants, with the three named quadrants being the critical ones. Consider the quadrant that is high on X and high on Y. These are items that are important to you and important to the other side. These are the *Contentious Issues* in the negotiation. Issues like price and payment terms will often be in this quadrant. You can

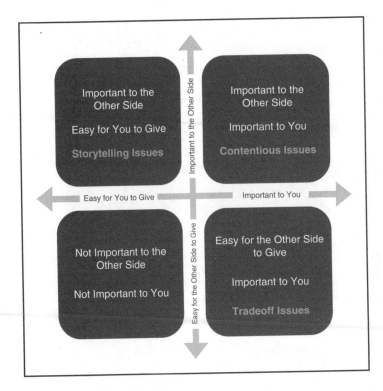

Figure 2.11: Issue Matrix

never avoid Contentious Issues; they will exist in every negotiation. However, you want to be certain that you do not only have Contentious Issues on the table because these will be the most difficult to negotiate. If you only have Contentious Issues on the table the discussion will likely be very heated and focus less on the other side's needs. Moreover, if you only have Contentious Issues on the table, every concession you make will cost you a great deal because everything you are discussing is incredibly valuable to you.

In fact, the most important items to include in any negotiation are the issues that are in the quadrant that is high on Y and low on X; these are the *Storytelling Issues*, as shown in Figure 2.11. These issues are important to the other side and easy, or not costly, for you to provide. Perhaps you even want to do these things. I do not suggest that the Storytelling Issues are the most important because I am nice or altruistic, but because Storytelling Issues allow you to claim more on the Contentious Issues and the Tradeoff Issues. Storytelling Issues also allow you

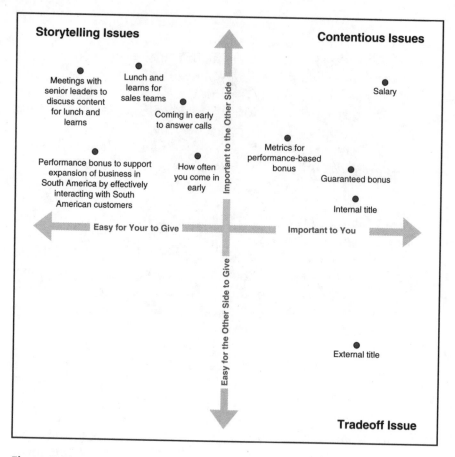

Figure 2.12: Issue Matrix for Example of Negotiating for Yourself

to create a rationale for your offer that focuses on the other side and the other side's interests. As we will learn in Chapter 6, it is essential to focus your rationale on the other side rather than on yourself, and Storytelling Issues will allow you to do this.

Your Storytelling quadrant in a customer negotiation will include the insight sessions and briefings for senior leaders, prep before analyst calls, and board meetings for the CEO and CFO, dedicated team, and all your differentiators. The Storytelling quadrant might also include a performance guarantee on a service level that you will achieve for a customer.

Tradeoff Issues are those that are important to you but less significant for the other side or not costly for them to provide. Tradeoff Issues might be as important to you as are some Contentious Issues. However, because they are less important to your counterpart than Contentious Issues, they are far easier to claim. In a customer negotiation, the Tradeoff quadrant might include the ability to use the customer's name or referrals that the customer will provide. You want to get more on Tradeoff Issues as you give up some on Contentious Issues, or as you give more on Storytelling Issues. If you do not put Storytelling Issues on the table, you have fewer tradeoffs to use to claim Contentious Issues and Tradeoff Issues.

You will notice that the fourth quadrant (low on X and low on Y) is not named. Issues that are not important to you or the other side are not very relevant in the negotiation. I suggest that you focus on the three critical quadrants as you build your plan for the negotiation.

While this Issue Matrix seems simple, many negotiators fall into a trap of only putting Contentious and Tradeoff Issues on the table. A great deal of research demonstrates that we are egocentric and focus largely on our own interests (Ross & Sicoly, 1979). This egocentrism causes us to focus on what's important to us and too often overlook issues that are important to the other side. This common trap leads us to miss many potential tradeoffs we could make that would allow us to get more in a negotiation. This mistake is made by experienced negotiators as well as by those who are more naïve.

I was once working with a group of investment banking partners and had all of them provide their objectives for client negotiations. They listed many different objectives—maximizing fees, ensuring the transaction closed, gaining referrals, and building their team's credentials. All these objectives would lead to Contentious or Tradeoff Issues being negotiated. However, they did not mention a single objective that would drive a Storytelling Issue.

Likewise, I was in front of the procurement executives for a Fortune 100 company and asked them to tell me their objectives for a negotiation with a supplier. They cited important imperatives like minimizing price, ensuring the supply was available on time, having the flexibility to reduce their commitment to the supplier if needed, being able to access more supply if demand required, and the customization of the materials being provided to meet their needs. All these objectives were very important to them, but all would have led to Contentious and Tradeoff Issues being put on the table. Even very experienced negotiators need to be reminded of the importance of negotiating the right issues, and to do this you have to reduce egocentric tendencies, know your objectives, focus on the other side, and develop Storytelling Issues that can be added to the discussion.

It is critical to review your Issue Matrix as you prepare to negotiate to make certain that you have the right issues on the table; in particular, you want to ensure that you have enough Storytelling Issues on the table to build a rationale that will focus on the other side's needs and allow you to get more on the Contentious and Tradeoff Issues. Next, I will discuss how to use an Issue Matrix to prepare for a negotiation that matters a great deal to you—negotiating with an employer or a potential employer regarding your own compensation package.

NEGOTIATING FOR YOURSELF IN EMPLOYMENT SITUATIONS

Remember that there is no such thing as a salary negotiation. You should never open a negotiation with only Contentious Issues on the table. You want to make certain that you have lots of Storytelling Issues included because this will help you secure more on the Contentious and Tradeoff Issues. For example, when negotiating for yourself, salary would be a Contentious Issue, while your differentiators that could help address the company's pressing business needs (such as your willingness to come in early to take calls from South America because you are fluent in Spanish, how many days a week you would do this, your willingness to conduct lunch and learns on cultural differences between North and South America, and meeting with senior leaders to discuss the content for these briefings) would all be in the Storytelling quadrant. A guaranteed bonus would be in the Contentious quadrant, but a performance bonus based on your ability to help the company expand business in South America by interacting with those customers on a weekly basis would be in the Storytelling quadrant. The metrics for this performance-based bonus might be in the Contentious quadrant, but your willingness to bet on your ability to interact effectively with these customers would be a Storytelling issue.

The Tradeoff quadrant might include issues such as your external title. While your internal title is often a Contentious Issue because of corporate policies and precedent concerns, your external title is often much simpler to negotiate. It is often easy to create a strong rationale for an elevated external title. For example, you may be able to secure the title of Chief Business Development Officer, South America, so that you will have the credibility to interact with CEOs of small companies in South America. Likewise, if you are being hired for a VP role in Human Resources, you may be able to secure the title of Chief Talent Officer so that you can credibly interact with senior candidates for your business. You may be a VP internally, but you might be able to secure a higher-level external title.

Ensuring that you have the right issues on the table will take the fear out of negotiating for yourself. We will continue to provide tips on negotiating for yourself in every chapter, but remember that the essential first step is to discuss the right issues. (See Figure 2.12.)

Summary

The first step in reducing your fear in a negotiation is to ensure that you have the right issues on the table. It makes sense that we are afraid to negotiate if we start with only one Contentious Issue on the table (such as price) or with a number of issues that are all contentious. A negotiation with only Contentious Issues will lead to a very difficult discussion where we are likely to damage our relationship with the other side and get relatively poor outcomes. No wonder we are afraid!

You can reduce this fear by spending time to ensure you have the right issues on the table. Think about your objectives for the negotiation and for your relationship with the other side in the short and long term. Remember that in any negotiation where you care about your relationship with the other side, you will have four common objectives:

1. To address the other side's pressing business needs
2. To build the relationship with the other side
3. To differentiate yourself, your company, or your product
4. To maximize your own outcome

You are far more likely to achieve the last objective if you remember the first three objectives and put the right issues on the table. For every objective you list, you should have at least one or more negotiable issues.

Once you have developed your list of objectives and their associated negotiable items, you want to analyze your list of issues on the Issue Matrix. In particular, you want to ensure that you have more Storytelling Issues than any other type of issue. Storytelling Issues will allow you to focus the rationale for your offer on the other side rather than yourself, and they will increase your ability to get more of what you want on Contentious and Tradeoff Issues.

As mentioned earlier, preparing for a negotiation involves putting the right issues on the table, doing the right analysis, and developing your plan. When you are ready to begin the analysis, you will want to consider your goal, your best outside option, and your bottom line. We will discuss each of these components in the following chapters.

3

Build Your BATNA

People are often afraid to negotiate because they fear that the other side will take advantage of them in the negotiation or force them to agree to something that is not in their best interests. This chapter will help you to eliminate this fear by building your power in the negotiation.

Your biggest source of power in any negotiation comes from your *Best Alternative to Negotiated Agreement (BATNA)* (Fisher, Ury, & Patton, 1981). Your BATNA is your best outside option; it is Plan B. Your BATNA reveals what are you going to do if you do not get an agreement with the other side. Your BATNA has nothing to do with the deal on the table; it is the other deal you will do if you do not complete this deal.

It is essential to build your BATNA before you begin any negotiation. If you are buying a house, you never want to fall in love with the house, or worse, let your spouse or partner fall in love with the house. You want to build your BATNA by identifying many potential houses that you might be willing to buy. If you are hiring an employee, you want to do a broad search so that you have other candidates you would hire if you did not hire a particular person. Just like you do not want to fall in love with a house, you do not want to fall in love with a candidate. The stronger your BATNA, the more power you will have in any negotiation.

Build Your BATNA Simultaneously

To maximize your power, you want to engage in *simultaneous BATNA development,* not *sequential BATNA development.* Too often, we explore one option and then, if it does not work out, we focus on developing another alternative; however, this limits our power. To maximize your power, you want to engage in simultaneous BATNA development, building your options at the same time, before you begin to negotiate, rather than one at a time.

For example, when renegotiating a commercial real estate leasing contract, you need to know where you would go if you did not stay in your current location. Have you sourced other office space? Typically, companies approach their existing landlord first and negotiate with them regarding the renewal. Companies tend to wait and see what type of deal they can get, and then if they don't like it, they seek out alternatives. But how will you know if you have a good deal if you do not know what other deal you could have had? You will optimize your power by first identifying other possible places before you approach the current landlord. It is critical to build BATNA simultaneously before you negotiate and to keep building and maintaining your BATNA throughout the negotiation.

The first question I always ask my clients when I am advising them on a negotiation is, "What is your BATNA: What will you do if you do not do this deal?" I was working with a CEO who was considering the potential sale of his company. When I asked about his BATNA, he said that if he did not sell to the strategic buyer who approached him, he probably would just continue to run the business himself. He pointed out that the potential buyer had approached him and that, prior to this, he was not planning to sell. It became obvious to me, though, that once liquidity was on the table, it was looking very attractive and he did not want to keep running the business himself. So I asked him again who would buy the company if the strategic buyer who approached him did not? He reiterated that he had no idea; he had not been looking for a buyer and had not talked to anyone else. I told him that before we had another conversation with the buyer who approached him, we were going to find out who else would buy his business. You need to build your BATNA simultaneously before you negotiate and continue to try to improve it while you are negotiating.

I was once working with the CEO of a restaurant company who was looking at potential locations in Miami to build one of his restaurants. I asked him if there was another property he was considering. He said, "Of course there is other property available, but look at this spot—it has great access to the highway, it has amazing signage, and look at the other tenants in the plaza." I asked again about other potential locations and he repeated, "Sure there are other spots, but look at this place—it is in the right neighborhood, it has awesome foot traffic, and it has incredible visibility from the road." I told him that before we went to speak to the landlord about this location, we were going to go find another location that got him this excited. You need to build your BATNA simultaneously, not sequentially.

This concept is very important when you are a purchaser of goods and services. Whether you work in procurement, run an IT department, or occasionally purchase services for your own home, you want to remember the importance of simultaneously building your BATNA. We often become very attached to our incumbent supplier and are reluctant to consider other alternatives. We are comfortable with the incumbent supplier and are certain about what they will do. This familiarity with this supplier creates an *incumbent advantage*. When I am a purchaser of goods or services, I want to try to reduce the incumbent advantage, but when I am the provider of the goods or services, I want to claim the incumbent advantage.

When I am the incumbent, I need to recognize that I never need to match a competitor's price; I am certain, I am known, and the buyer is comfortable with me, so I should be able to claim a higher price than other competitors. This is the incumbent advantage. Of course, if I am the purchaser of goods or services, I want to reduce this advantage by generating options and developing alternatives.

RFPs and RFQs

RFPs (Requests for Proposals) and RFQs (Requests for Quotes) are excellent tools for building your BATNA. I encourage my clients to view RFPs and RFQs as BATNA generation tools, but I stress that they are not purchasing tools. Rather than buying through the RFP process, you want to use competitive bidding processes to build options and then negotiate. When I teach CEOs of mid-cap and small-cap companies, I am often surprised by how many of them report that they have single-source suppliers and do not regularly use RFPs to build BATNA. A sole source supplier is risky; most obviously, the supplier can hold you hostage on price if you have no other alternatives. The risks go beyond pricing, though. Your sole supplier may not be motivated to provide innovative solutions or meet timelines because they do not feel any competitive pressure to serve you in these ways. I had one client who was complaining that their supplier was not delivering on time, but when I suggested that they shift the order to another supplier, they said they had no one else. Competition controls pricing, but it also ensures you get quicker timing of goods, innovation, and service. Additionally, depending on a single supplier can threaten the security of your supply chain because this supplier may have a shortage of supply, encounter a catastrophic event, or go out of business. If you only have one supplier, any of these events can shut down your production.

I encourage my clients to build their BATNA and avoid sole supplier relationships—except with their negotiation adviser, of course!

Even sophisticated companies who use RFPs on a regular basis often make mistakes that weaken the power they generate from their RFPs. One of the biggest mistakes that companies make is trying to purchase through the RFP rather than using the RFP as a BATNA-generation tool.

RFPs are excellent BATNA-generation tools. They have a number of other purposes as well. They focus the incumbent on the fact that there is competition, and they allow a buyer to learn more about the market: what is new, what kind of technology others are offering, and what is possible. They make you better informed about the range of possibilities and inform the incumbent that you have alternatives.

A second error occurs when companies claim to use RFPs but only send the bid to three suppliers. Whenever I see this, I suspect that the company is simply checking a box from procurement that says they are required to obtain three bids, and are not really viewing the RFP process as a BATNA-generation tool. I also know when I only see three bids that the buyer did not use the RFP process as a learning opportunity to investigate what else was available and to learn what others could do. I encourage my clients to use the RFP to generate a number of alternatives and then select three to five of these options to progress through to the negotiation phase.

The most costly error in an RFP process is when people use the bid from the supplier as a starting point for the discussion. They will carefully examine the submitted bid and respond by saying, "Your bid is too high," "Your bid is 20% higher than everyone else's," or "I need you to sharpen your pencil on your bid." All of these statements are problematic because they all allow the supplier to anchor the discussion and start the negotiation with their bid. You want to build your BATNA through the RFP and determine which set of suppliers you will advance to the negotiation phase. Then you want to take control of the negotiation and establish the starting point by making the first offer. You should never discuss the supplier's bid. Instead, you should highlight the intense competition the RFP process generated and the number of other suppliers who are interested in working with you. You want to use the RFP to highlight competition and then start the conversation.

Many companies focus too heavily on the initial bids from suppliers. Some companies extensively score these submissions and share these scores throughout the organization. I advise my clients to be very careful in scoring RFP responses and stress that the pricing submitted in an initial bid should never be scored, because this pricing has not been negotiated. I encourage my clients to do very light scoring of RFP responses; at this stage, purchasers should only be looking at whether the supplier can meet the desired threshold for goods, services, and timeline—or not. Reference checks should play a significant role in determining who to advance to the negotiation phase, and initially submitted prices should play no role at all.

I base my recommendation to avoid focusing on initially submitted pricing on the fact that in an RFP situation, the incumbent who knows they are facing competition will often submit the best pricing. The incumbent is bidding with certain information while all other bidders are facing some uncertainty in crafting their bids. Paying too much attention to the initially submitted bids contributes to the incumbent advantage. The goal of the RFP is to reduce the incumbent advantage, so initial bids should be scored on meeting the thresholds required for inventory, service, and timeline with a high weight for the references secured for each of the suppliers. Remember that at this phase, you are selecting who to advance to the negotiation round of the process, not from whom you will buy or how much you will pay.

Since the RFP is designed to generate alternatives, you do not want to design any rules around it that will limit your alternatives. When developing the RFP to send to potential suppliers, you do not want to restrict yourself to picking the lowest bidder or eliminating the highest bidder. Remember, at this phase, you are identifying options, not choosing providers.

Generating BATNA in Our Everyday Lives

We can all learn from the mistakes sophisticated companies make in RFPs and use the suggestions provided to improve our own interactions with suppliers, contractors, and other service providers, whether we are negotiating on behalf of our company or procuring suppliers to work on a project at our house.

Common Mistakes Sophisticated Companies Make in RFP Situations

1. Sending the RFP to only three suppliers
2. Sending the RFP to the same suppliers each time
3. Using the RFP as a buying tool, rather than a BATNA-generation tool
4. Creating restrictions around the RFP that reduce your flexibility, such as the highest bid is eliminated or the lowest bid wins
5. Spending too much time scoring the initial RFP responses
6. Sharing the initial bids—including pricing—with internal customers
7. Using the supplier's initial bid as the starting point for the negotiation

For example, I used all these ideas when I installed a pool at my house. My pool negotiation started with an internal negotiation between my husband and me because my husband hated swimming pools and I had wanted a pool since I was five years old. When I finally convinced my husband that we should install a swimming pool at our house, I sent an RFP to a number of different pool installers. I didn't know much about pools, so I used the RFP process to learn about the installers' offerings: what materials were being used, what kind of heater was most common, and what the difference was between the saltwater system and the traditional chlorine system. I sent the RFP to a wide variety of potential installers, even though there were four installers who controlled much of the market in my town. As we waited for the initial RFP responses, I checked the references of a number of installers. At the same time, I called the various installers to talk to them about the timeline for the project. We contacted them in early October because I wanted the pool to be completed by May 1. Each of the installers assured me that this deadline could absolutely be achieved.

Based on this research, I created the list of the three installers I would include in the negotiation round. Note that I picked them based on their references, not their bids. I did not pay much attention to their initial bids because these were nothing more than their starting points.

I then contacted the three I had advanced, saying that I was "excited by the number of installers who wanted to put in our pool." I suggested that "this was probably because our pool would be the first pool put in the neighborhood in a number of years" and that "everyone recognized that the neighborhood had a lot of new young families, so whoever installed the first pool would have a big advantage in getting the contracts for the rest of the pools on the street." Given this situation, I suggested that installing my pool would provide tremendous publicity for a pool installer.

Since there are no advertisements or billboards allowed in a five-mile radius from my house, I suggested that if I allowed the installer to park their large truck in my front driveway, I should probably get the pool installed for free because their large truck would provide unprecedented signage opportunities. I said that, "although there were many other companies interested in installing the pool, I was interested in working with them but that I needed their offer to look like X." The offer I made included the heater, saltwater system, warranty, price, and a timeline for the completion of the project. The timeline was very important because I wanted to make certain the pool would be ready to swim in by May 1, which, as I mentioned, all the installers had assured me initially was absolutely possible. Have you ever worried that a supplier may be over-promising, though? A great way to test this is to use a contingency in your offer, essentially asking the other side to bet on what they are telling you. Given this, my offer also included a contingency on the timeline. I reiterated the importance of having the pool completed by May 1, and I said that for every day that the pool was not completed after May 1, there would be a $500 per day deduction from the final price.

Despite the fact that all of the suppliers initially stated that my timeline was feasible, when I called each of them to make my offer, one of them pushed back on the timeline and expressed significant concerns about meeting the May 1 deadline. In fact, this installer never called me back after he heard the offer I made. I do not think that this contractor was confident that he could finish the pool by October, let alone May. Another installer said that he would be interested in building the pool and would be willing to accept a contingency on the deadline but said he thought the penalty should be $50 per day rather than $500. I asked him if this was because he did not think he would finish it on time. He assured me that this was not the case and said that there were just so many factors outside of his control that could cause a delay, such as the weather and other contractors. He said that he would be willing to make the penalty $500 a day if I excluded any delays caused by the weather or other contractors. I told him that I did not understand what would cause a delay besides the weather and other contractors. The third installer selected from the initial round responded very differently to the bet on the timeline and said "no problem at all." Clearly, he was confident that he could complete the pool on time. It turned out that this contractor had the best references of all of the respondents. As you might expect, this installer's initial bid also included the highest price. This did not matter to me, though, because I was not discussing his offer. I was making the starting offer, focusing on the competition, the tremendous interest others had in installing the pool, and including a starting price that was lower than any price I had received from an installer.

I would never lie and say that I received this offer from someone; instead I made the offer and said that "I would like their offer to look like this." You should never be dissuaded by a high offer from a particular supplier because this initial RFP response is simply their pre-negotiated offer. You should make the final decision based on the offers you secure after you negotiate, not on the initial bids submitted.

In my pool purchase, I went into the negotiation phase with my offer and anchored the starting point for our discussions. I made a multi-issue offer that focused on the price, deadline, and many other elements. I never spoke about the installer's initial bid, and I never asked the installers to take something off or sharpen their pencils. Any reference to their original responses would authenticate their bids. A huge advantage in an RFP is information asymmetry. You know what every supplier bid, but they do not. If you go back and talk about their bids, you are implying that their bids were reasonable. Even if you communicate that their bid was higher than everyone else, you have also communicated that their bid is a realistic starting point for your discussions. You should never discuss their bids.

Build BATNA and Maintain BATNA

One of my clients is the procurement department for a large global company. They found themselves in a negotiation with their single biggest supplier who represented the most significant line item in their budget. The supplier was not only expensive, but also had terrible customer service, was often late on deliverables, and made errors in their work. The senior vice president for Procurement asked me to help his team prepare for this very high stakes negotiation. The first question I asked the team was "What is your BATNA?" They responded by saying that there was no alternative and insisted that no one else across the globe could provide the data that this company provided. I asked them if there were suppliers who could service certain regions instead of the entire globe. They said that some other companies could provide data by region but that there was absolutely no one else who could provide the data across the globe. I encouraged my client to develop the RFP with a focus on the data by region and by product rather than focusing on the entire globe. I said that it was critical that the incumbent supplier recognize that there was competition and that other suppliers could do the work.

Once the RFP was sent, the company noticed that the incumbent supplier's behavior improved dramatically. The supplier was on time with deliverables, their work was better than before, and they were much more responsive than in the past. My client was delighted, thanked me for my work, and asked me to send them my invoice.

I stressed to them that we were not finished, though. They were surprised and reiterated that their incumbent supplier was now "behaving," and they were so happy that they had done the RFP. I repeated that we were not finished yet and added, "You have to cut off a thumb." They replied, "What thumb? We do not want to cut off a thumb." I explained that we had to award some piece of business to someone else; if we gave all of the business back to the incumbent, we would only reinforce their perception that my client had no other alternatives. The client was shocked. They were happy with the incumbent supplier now and did not want to make a change.

They also mentioned that they had scored the initial bids and shared the bids and scoring with their internal customers who owned the business. These buyers wanted to continue with the incumbent supplier, especially since the incumbent was the cheapest alternative. Now I was shocked. I had no idea that they had shared the bids with their internal customers. I asked them if they had really shared the initial RFP responses and they said, "Of course we shared the responses. We scored them and shared them in their entirety with the internal buyers." This was clearly a mistake. The initial RFP responses are nothing more than that—initial responses. I noted that the team could have shared the parameters of the bids with the internal team to get them to score the suppliers' approaches or capabilities, but that prices should never have been shared. They asked how the internal customer could have selected the supplier they wanted if they did not see the price. I reminded them that the goal is never to select the "winner" through the RFP process. The RFP process is a BATNA-generation tool, not a negotiation tool; the objectives are to create competition, learn about alternatives, gain information, and select who should advance to the negotiation phase—not to select a winner.

The prices the team shared were pre-negotiation prices, so they had no meaning and could not be used to predict what you might be able to negotiate. As I explained, if they were sharing pre-negotiated prices, what function was the procurement department going to play? Their job was to negotiate. As I said before, the incumbent will often come in with the best price; the incumbent has insider knowledge and certainty on costs and margins, so they may have the best initial bid price. This does not matter, though, because none of the initial bid prices are relevant. The negotiated offers you generate can certainly be scored and shared with internal buyers, but the initial bids should not.

I explained that since they had shared the bids, their job would be more challenging because they would need to have the internal negotiation with their buyers to convince them why they needed to consider awarding a piece of the business to another supplier. I finally talked them into this, and they went back to the internal buyers to negotiate. After that discussion, they negotiated with a number of the suppliers. In the end, my client did not just cut off a thumb; they cut off a thumb and two fingers, awarding 33% of the business to other suppliers. In the beginning, this client had said there was no one else in the world who could do the work but, in the end, they awarded one-third of the business to other suppliers.

My client's procurement department won a significant corporate award that year for the very first time. They received the award based on a number of factors. The company definitely appreciated the significant cost reduction the team had negotiated, but the procurement team received even more credit for the service improvement, responsiveness, and innovation that they drove through this process.

There is power in creating competition, so I recommend that my clients build and maintain BATNA. I tell my procurement clients all the time that they are the BATNA generators. No one else in the company may want to build BATNA for suppliers, but the procurement and supply chain groups need to focus on this objective. Engineers may like to use the current supplier with whom they are comfortable, and the plant manager and brand manager want to use the incumbent they can rely on. Often no one else has a desire to build options, but the BATNA generators in procurement and supply chain need to pursue this mission.

Another one of my clients is the procurement department of a Fortune 10 company. The executives in this department are a savvy group of negotiators who are comfortable using power; however, they would always say that their most difficult negotiations were the internal negotiations they needed to have to convince their internal buyers to consider alternatives. When I first started to work with this client, I was stunned by how many sole source contracts they had in place. The procurement executives must be the BATNA generators who are constantly striving to develop and maintain alternatives. When my Fortune 10 procurement executives would try to build options, they often encountered pushback from the engineers, plant managers, and brand managers in their company. The procurement group would stress that the supplier could raise the price and insist that alternative suppliers would offer a better price, but the internal buyers seemed unfazed. I pointed out to the procurement team that because these engineers and other managers were not evaluated on the price being paid, price was largely irrelevant to them. The other leaders in the business were being measured on the work getting done and preferred the certainty of using the same suppliers over and over again. I encouraged the procurement team to highlight the risks of a sole supplier, suggesting that others in the company might care about the delays and poor service that could result from a supplier with no competition. I suggested they also stress how a single supplier threatens a company's entire supply chain, particularly if the supplier is a critical one. If this single supplier has a catastrophic event, such as a hurricane or flood near a facility, or goes out of business, the company would have no supply. The engineers and other leaders in a business may care much more about these threats than about the price being charged and may be convinced that the company should build and maintain BATNA.

If possible, you want to use competitive bidding to build options and then maintain options by splitting the work between two or more suppliers. As an analogy, I often tell my construction clients that they should not have one painter on a project, but rather, they should have one painter for the even-numbered floors and a different painter for the odd-numbered floors. This way they have the ability to hold the painters accountable because it is clear who painted each floor, but at the same time they maintain competition and have readily available alternatives.

When we installed our pool, we sent an RFP to a number of masons to do the stonework on the patio and to build a stone wall around the backyard. I followed all of the strategies I detailed earlier, but in my negotiations with the three finalists, I could never get the mason with the best offer on the hardscape to provide the best price on the wall, or the one with the best offer on the wall to provide the best price on the hardscape. I underscored that I would happily award the work to two different masons, but then they would never be able to show off the project to potential clients because they would be showing off their competitor's work. In the end, I hired one mason for the wall and a different mason for the hardscape. I must admit on this one-time project, it was not my intent to maintain BATNA (as it was a short-term project, and I did not think that I would have a future need for a mason). However, it was fabulous to have this competition. Having two different competitive masons on site every day resulted in built-in quality control. Every morning when the masons and their teams arrived on site, the first thing they would do was inspect the other mason's work from the prior day. They would point out every glitch and flaw. I have a curve in my wall that is apparently hard to achieve (I know nothing about masonry, but this is what I have been told). When people see the wall, they always ask me how I got the mason to do this. Of course, I did not get the mason to do it—the other mason did!

Therefore, I encourage you to build BATNA and maintain BATNA. Companies often tell me that they want to give the work to a single supplier so that they can secure the advantage of scaling their purchase and drive volume discounts. Clearly, volume discounts are an excellent thing to obtain, but you always want to remember that having a strong BATNA is the biggest source of power and will drive more discounts than anything else. Certainly, it may be advantageous to use five suppliers rather than fifteen to obtain a volume discount—but having one supplier instead of three will decrease your power significantly.

I observed this in a very direct way a few years ago. I had a CEO client who was obsessed about having his team negotiate well. He insisted that everyone in the company be trained in negotiation and that his team use the strategies in all of their customer and purchasing negotiations. The CEO also had every negotiation plan reviewed by a more senior leader based on different thresholds so that the team was both trained and held accountable.

The company was a relatively small public company that negotiated with big telecom providers and was wildly successful in their negotiations with customers and suppliers. My client was later acquired by a much larger public company. When the acquiring company announced the deal to the street, they highlighted how there would be many synergies. They argued that the small company would benefit from the deals negotiated by the large public company because of the "buying power" the large company could provide. In fact, though, what was revealed during the integration was that my client, the small company, had much better prices negotiated in every single area than the large company had achieved with all of their "buying power," including superior prices on shipping, telephone services, audit, tax work, and everything else. This example demonstrates that the power of BATNA and good negotiation strategy can exceed the buying power associated with volume. This is another example of why you want to build BATNA and maintain BATNA.

On another occasion, I was working with a company selecting their shipping supplier. They were debating whether to use FedEx or UPS. I suggested that they use both. I proposed that they split the country and use UPS for half the country and FedEx for the other half. This way, they would have relationships established with both suppliers, create a sense of competition to ensure the highest quality service was maintained, and reduce the barriers to making a change if a deterioration in service required this. There is no better way to ensure that you have excellent service, great innovation, and quick timing than to create a sense of competition. You want to build this sense of competition by building your BATNA and maintaining your BATNA for your advantage.

Building BATNA as a Seller

We have been discussing building your BATNA as a purchaser, but the concept of BATNA development is also important when you are selling services or goods. In these situations, your BATNA is often your pipeline; who will you sell to if not this party, or who will you do work for if not this client? Focusing on footprint expansion with existing clients and developing relationships with senior leaders at potential clients will help you to build your BATNA. You want to focus on developing your pipeline and making it as strong as possible. This is also true when you are selling your own talents in an employment situation. Please see the following box to learn how to build your BATNA in employment situations.

NEGOTIATING FOR YOURSELF IN EMPLOYMENT SITUATIONS

What is your BATNA when you are negotiating with an employer? Your BATNA is the other job you would take if you did not have this job. Clearly, when you are securing a new job, it is advantageous to get as many offers as possible. I always encourage my students at Kellogg to continue to engage in recruiting after they have secured an offer from an employer. I remind them that their BATNA will be their biggest source of power in their negotiations with employers and encourage them to generate as strong a BATNA as possible before they begin to negotiate. Employers like to hire people who have other offers and the inferred value of candidates increases when others want to hire them. For all of these reasons, I highly recommend that people build their BATNA when looking for new jobs and that they try to generate as many options as possible before they begin to negotiate.

Many people also suggest that once you are in a role you should constantly be improving your BATNA by securing outside offers. There is research suggesting that you will get paid more if you have other employment offers (Gallo, 2016). However, if you are constantly pursuing other offers, at some point your employer may suggest that you take one of these. Also, if you pass on many offers, you may not be able to secure an offer when you need one in the future. There are times in a person's career when they should definitely get outside offers, and I want them to maintain their ability to secure offers at these key moments, such as when an associate at a law firm is being considered for partner, when a person is up for a big promotion, or when someone is very dissatisfied in their role and the company is not responding to their requests for a change. In these cases, securing an outside offer is essential, and you do not want past behavior in securing and passing on offers to negate your ability to generate offers at these key points. Although I do not encourage people to get an outside offer every year to build their BATNA, I do suggest that they always know where they would be working if they were not in their current role. Rather than constantly securing outside offers, I encourage people to put their energy into developing and harnessing their networks to generate interest in them. It is key to always know where you would work if you did not have your current job. This BATNA not only gives you power when you negotiate, it also gives you the ability to maintain your ethical standards.

People often feel "forced" to engage in unethical behavior because they are afraid that they will lose their job if they do not do what is asked. When you have other alternatives, though, you can choose how you will behave. BATNA gives you power in negotiations and in making choices about your own behavior. You are much less likely to feel forced to do something if you have robust outside alternatives. Your BATNA is your strongest source of power in any negotiation, and it allows you to maintain your ethical standards, so leverage your network to know about opportunities, have people interested in you, and know where you would be working if you were not in your current role.

Summary

Your BATNA is your biggest source of power, so you want to ensure that you are building it. Your BATNA is not your only source of power, though. If you are engaged in a two-party negotiation, other sources of power include information, time, and ratification. We discussed the power of information in the last chapter; the more you know about the other side's interests, priorities, and challenges, the more power you will have as you approach the negotiation. Likewise, the better that you understand your own priorities and preferences, the more power you will have as well.

Another source of power is time; a negotiator who is in a hurry loses power to the other side. The challenge is that sometimes you really do have a deadline, such as the end of the quarter or the year. When time is a factor to you, you want to ensure that it is a factor to the other side as well, so that you don't lose power. I often advise my clients to make time matter to the other side by offering some element of the offer that is time-bound, such as, "If we can get this settled by the end of this month, I can guarantee that you can continue with the team that you have on site. This team is in tremendous demand, though, so if we cannot agree by then, there is a chance they would be assigned to another client—but I would secure a new team for you." Some clients try to offer a discount that is time-bound, but I do not encourage them to do this because I think it is hard to maintain credibility with offers like this. It is likely that when the customer comes to you the month after the stated deadline, you will still offer the discount and lose credibility. On the other hand, if you use an issue like the guarantee of the ongoing team, you can credibly state that the team is still available if needed. The key is to try to neutralize time pressure by making it matter to the other side when it matters to you.

A fourth source of power is ratification. This occurs when you limit your authority in the negotiation by saying that you have to check with someone or that you do not have the authority to agree to anything more. Ratification is used at the end of a negotiation as a closing strategy, and we will discuss it in much more detail in Chapter 9.

If you are engaged in a multiparty negotiation, there is an additional source of power in the coalitions you build with others. Though there are other sources of power in negotiations, your BATNA is always your biggest power source. There is no stronger power than having an exceptional alternative. This chapter emphasized the need to build your BATNA simultaneously rather than sequentially, and it explained how to do this. Your BATNA is also the single biggest determinant of your reservation point, or your bottom line, which will be discussed in the next chapter.

4

Define Your Reservation Point

One reason that people are often afraid to negotiate is because they are worried that they will lose the deal. In Chapter 3, we discussed building your BATNA, which is your best outside option for the negotiation. Your BATNA will provide you with your biggest source of power in any negotiation. By developing a strong outside alternative, you can reduce your fear of losing the deal.

Your BATNA is also critical because it drives your *reservation point*. Your reservation point is your bottom line; beyond this point, you would prefer to walk away with an impasse rather than accepting an agreement. Knowing your reservation point will reduce your fear that you will accept a poor outcome, or take a deal when you should have walked away.

Your BATNA vs. Your Reservation Point

Your reservation point defines the worst outcome that you would be willing to accept. Your reservation point is determined by your BATNA plus or minus any idiosyncratic factors that make you prefer one option over another.

Consider, for example, that you are negotiating with your landlord regarding your lease for the coming year. You know that you need to develop your BATNA, so you visit a number of other buildings and find alternative apartments. Your favorite of these is a nearby apartment you are confident you can get for $2,100 a month. Your current landlord has stated that your rent will be $2,300 a month for the coming year. While your BATNA is an apartment for $2,100, this is not necessarily your reservation point. Your current apartment has a view of the lake and has a walk-in shower, two features that you really like. You also think it would be a hassle to move, so you decide that if you can convince your landlord to rent your current apartment to you for $2,200 a month or less, you would stay in your existing place. Whereas your BATNA is the alternative apartment at $2,100, your reservation point is $2,200 because of the features that you like more in your present place, and the effort involved in moving. Your reservation point is determined by your BATNA, plus or minus idiosyncratic factors such as these.

In this chapter, we will discuss how to create a Scoring Tool to ensure that your reservation point is determined across the whole package of issues—location, view of the lake, walk-in shower, moving effort, and price—rather than being based on price alone.

The Importance of Knowing Your Reservation Point

You always need to know your reservation point because you must know when to walk away. You do not want to accept an agreement that is worse than your reservation point. Moreover, you also need to know when you should not walk away. An agreement that is better than your reservation point may not be what you wanted to achieve and may fall quite short of your ambition, but it may be much better for you than having an impasse.

It is essential to know the point at which you would walk away because there is often a lot of pressure on you to agree. The other side may be talking about how much time has been spent on the deal and how long the two of you have worked together; you may have people on your own side stressing that you should "not lose this deal." If you do not know your reservation point, you may agree to a deal that is worse for you than if you had walked away.

Since your BATNA determines your reservation point, the more attractive your BATNA is, the more attractive your bottom line will be. You want to work hard to build your BATNA by simultaneously generating alternative options, as we discussed in the previous chapter. Building your BATNA will allow you to optimize your reservation point.

An Individual's Reservation Point vs. the Company's Reservation Point

It is important to recognize that an individual negotiator's BATNA may not be the same as the BATNA for the company they represent. For example, consider the BATNA of a salesperson selling bottled water to Kroger, a large supermarket chain. If the salesperson responsible for the Kroger account only has the Kroger account, he would have very weak BATNA. If he does not sell the 16-ounce case to Kroger, he may not receive his annual commission. He may be desperate to close the Kroger deal; he has very weak BATNA, and so he has a low reservation point and would be happy to close the deal, regardless of the price Kroger pays. On the other hand, the bottled water company has much stronger BATNA. If the company does not sell to Kroger, they could sell the 16-ounce bottle cases to other large chains, such as Albertsons, Costco, or Target. During warm weather months, it may be challenging to meet the demand for 16-ounce cases, so the company may have a very strong BATNA while the individual salesperson does not. Because the company has a strong BATNA, the company's reservation point is much higher than that of the individual salesperson.

The national sales manager does not want the salesperson to craft a bad deal with Kroger because the company has strong alternatives to sell the product elsewhere. This situation is common and may lead to conflict between the salesperson and sales leadership. Often, leadership will attribute the salesperson's desire to close what they perceive as a lousy deal to the salesperson being "soft" or "too focused on the customer." These attributions are incorrect, though. What is really happening here is that the BATNA, and thus the reservation point, of the salesperson and the leadership team are different.

It is critical in situations such as this that the company's reservation point provides the bottom line. Although this may disappoint the salesperson, the company will be better off focusing on its own BATNA and reservation point, rather than an individual salesperson's perceived reservation point. This is why it is important to ensure that sales teams are limited in the lowest offer they are allowed to negotiate, and that they need to ask sales leadership to approve any offer outside these boundaries.

Determining Your Reservation Point Across All Issues

Your reservation point, however, should never be based on price alone. Your BATNA involves many dimensions which need to be included in defining your reservation point. Imagine that you are leasing office space in a beautiful building in San Francisco overlooking the Bay; your BATNA is the other space you would lease if you did not rent this space. You cannot compare the two on price per square foot alone, though. This space has a view of the Bay, with great signage opportunities and a price of $350 per square foot, whereas your alternative has no view and poor signage options—but it has the ability for you to expand, easy access to public transportation, and is priced at $300 per square foot. You cannot compare the two alternatives based on price alone, and you would not want to establish your reservation point based purely on price.

To ensure a focus on the entire package of issues I encourage my clients to create a *scoring tool*. This tool allows a negotiator to quantify all of the issues in the negotiation and establish a reservation point across the whole package of items (Raiffa, 1982). Without a scoring tool, a negotiator may become obsessed with the single most quantified issue and lose focus on the rest of the package. For example, when we do not have a scoring tool, we focus on price per square foot in a commercial real estate deal, on salary in employment negotiations, and on sales price with customers. Even expert negotiators tend to fall into the trap of focusing on the single, most quantified issue. A scoring tool helps you to avoid this trap.

TRAPS EXPERT NEGOTIATORS ENCOUNTER

Even expert negotiators get trapped.

1. Negotiating the wrong deal—negotiating what is standard or typical rather than putting the right issues on the table
2. **Focusing primarily on highly quantified issues**

Scoring Tools

When you are developing a *scoring tool*, you can decide to use any metric that you would like to quantify your negotiation issues: you could use points, currency, or other ROI measures relevant to your organization. Of course, you need to use the same metric for all of the issues. There is one caution I would provide when you are using currency in your scoring tool, though: often when you use currency, issues that are naturally quantified in terms of currency become disproportionately weighted in the scoring tool. For example, if you are creating a scoring tool for an employment negotiation, the issue of salary is already in dollars, but title, location, and promotion opportunities are not. If the salary is $200,000, it may get over-weighted in your analysis even though the most important issue to you is your ability to secure a future promotion. If you are struggling to get the right value on the non-currency issues, I would recommend using a different metric, such as points, in your tool.

There are six steps to creating a scoring tool (Raiffa, 1982):

1. Develop your list of objectives.
2. Identify at least one negotiable issue for every objective.
3. Fractionate the issues—break the issues down into smaller issues.
4. Prioritize the issues.
5. Weight the issues by dividing 100% across the issues.
6. Assign a value to each option within each issue. This value will then be multiplied by the weight of the issue to generate the score for the option negotiated for each issue.

I will use a personal example of mine to illustrate the power of a scoring tool and the steps required to create one. This negotiation occurred when I was hiring a nanny to care for my two boys; they are now grown young men, 19 and 24 years of age, but this favorite example nicely demonstrates how to build a scoring tool. If you have ever hired a babysitter or child care provider, you know that the typical discussion revolves around price per hour. My objectives in this negotiation, though, were much broader than wanting to settle on a rate per hour; my objectives were to have long-term, high-quality care for my two sons in a stimulating, loving environment. I also cared about a long-term arrangement because I learned early on that the costs of switching caregivers were very painful to me and my boys.

I also wanted to address the potential nanny's needs and to differentiate our family as a choice employer, so that a nanny would want to work for us versus someone else. Clearly, price needed to be negotiated, but that alone was not enough to achieve all of my critical objectives. Remember that the first step in a negotiation is to make a list of your objectives; then, for every objective that you have, you should have at least one, if not more than one, negotiable issue.

For the objective of long-term care, I thought I could add in some issues that created stickiness. I added vacation time (it could increase the longer the nanny was with me), health benefits, and dental benefits (this negotiation was completed prior to US health reform). I thought that these issues would also likely address the pressing needs of my potential nanny.

I wanted to hire a highly qualified individual who was passionate about education. Such a person might be seeking to improve their development opportunities and future employment possibilities. To address these needs, I added the option to pay for the nanny to obtain a master's degree in education. While doing so would address my potential nanny's needs for development and future options, it would also address my objective for high quality and my objective for length of employment, because I was offering to pay for one course per semester—making the overall degree an 8- to 10-year commitment. I knew that once the nanny completed her (at this point in time, all of the candidates who responded to my advertisement for the role were women) master's degree, she would likely want to obtain another role, but I thought I could keep her for many years while she completed her degree. By the time she finished her studies, my children would be older and would not need a nanny's care. The reason I chose a master's degree in education, and not just any master's program, is that it ensured I was able to hire someone who was passionate about education, which I thought would add quality to my boys' environment.

The option of a higher degree was also a superb sorting mechanism. I was hiring during a time of economic downturn, and I did not want to hire someone who did not have a passion for education, or someone who would leave for another type of job when the economy improved.

This would threaten my objective of long-term care, so I wanted to identify candidates with a sincere interest in education; the option to pursue an advanced degree helped me do this.

I live in a high "nanny competition" area of Chicago's North Shore, where people go nanny shopping at the park and play dates are sometimes staged nanny interviews. If I had an agreement that focused solely on my nanny's rate per hour, my objective of long-term care would be threatened. After all, other parents could offer more per hour, and I might lose my nanny. From my perspective, the hourly rate, benefits, and master's degree all cost me money, but in a highly competitive nanny area, providing an educational benefit was a way to offer the nanny more than money and differentiate our family as an employer of choice. Having issues like the master's degree and benefits on the table would make it more difficult for someone to hire away my nanny and would make the agreement one that better satisfied both of our interests. (See Table 4.1).

Once I crafted the list of issues for each of the objectives, the second step was to *fractionate* the issues. You want to try to break the issues down into smaller elements. Too often, we negotiate issues at the big bucket level. We negotiate something such as timing as though it is one issue rather than breaking it down to find underlying sub-issues. When we do this, we often miss differences in the preferences of the two parties. For example, an accounting firm may be negotiating with a client on the timing of a project, and each side may have significant differences in their views. But the timing of the project should not be one issue; timing should be fractionated into the numerous sub-issues that underlie overall timing, such as how quickly the firm can start the work, what the deadline is for completion, whether the work can be initiated and returned to later or whether it needs to be completed in a continuous time block, the time of year, and the overall duration

Table 4.1: Objectives and Issues in My Nanny Negotiation

Objectives	Issues
■ Addressing the nanny's pressing needs ■ Long-term care for children ■ High-quality care for children ■ Differentiating our family as a choice employer ■ Building a strong relationship with the nanny	■ Hourly rate ■ Vacation time ■ Health benefits ■ Dental benefits ■ Pay for nanny's master's degree in education

of the project. When the conversation focuses simply and vaguely on "timing," the two parties may miss critical differences in their preferences. The firm may be very focused on the time of year because they have busy seasons and less busy seasons, while the client may be very focused on duration; the client may be happy to have the work done at another time of the year if it means that the overall amount of time on site with the project will be shorter. It is very important to break an issue down and identify underlying issues. Too often, we negotiate at the big bucket level, and when we do not agree, we simply compromise. You should never compromise before you fractionate the issues.

As an example, consider the topic of vacation time in the negotiation with my nanny. On this single issue, my nanny and I had opposing preferences since she wanted a lot of time off and I wanted control over the schedule. If I gave her a day off, I would lose control over the schedule. So, on this single issue, we have opposing preferences. But we can fractionate this issue into two sub-issues: number of days off and who chooses the days. Here, we have very different preferences. My nanny wanted to have a lot of days off, but she did not care much about which days they were. On the other hand, there are many days off I could give to my nanny as long as I could select the days based on our family schedule; she could have two weeks at the holidays, two weeks at Spring Break, and four weeks in the summer. In total, my nanny could have up to eight weeks off if I selected all of the days, but if I did not pick the days, I would not even want her to have four days off because I did not want to lose control of the schedule. If we compromised on the single issue of vacation time, she might get seven days off with me picking four of them and my nanny selecting three of the days. But this would clearly be suboptimal: she would get more, and I would get more, if we fractionated the issues. You should never compromise until you fractionate the issues and identify the sub-issues.

Once you have identified all of the issues, you are ready to progress to the fourth step which is to prioritize the items. You should rate the issues from the least important to the most important. But it is not enough simply to prioritize the issues; you must go one step further.

The fifth step is to weight the issues. You want to allocate 100% across the items. How much more important is your most important issue than your second most important one? Is your most important issue worth 35% and the second most important worth 33%, or is your most important issue worth 40% and your second most important worth 20%?

Now you are ready for the final step: to identify the options for each issue and value each of the options. This value will then be multiplied by the weight of the issue to generate the score for the option negotiated for each issue. Once this is in place, you can use your scoring tool to evaluate your BATNA. This will help you to define your reservation point.

Your BATNA never looks exactly like the deal on the table, so you want to value your BATNA across the entire package of issues, and your scoring tool allows you to do this; in addition, it helps you identify priorities and evaluate different tradeoffs. Without a scoring tool, you may become overly focused on highly quantified issues and other very salient items, ignoring the rest of the package. A scoring tool will help to ensure that you maintain a package focus. This is essential in every negotiation, including a negotiation for yourself.

NEGOTIATING FOR YOURSELF IN EMPLOYMENT SITUATIONS

We have been discussing employment negotiations in each of the chapters. You already know that when you are negotiating for yourself, you should ensure that you have the right issues on the table. (It should never be a salary negotiation but rather an employment discussion.) You need to focus on addressing the employer's pressing business needs, differentiating yourself, and highlighting how an agreement with you does not establish precedent for others. You also want to strengthen your BATNA and be aware of your options. Likewise, it is very important to assess your reservation point.

Your BATNA is the single biggest determinant of your reservation point; your reservation point should be determined by your BATNA plus or minus any idiosyncratic factors that make you prefer one option over another. For example, if you are negotiating a potential new job with a different company, your BATNA is the package that you presently get from your current employer. While your BATNA drives your reservation point, your reservation point may be slightly different than your current package. You may think that if you take the new job, you will have to work really hard to prove yourself, build capabilities, and establish new relationships. Thus, you may assess that while your BATNA is your current package, your reservation point is your current package plus 20%. On the other hand, you may be really frustrated in your current role and dislike your boss. In this case, your BATNA is still your current package, but your reservation point might be your current package minus 10%.

It is critical to know your BATNA and to assess your reservation point. Often, people become very frustrated by something at work and may quit their job without considering their BATNA or analyzing their reservation point. Likewise, people may agree to take an offer that they later regret because it was actually worse than their reservation point.

It is also essential to have a scoring tool when you are negotiating for yourself so that you do not become obsessed by highly quantified issues (such as salary) or very salient issues. An example of the tendency to focus on salient issues rather than the entire package comes from an experience with one of my former Kellogg MBA students. This student was incredibly talented with a superb background, and he had a lot of success in the recruiting process. He received six employment offers, and he asked me for assistance in negotiating his offer. I was more than happy to help him, and told him, as I tell all my students, that the price of admission for my assistance was a well-developed scoring tool. He said that he would work on it and get back to me. I ran into him a few weeks later and asked him if he was still interested in meeting with me. He said that he was still working on his scoring tool. A few weeks passed, and I asked him the same question again. He told me that he did not need help anymore because he had already accepted his offer. I asked him which offer he had selected. I knew that he had just had a baby, and he had told me in our initial meeting that his single most important issue was spending time with his new child. He also had geographic preferences, mentioning that he would prefer to be in the San Francisco Bay Area because he and his wife enjoyed hiking and other outdoor activities.

He had one consulting offer and five corporate offers. The only offer he had in San Francisco was the consulting offer, and he decided to accept it because it was in San Francisco. The firm he went with has a reputation for Monday to Thursday travel, and he was working in an industry specialization that was not found in the Bay Area. So, of course, although he took the role to be in San Francisco, he was not actually going to be in San Francisco four days out of every week.

Moreover, he had said his most important priority was to be home with his new baby every evening by a reasonable time, yet he committed to a role where he would travel for four nights every week.

When I spoke to him a few weeks before graduation, he seemed anxious about the choice he had made and was very concerned about the travel and the time away from his young son. He made his decision based on the very salient issue of geographic location and overlooked the rest of the package. Had he created and used a scoring tool, he would have avoided this trap and steered clear of a painful mistake. Scoring tools allow us to quantify issues, evaluate priorities, and carefully analyze the tradeoffs that we are willing to make; scoring tools also help us to develop more creative solutions because they allow us to consider different offers that we find equally attractive.

When you are negotiating for yourself in employment situations, it is critical to build your BATNA by knowing what you would be doing if you did not accept this role. It might be taking a different job, or it might be keeping the role that you already have. Your reservation point might not be exactly the same as your BATNA, but your BATNA will be the single biggest determinant of your reservation point. I strongly recommend that you evaluate your BATNA using a scoring tool so that you can quantify all of the issues in the negotiation and not become obsessed by the most quantified issues. This scoring tool can help you to focus on the entire package in the employment negotiation—role, responsibilities, opportunities for development, visibility, exposure, location, flexibility, impact you can have, experience, positioning for the next role, title, pay, equity, vacation time, and everything else. This will ensure that you do not become fixated on the easily quantified issue of salary, or on a salient issue like location, and overlook the other components of the package.

Having a scoring tool will help you to focus on the entire package of issues and be better prepared to negotiate for yourself. Being well prepared with many issues on the table, a clear understanding of your BATNA, an assessment of your BATNA using your scoring tool, and knowledge of your reservation point will reduce your fear when you are negotiating for yourself. As we continue to build strategies in the upcoming chapters, we will take the fear out of these critical negotiations and help you to advocate for yourself in effective ways that build the relationship and maximize your outcome.

Summary

We have been preparing for a negotiation by putting the right issues on the table, building our BATNA, and assessing our bottom-line reservation point. In this chapter, we learned that our BATNA will be the single biggest determinant of our reservation point, but that the two might not be exactly the same because there might be idiosyncratic factors that would cause you to prefer one option over another. We also learned that in establishing your reservation point, it is critical for you to focus on the entire package of issues and not just the single most quantified issues or the most salient issues. A scoring tool can help you to quantify the whole set of issues.

We have prepared a great deal thus far, but we are still not ready to negotiate. In fact, one of the most important steps in the preparation phase has not yet been completed. We have not yet considered one of the most critical components of the negotiation: What is our goal? We have spent time thinking about what we have to get (our reservation point), but we have not spent time considering what we want to get (our goal). Often people are afraid when they negotiate because they are negotiating too close to their own bottom line. The next chapter will help us to reduce fear in the negotiation by focusing on how to establish an ambitious goal. This will allow us to negotiate closer to the other side's reservation point rather than hovering near our own bottom line.

5 Establish an Ambitious Goal

One of the most important elements of your initial analysis is to determine your goal for the negotiation. What do you want, what are you trying to get, and what are you striving to achieve in the negotiation? Goals are very important because research demonstrates that goals drive negotiation outcomes (Galinsky, Mussweiler, & Medvec, 2002), so it is critical to establish an ambitious goal.

I think people are often afraid to establish bold goals, because they worry that doing so will cause them to lose the deal, offend the other side, or damage their relationship with the other party. These concerns are unfounded, but these misconceptions cause people to worry about establishing ambitious goals. The reality is that an aggressive goal will not cause you to lose the deal; you do not walk away from the deal if you are not achieving your goal—you only walk away if you have not secured your reservation point.

In addition, people fear that an ambitious goal will offend the other side and cause them to walk away. I always remind my clients that a goal cannot offend anyone because a goal is never shared with the other party—it is in my own head. My goal affects my own mindset about what is possible, what I am shooting for, and what I want. Oftentimes, the biggest constraint in any negotiation is our own thinking and how what is in our own heads limits our sense of what is possible to achieve.

Clearly, my goal will shape my first offer (Galinsky & Mussweiler, 2001) which is shared with the other side; my first offer can offend the other party, so I have to be thoughtful as I develop my offer. My first offer should be ambitious but not outrageous, a distinction we will discuss in the next chapter. Nevertheless, an aggressive goal cannot hurt me as long as I do not walk away if I am not achieving my goal. An unexpressed bold goal will not offend anyone or damage your relationship with the other side. So, we should not fear having an ambitious goal, but we definitely should be afraid not to have one.

The Importance of the Goal

Our goal is in our own head, driving our behavior in the negotiation, anchoring our expectations, and determining our outcomes. Our goal sets the upper limit for us in a negotiation. We are very unlikely to get an outcome better than what we are trying to get. The goal establishes the ceiling—the best outcome we will achieve. Failing to set an ambitious goal will cost us a great deal in every negotiation (Galinsky, Mussweiler, & Medvec, 2002).

While having an aggressive goal is essential, many negotiators do not establish ambitious goals for themselves. Often, they focus on what they *have* to get rather than thinking about what they *want*. This mistake costs organizations hundreds of millions of dollars, euros, yen, and pounds per year. When we do not establish ambitious goals, we leave a great deal of money on the table.

The suboptimal agreement that results from a failure to establish an ambitious goal often reduces the outcomes for both you and the other side. Often we are afraid that we will damage the relationship if we establish an ambitious goal. As you will see in this and future chapters, you are actually far more likely to damage your outcome, the other side's outcome, and your relationship with your counterparty when you negotiate around your bottom line reservation point than when you establish an ambitious goal.

Why People Do Not Establish Ambitious Goals

Why don't we establish aggressive goals? An information asymmetry underlies our failure to establish ambitious goals. When you are going into a negotiation, you tend to know everything about your own side—you are aware of your strengths, but you also tend to be acutely aware of your own weaknesses. You know how badly you need to close the deal by the end of the quarter; you know that you will not make your numbers without this order; you know your people will be laid off unless you generate this specific business. While we are conscious of our strengths and acutely cognizant of our weaknesses, we generally know far less about the other side.

Typically, we are aware of our counterparty's strengths because they openly share this information with us, telling us how much others want to work with them and how our competitors desire their business. However, we often do not know much about their weaknesses. So while our own weaknesses are very salient to us, we know very little about the vulnerabilities of the other side. This information asymmetry may lead us to fail to establish aggressive goals because our goal should be based on the weakness of the other side's alternatives.

I encourage my clients to focus on the weaknesses of the other side and to make a list of their limitations. What other options does the other side have? What will they do if they do not get an agreement with you? How risky will it be for them to switch suppliers? What will happen if they lose you as a customer? Who will get fired if the deal falls apart? I want these disadvantages to be salient to my clients because I believe that your goal for the negotiation should be based on the weaknesses of the other side's alternatives.

Specifically, I think your goal should be based on the weaknesses of the other party's best outside option (their BATNA). Your counterparty's BATNA reveals what the other side will do if they do not get an agreement with you. Your goal should be based on the weaknesses of their BATNA, so you need to analyze the other side's BATNA carefully in order to establish your goal. When you analyze the vulnerabilities of the other side's BATNA, you are able to estimate the other party's reservation point and use this analysis to establish your goal.

A Trap Experts Encounter

Unfortunately, I find that even very skilled negotiators often do not analyze the weakness of the other side's BATNA in order to establish an ambitious goal. In my course on the traps that expert negotiators encounter, I highlight the trap of failing to establish an ambitious goal. Experts fall into this trap because they often focus on what is normally achieved in a particular type of negotiation and base their goal on this. Because experts negotiate so often, what is typically achieved is very salient to them and may become the marker for what they strive to get in a specific negotiation.

TRAPS EXPERT NEGOTIATORS ENCOUNTER

Even expert negotiators get trapped.

1. Negotiating the wrong deal—negotiating what is standard or typical rather than putting the right issues on the table
2. Focusing primarily on highly quantified issues
3. **Failing to establish an ambitious goal**

We often do not assess the weaknesses of the other side's BATNA because we tend to focus on ourselves rather than the other side (Ross & Sicoly, 1979). I was once working on a negotiation strategy with a partner from a consulting firm. The first question I asked him was "What will the client do if they do not hire your firm?" He said, "I guess they will just hire another firm—there are a lot of other firms they could choose." I pushed him on this, asking which specific firm they would select. He said he didn't know and that there were "a lot of other firms." I pushed him further, and he finally revealed that he thought the client would use McKinsey if they did not use his firm. I asked him whether the client would prefer to use his firm or McKinsey, and he said he thought they would prefer his firm because it had done more of this particular type of project, but that if they did not select his firm, he was sure they would choose McKinsey, particularly since McKinsey was on-site and embedded at the client.

I asked him how much McKinsey would charge for this project, and he reported that they would likely charge at least $1 million for the work. I then asked him how much he had asked for in his meeting with the client the day before, and he said $350,000.

You and I can both see that there are at least 650,000 problems with this offer; the client's BATNA was to spend at least $1 million with a firm they did not prefer. Based on this, we would estimate that the client's reservation point was at least $1 million. So why did the partner only ask for $350,000? What was the basis for this offer? It is likely that the partner's offer was based on a focus on his own costs for conducting the project (estimated at $300,000), his own BATNA, and his reservation point, rather than an assessment of the weakness of the other side's BATNA and an attempt to estimate the client's reservation point.

This tendency to focus on our own costs and our own reservation point is pervasive. Whenever I teach a course, I always ask the participants how many of them have companies that engage in "cost-plus pricing." Not surprisingly, more than 75% of the people in most of my audiences raise their hands. I refer to cost-plus pricing as reservation point pricing; the pricing is based on their company's costs, but it completely ignores the other side's weaknesses and vulnerabilities. When you focus on your own costs, you are negotiating around your own reservation point, meaning that you are negotiating in the range of the worst deals you would be willing to accept rather than focusing on the deal you want. Your own costs are critical to establishing your reservation point, but they should be completely irrelevant to your goal because your goal should not be based on anything about you; your goal should be based on the weaknesses of the other side's BATNA. If my clients want to persist in cost-plus pricing, I often tease them by offering to print business cards for them that say "I negotiate the worst possible deals." That is what you will do if you set your goal based on your own reservation point. Instead, you want to establish ambitious goals based on the weakness of the other side's BATNA.

Your Goal and Your Reservation Point Should Not Correlate with Each Other

Because your goal is based on the weakness of the other side's BATNA, whereas your reservation point is based on your own BATNA, your goal and your reservation point should not correlate with each other. They should be completely independent of each other, and you need to have both in mind before you begin to negotiate.

One of my clients who owns a professional baseball team was negotiating with the owner of the stadium where his team plays. As he prepared for the negotiation, he complained to me, "It's going to be a terrible negotiation because I have no power at all." I suggested that we improve his power by building his BATNA and consider other cities where his team could play. He responded that he "did not want to move the team." I proposed that we take a trip to see other potential stadiums. He reiterated that he "did not want to move the team." I suggested that we at least meet with team owners who had moved their teams to learn more about their experiences. In response, he clearly conveyed that he "did not want to move the team," and he said this is why the negotiation would be so difficult.

I am a BATNA generator, and I always try to build my clients' BATNA, but it was clear to me that he did not want to have his BATNA generated. The failure to build his BATNA would weaken his power in the negotiation, but should not affect his goal in any way. I explained to him that as long as he never repeated the words he just stated to anyone else, including his best friends, business partner, wife, and mother, he could still establish an ambitious goal for the negotiation. He seemed confused, strongly reinforcing, "But I said I do not want to move the team, so I have no power at all." I explained that the fact he did not have a BATNA meant that he had a weak reservation point and clearly lacked power, but that this had nothing to do with the goal he should establish. Since his goal should be based on the weakness of the other side's BATNA, I asked him to consider what the owner of a professional baseball stadium would do without a team. Perhaps they would rent out the stadium to Little League teams or have flea markets there on weekends—neither sounded like a good BATNA at all. While the team owner's BATNA was weak, and he did not have an attractive reservation point, the other side's BATNA was exceptionally unattractive, and this meant that my client could establish a very ambitious goal. There would simply be a large range between his reservation point (based on his own weak BATNA) and his goal (based on the weakness of the other side's BATNA).

This clarifies the idea that your goal and your reservation point should not correlate with each other; they are independent of each other because they are based on completely different pieces of data. Your goal is based on the weakness of the other side's BATNA, but your reservation point is based on your own BATNA. Many negotiators do not consider these two concepts distinctly as they prepare. They often focus on their own reservation point and establish their goal to be something slightly better than their bottom line. This leads them to negotiate right around their own reservation point; as I like to say, this leads people to spend a lot of time negotiating "lousy deals."

The Bargaining Zone

Much has been written about the bargaining zone in a negotiation. The *bargaining zone* defines the range of possible agreements; in fact, some refer to it as the "zone of possible agreements" or the ZOPA (Lewicki, Barry, & Saunders, 1985). The bargaining zone is established by the range between the buyer's and seller's reservation points (see Figure 5.1). While many people discuss the concept of bargaining zone, we often do not discuss the deep, dark secret: that we often do not negotiate across the entire bargaining zone. We often negotiate in one portion of the bargaining zone that is immediately around our own reservation point. This is why I say that we are often negotiating "lousy deals." In order to capture the advantage of the entire range of the bargaining zone, we need to analyze carefully the other side's BATNA, look for the weaknesses in their BATNA, use this information to estimate the other side's reservation point, and establish an ambitious goal. We want to negotiate around the other side's reservation point, not around our own reservation point.

I frequently speak to chapters within an organization known as the Young Presidents' Organization (YPO). This is an organization of very successful CEOs who have ascended to the top job by the time they are 40 years old; they are truly an impressive collection of serial entrepreneurs, family business owners, and sharp hired guns. I have spoken at many of the YPO chapters all over the world, and conducted sessions for YPO International as well.

I was speaking at one of the international events when I met a CEO who asked to me to work with his international sales group on their negotiation strategy. I agreed to conduct a two-day training for his sales team. The moment I arrived at the session, though, I could tell that the VP for Sales was not excited about the session. When he first walked in the room, his attitude suggested that he did not think the session was necessary and that it was definitely not his idea. The CEO, who had already attended a full two-day course with me, introduced me with a very strong endorsement. Unfortunately, though, the CEO had to depart for a trip that afternoon, so I was left with the entire international sales

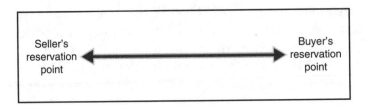

Figure 5.1: Bargaining Zone

organization and a VP of Sales who clearly did not want to be hosting the class.

On the morning of the first day of the session, the VP participated in a negotiation simulation and got the worst negotiation outcome of anyone in the room. Later that day, the participants completed a second negotiation case, and again the VP of Sales scored the worst outcome. The next morning, the participants completed a third negotiation, and once again the VP achieved the worst outcome. When we were discussing the third case, the VP said something I will never forget because it so nicely underscores the fact that individuals often focus on their own reservation point instead of establishing an ambitious goal. He said, "I am known in this company as the closer. I close more deals than anyone else, and I close very quickly. I have been thinking over the past two days that I must be closing a bunch of lousy deals, though, because I go in focused on my reservation point and negotiate right around my own bottom line."

I thought it took an incredible amount of courage for the VP to admit this in front of his entire team, but I think he said it because he thought this might be a fairly pervasive problem across the company. This was not a company that lacked a negotiation strategy or negotiation experience; their team was filled with many individuals with a lot of experience. However, the tendency to focus on their reservation point and engage in "cost-plus pricing" was destroying the company's margins. The sales team had a strategy, but they lacked ambitious goals. Goals set the ceiling in negotiations. We generally do not do better than the goal we establish, and therefore if we do not establish ambitious goals, we will leave money on the table.

Are You Rewarding People Who Establish Ambitious Goals?

Organizations need to be careful in establishing their sales incentives to ensure they do not reward negotiators who focus on their reservation point. If organizations incentivize their sales teams only on revenue generated or market share achieved, then their sales team will often focus on their own reservation points rather than establishing ambitious goals. I encourage my clients to reevaluate how they are incenting their sales teams, pushing them to analyze whether they are incenting sales executives to maximize outcomes or just to close deals. If they want to motivate sales executives to maximize outcomes, they need their sales teams to establish ambitious goals and should incent them on margin, percent of goal achieved, and driving profitability for the organization rather than on revenue or market share.

Rewarding people based on the achievement of a goal can be tricky because people often express concern about establishing ambitious goals if they will be measured against these metrics. I had a client tell me that they were afraid to establish the ambitious goal that I was suggesting because they feared they would be accountable for this goal and negatively evaluated if they did not achieve it. You do not want to have a performance metric tied to the achievement of a goal potentially reducing the goals that people establish. You may not want to measure people's performance against a super ambitious "in a perfect world" goal, and if you are the one being measured, you may not want to share this exceptionally aspiring goal with management or with your board of directors. I recommend measuring people against more realistic goals while encouraging them to establish very ambitious goals based on the weakness of the other side's BATNA.

Goals Should Be Based on the Weakness of the Other Side's BATNA

It is important to remember that goals should not be correlated to your company's costs, should not be based on the last agreement signed, and should not be tied to what people typically achieve in this type of negotiation. Goals should be based on the weakness of the other side's BATNA. Of course, the more you differentiate yourself on characteristics that matter a great deal to the other party, the weaker their BATNA will be. Naturally, this requires both translating your differentiators into negotiable issues, as we discussed in Chapter 2, and careful analysis of the other side's BATNA. This was demonstrated very clearly to me in a set of negotiations I assisted in during the midst of the COVID-19 crisis. The shutdown associated with the pandemic hurt many businesses, but few fared worse than small restaurants and retailers. Many of these businesses were trying to renegotiate their commercial real estate leases in order to survive. I was working with a private restaurant chain with locations across the United States to try to renegotiate all of their lease payments. In our first conversation, I uncovered that the skilled team charged with this assignment had reviewed all of their leases and their other fixed costs and established what they "needed to get" in these negotiations. They knew their reservation point and understood what they had to get from each landlord to maintain each of their locations. However, I encouraged them to spend some time thinking about what they wanted to get, not just what they needed to achieve. I suggested that they focus on the weaknesses of each landlord's options to establish their goals. I also suggested that it was critical that we differentiate their restaurants from other potential retail tenants in each of these discussions and that by translating the chain's differentiators into negotiable issues, they would be able to emphasize the weakness of their landlords' alternatives.

A BATNA Analysis Tool

Many negotiators, even very experienced negotiators like the real estate team for the restaurant chain, do not focus on the weaknesses of the other side's BATNA to establish a goal. This is why I recommend to my clients that they create a *BATNA Analysis Tool*. This is a tool specifically designed to evaluate the weaknesses of the other side's BATNA. A BATNA Analysis Tool involves 10 questions that are focused on assessing the weaknesses of the other party's options. Each question is scored on a 1–10 scale, where a "1" consistently indicates that the other side has weak outside options and a "10" means that the other party has strong outside alternatives. Once each question is answered, the scores from all questions are summed up and then divided by 10 in order to generate the average BATNA analysis score. If the average score is 1–4, you know that the other side has weak outside options; this means that you should have an aggressive goal. You would expect the goal to be more ambitious than the typical goal that would be established for this type of negotiation. If the average score is a 5–7, you know that the other side has an average BATNA and would expect that the goal for the negotiation would reflect the typical level of a goal for such negotiations. On the other hand, if the BATNA Analysis Score is an 8 or higher, you know that the other side has strong outside options; although you would pursue the typical goal in this negotiation, you recognize that it might be challenging to achieve this.

I have included in the following figures an example of a BATNA Analysis Tool for customer negotiations and one for supplier negotiations. I recommend to my clients that they review the examples of questions to include and then customize their own BATNA Analysis Tools for their customers, and another tool for their suppliers. Take a look at the following illustration in Figure 5.2 for an example of a BATNA Analysis Tool designed for one of my clients for their negotiations with customers.

Likewise, if you are a purchaser of goods or services, you would also want to have a BATNA Analysis Tool to evaluate to whom a supplier would sell to if they did not sell to you (see Figure 5.3). A very wise client of mine once suggested that in a supplier negotiation, the BATNA Analysis Tool should be completed for both the company and for the individual salesperson who is selling to your business. Generally, the BATNA Analysis score for the individual salesperson will be weaker than the score for the company overall. This lower score is critical to consider as you establish your goal for the negotiation with the salesperson selling to you.

You can revise these tools to include questions specific to your company or industry, but you want to use the same 10 questions across all of your customer negotiations in a specific segment and all of your supplier negotiations in a particular area. The same 10 questions should be used for every account so that you can evaluate on a relative basis which accounts should have more ambitious goals.

Often companies establish a goal for their whole book of business but do not establish a specific goal for each account. They may have a goal of a 70% margin or a goal of a 12% increase for the year. It is fine to have an average goal highlighting what you want to achieve across the entire book of business, but you also should specifically establish goals for each account based on the weakness of the other side's BATNA. If you do not do this, your sales team will always be able to rationalize why certain accounts will not deliver the average goal; they can easily identify those accounts where you will get less than the average goal. But I doubt that anyone will suggest that, on certain accounts, you should shoot for more than the average goal. If across all of your accounts you ask for the average goal or less than the average goal, clearly you will not achieve your overall goal. In order to achieve the average goal, you have to conduct BATNA Analysis on each account so that you can

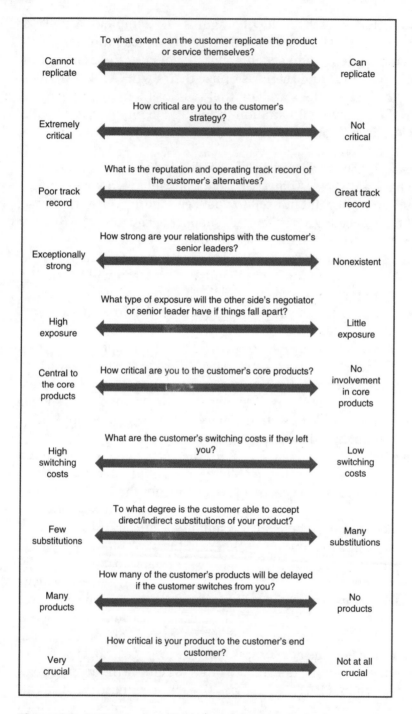

Figure 5.2: BATNA Analysis Tool: Customer Negotiations

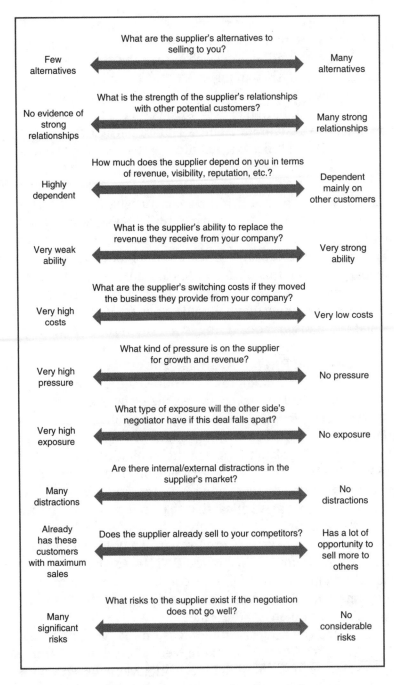

Figure 5.3: BATNA Analysis Tool: Supplier Negotiations

establish which accounts have a very poor BATNA where you should be asking for much more than the average goal.

So, in our leasing negotiation described earlier, the restaurant team completed a BATNA Analysis Tool for each of their locations. This tool assessed how much each landlord needed their business, how much empty retail space the landlord had or was expecting to have, and how much of a magnet this restaurant chain was for a particular location, attracting other retail and office clients into the space and sparking a rise in rent per square foot.

After completing the BATNA Analysis Tool for all of their locations, we examined the scores to establish the goals for what we would try to get. If the score was a 1, 2, 3, or 4, we established very ambitious goals, trying to get 12–16 months of rent abatement coupled with a discounted rental rate after this. If the score was a moderate 5, 6, or 7, we established a goal of getting 6–10 months of rent abatement where we would pay some of the fixed costs such as taxes. If the score was high (an 8 or above), we knew that it would be hard to get a great deal. We approached these discussions trying to get the rent abatement of 6–10 months, but we recognized that we were less likely to achieve this. We also allowed the BATNA Analysis scores to define the order in which we approached the landlords. I encouraged the team to begin with the landlords who had the lowest scores; the team was more likely to achieve success in these initial discussions and establish a precedent that other landlords had worked with the chain. Before we started to work together, they had spoken to a few of their landlords but had not been successful in getting rent abatement or ongoing rental rate reductions. They were frustrated by these conversations, and when we first started the project, they were skeptical that the strategies would work. But when we looked at the BATNA Analysis scores for the landlords that they first approached, it was clear why they had not been successful; these landlords had some of the highest BATNA Analysis scores of any of the landlords in their portfolio. Of course these landlords had been challenging—they had strong outside options and did not need the restaurant chain as much as others did.

When we restarted the project with a focus on the landlords with weak BATNA Analysis scores, and where we had established ambitious goals, we achieved outcomes that the team never believed would be possible. Analyzing the weakness of the other side's BATNA and establishing ambitious goals paid off well for this restaurant chain. They were able to adjust many of their leases, resulting in a huge savings in fixed costs for the company and allowing them to survive the mandatory closure of restaurants in their markets and the reduced capacity when they reopened to allow for six feet between each table. Lowering their lease commitments was key to their survival, and establishing ambitious goals based on the weakness of each landlord's BATNA helped them to do this.

If we do not have a BATNA Analysis Tool, we tend to think of the other side's alternatives in a superficial way such as, "They will rent to someone else" or "They will use somebody else." We need to be very specific about to whom they would rent, who they would use, who they would buy from, or to whom they would sell, and then analyze the weakness of that option compared to our offering. Using a BATNA Analysis Tool is a great way to really dig deep and analyze the weakness of the other side's BATNA. The 10 questions assess what is happening in the other party's business and uncover the weakness of their alternatives.

The BATNA Analysis Tool Guides Goals and Much More

A BATNA Analysis Tool enables you to establish ambitious goals. As you can see from the leasing example, it also helps you to establish an order to approach a series of negotiations. When my clients have a number of negotiations with other parties, I often recommend that they begin their negotiations with the parties that have weak BATNA rather than starting randomly or beginning with their biggest customers. This increases the likelihood of early success, builds confidence in the negotiators, and creates new precedent. The BATNA Analysis Tool also helps negotiators to consider how to weaken the other side's BATNA over time, add issues to the negotiation to highlight the weakness of the counterparty's BATNA, and identify opportunities to bundle discrete deals together. In addition, it is a powerful tool to align the negotiation team and assess negotiators' performance.

Building a Plan to Weaken the Other Side's BATNA Over Time

A BATNA Analysis Tool is also useful in identifying where the other side has strength. The other party may have an overall score of 4.3, but they have a high score on a few individual items. This is critical to analyze and use in developing a plan on how you will weaken your counterparty's BATNA over time. For example, you may notice from the BATNA Analysis that you do not have well-established relationships with senior leaders from the other party. Once you identify this, you can build a plan focused on developing these relationships to weaken the BATNA of the other side over time and decrease their power.

Adding Negotiation Issues to Highlight the Weakness of the Other Side's BATNA

Closely analyzing the individual questions in the BATNA Analysis Tool also helps you to identify issues that you should add to the negotiation to underscore the weakness of the other side's BATNA. For example, if you recognize that the other party needs a project completed very quickly and their alternative does not have the capacity to start soon, you might want to add a number of issues to the table to emphasize the fact that their other alternative would take a long time. For example, you could negotiate the start date, the completion date, and a financial guarantee that the project will be completed by a particular date. All of these issues will highlight the weakness of the other party's BATNA.

Identifying Opportunities to Bundle Discrete Deals Together

The BATNA Analysis Tool can also be used to uncover opportunities to bundle deals together. Frequently, when large companies are negotiating with other large companies, there may be multiple negotiations that are taking place across the two enterprises. I encourage my clients to conduct an analysis of the other side's BATNA for each of these discrete negotiations. If my client determines that the other party's BATNA is weak for one negotiation and strong for another one, I encourage them to bundle the two deals together. This allows my client to leverage the negotiation where the other party has weak options to get more on the negotiation where they have strong alternatives.

For example, one of my large enterprise clients historically has had different divisions individually approach the same customers. After learning about the BATNA Analysis Tool, they recognized that if two divisions were about to approach a customer, they would gain an advantage by analyzing the customer's BATNA for each of the individual deals. If they found that the customer had weak BATNA for one deal and much stronger BATNA for the other, they identified that the company would be best served if they bundled these two deals together rather than negotiating each one separately. This resulted in far better outcomes for my client.

Aligning Your Team

I have found that a BATNA Analysis Tool can also help you to align your internal team prior to a negotiation. It helps to focus all of the team members on the weakness of the other side's alternatives and quantify this weakness. I encourage each team member to complete the BATNA Analysis Tool individually and then compare responses. This shared analysis, focus on the weakness of the other side's options, and quantification of the weakness of the other party's BATNA often helps to eradicate the team's fears that they will offend the other side or lose the deal if their goal is too ambitious.

In order to align the team, you should distinguish between the *deal team* versus the *table team*. The deal team includes the broad cross-functional group that is involved in planning for the negotiation, developing the strategy, overseeing the progress, and approving the deal. The table team is a subset of the deal team who will actually be at the table negotiating. In an optimal situation, all of the members of the deal team would individually complete the BATNA Analysis Tool so that all of their perspectives inform the evaluation. Often a team member who is slightly more removed from a deal will see the weakness of the other side's options more clearly than someone who is frequently interacting with the other side. Someone who is in close contact with the other side, such as the salesperson who owns a client relationship, will sometimes overestimate the strength of the customer's BATNA because they have heard the customer speak so often about the strength of their alternatives. A more distant team member is often more objective in their assessment of the other side's weaknesses. By having each person independently complete the BATNA Analysis Tool, you capture all of this unique expertise.

I was teaching a negotiations course in a large technology company one Friday afternoon. One of the participants was working on a very significant customer negotiation that involved a large deal team from across the business. The table team was going to initiate the negotiation with the customer the next week and was discussing the offer they were going to extend. The woman in my class was a member of the table team but she did not own the responsibility for the customer relationship. She completed the BATNA Analysis Tool in the class session and uncovered that the customer's BATNA was very weak with an overall score of 2.6. She became quite disturbed by this analysis because she said that the team was discussing a very modest goal for the negotiation with this customer. She said she thought the team needed to establish a much more ambitious goal but that she did not think the sales leader who owned the customer relationship would agree to do this. I encouraged her to have the team members individually complete the BATNA Analysis Score so that she could use their careful examination of the customer's BATNA to inform the discussion.

While we were in the class, she sent the BATNA Analysis Tool to a number of the members of the broader deal team, including every other member of the table team who would be meeting with the customer the following week. She asked them all to take 2–3 minutes to complete the BATNA Analysis Tool and send her the score they calculated. All of them sent a score between 2 and 2.8. This meant that the customer had very weak BATNA and that the team should be ambitious in establishing their goal for the negotiation. The woman in my class scheduled a virtual meeting late on Friday afternoon to discuss the analysis and encourage the team to modify its goal. As a result of this, the team more than doubled the goal they had initially been discussing and completely modified their opening offer because of this updated goal. The team went into the negotiation the next week with their much more ambitious goal and ended the negotiation with 50% more than what they were initially planning to ask for in their offer. As this example reveals, a BATNA Analysis Tool takes the fear out of establishing an ambitious goal.

Assessing Negotiator Performance

A BATNA Analysis Tool also provides a window for senior leaders to assess the skills of their own negotiators; it is like a glimpse behind the black curtain into the way that their team members negotiate. Leaders often evaluate their salespeople on revenue achieved. However, the reality is that some sales team members were assigned easy accounts where the customer had weak alternatives and desperately needed the company's goods or services. Anyone could have generated revenue on these accounts. Other team members may have been assigned much more challenging accounts where the customer had really strong alternatives. If you compare performance on revenue alone, you miss this discrepancy. The BATNA Analysis Tool allows you to compare people's performance at a much deeper level. It allows you to assess how well individual negotiators performed relative to how well they should have performed. The key questions are, did the salesperson generate all of the revenue possible at the right margin, and did the salesperson position the account to become more dependent on your company over time? Are they building relationships with senior leaders and providing services that will make it harder for the customer to move to someone else in the future?

I encourage my clients to integrate the BATNA Analysis Tool into their organizations' customer relationship management tools (CRMs). This allows the management team to run reports based on BATNA Analysis scores and link these to revenue and margin reports. This will delineate which salespeople or teams are dealing with accounts that have high BATNA Analysis scores versus low BATNA Analysis scores. This allows sales leaders to quickly evaluate how team members are performing given the BATNA of the customer. It will accentuate top sales people who are effectively weakening the customer's BATNA over time and underscore cost-plus pricing among salespeople and teams who consistently establish relatively poor deals with accounts that have low BATNA Analysis scores.

One of my clients, Acumen Solutions, has built their BATNA Analysis Tool into their SalesForce application. Acumen was very well positioned to do this because they consult on SalesForce implementations for companies around the world. CEO David Joubran says that the BATNA Analysis Tool has helped him to "evaluate his sales team in a much deeper way." He used to evaluate sales results, but now he has the opportunity to evaluate the sales team's process as well. Are team members establishing appropriate goals? Are they effectively expanding their footprint within accounts and establishing strong relationships with the customers' senior leaders? Are they emphasizing Acumen's expertise? The BATNA Analysis Tool provides insight into all of these questions.

Errors in BATNA Analysis

Clients often ask me what happens if they incorrectly estimate the other side's BATNA. I always tell them that it is very likely that they will be incorrect in estimating the other party's BATNA, but that only one kind of error is problematic. I explain that I am only worried if they overestimate the strength of their counterparty's alternatives—not if they underestimate their options. Underestimating the other side's BATNA and establishing a goal that is overly ambitious is not a problem. This will lead you to make an offer that may be too aggressive, but you can adjust in the negotiation when you recognize that your originally established goal is not attainable. Remember, you do not walk away if you are not achieving your goal. But if you overestimate the strength of the other party's BATNA, then you will set too low a goal and make an offer that is not aggressive enough. This is a tremendous problem because you cannot recover from a first offer that is too conservative. You may have experienced this problem before when you make an offer that the other side immediately accepts and you experience that "oh shit" moment when you know you could have gotten more. We will discuss the need to leave room to concede in Chapter 9; having an ambitious goal enables you do this.

Setting Goals in Everyday Negotiations

I encourage companies to have a BATNA Analysis Tool for all of the negotiations they regularly encounter with customers, suppliers, tenants, and others. I will also encourage you in the following section to have a BATNA Analysis Tool when you are negotiating for yourself across your career. Although you will not have a BATNA Analysis Tool for every negotiation you encounter in the everyday world, you should still establish ambitious goals in each of these negotiations, based on the same type of analysis. Specifically, you want to establish your goal by analyzing the weakness of the other side's BATNA, even if this BATNA is assessed on the fly in an everyday negotiation rather than being carefully analyzed with 10 questions in a BATNA Analysis Tool.

A story from a number of years ago reminds me of this message. When my boys were young, we loved to have "family game nights," and sometimes we would invite other families with young children to join us. We had invited a Kellogg colleague of mine with his wife and two sons to come over for dinner and play board games on a Saturday evening when my boys were seven and three. It was St. Patrick's Day, so I decided that we should have some fun leprechaun cookies for dessert. I stopped by a local bakery to pick them up. As the boys and I left the car, I grabbed $20 from my wallet to purchase the cookies. As we entered, I was looking at the many cookie options in the case by the door and realized that my sons had wandered over to the large, refrigerated case on the wall that held the gigantic St. Patrick's Day cakes. These were two-tiered cakes with a leprechaun on top, a pot of gold on the bottom layer, and a pathway of gold chocolate coins cascading across the layers. The cakes were stunning and had clearly caught the eyes of both of my sons, who had their hands on the case's glass door trying to get a closer look. "Mommy, look at these cakes!" they exclaimed. I explained we were getting cookies and tried to sway them back to the cookie counter, but their eyes were glued on the cakes. The cakes were $69, and I only had a $20 bill in my pocket. I told them about all of the great cookie designs—there were leprechauns, shamrocks, and rainbows with pots of gold at the end. Still, they stood staring through the glass door at the cakes. I noticed there were quite a few of these cakes. I also looked at my watch and observed that it was 3:00 p.m. and that the bakery would be closing in an hour. As I was looking at the cakes, I realized that nearly all of them had a little plastic button in the icing that indicated whether the cake was white, yellow, or chocolate. I say nearly all of them, because I noticed that this plastic piece was missing from one of the cakes. I recognized that the fact it was missing could give me a negotiation opportunity. Always a mom who would rather negotiate with others than with my own children, I told my boys, "Mommy only brought $20 into the bakery with her and this cake is $69. If mommy can purchase this cake for $20 or less, then we will take the cake, but if not, then we are getting the cookies like we planned and leaving because we need to get home." I then picked up the cake with the missing button. My quick analysis suggested to me that the bakery had weak BATNA on selling this cake.

There were at least seven other cakes on the shelf with flavor buttons attached. You could not ascertain the flavor of the cake without the button because the cakes were so large that they were placed on wooden boards, so it seemed to me that it would be difficult for the bakery to know the flavor of this cake. The bakery would be closing within the hour and would not be open the following day, so the cakes that were not sold within the next hour would be unlikely to be sold at all. Given this quick analysis of the weakness of the other side's BATNA, I established an ambitious goal and proceeded to the register. As I set the cake down, I asked "What flavor is this cake?" The bakery employee looked at the cake, turned it around, and said, "Oh, I guess we don't know what flavor that one is because the flavor button is missing. There are other cakes in the case, though, if you want a chocolate one, a white one, or a yellow one. The buttons on the side tell you the flavor but this cake does not have one." I said, "Gosh, I guess you are unlikely to sell this cake if you do not know the flavor. I mean who is going to purchase a cake without knowing what flavor it is, especially when there are seven others in the case, and you are closing soon. I'll tell you what, I am having guests for dinner tonight and I don't know what flavor they prefer, so I will take a chance and take the cake off your hands for $10 if you want." We negotiated a bit but, much to the delight of my two boys, I was able to get the cake for less than $20, so we took it home. We opened the box to pull it out after dinner and all four of the kids shrieked in delight when they saw the pot of gold and the chocolate coins. My colleague said, "Wow, what a beautiful cake," and my three-year-old mortified me as he replied, "And my mommy got a really good deal on it."

Why did I get a good deal? Because I set an ambitious goal based on the weakness of the bakery's BATNA. In complex business negotiations, you should analyze the weakness of your counterparty's BATNA using a BATNA Analysis Tool. In more spontaneous everyday negotiations, it is unlikely you will use a BATNA Analysis Tool, but you should still analyze the weakness of the other side's alternatives. Ambitious goals are critical to securing optimal negotiated outcomes. This is true in everyday negotiations, such as the one in the bakery, and in business negotiations. This is also true when you are negotiating for yourself.

ESTABLISHING AMBITIOUS GOALS WHEN NEGOTIATING FOR YOURSELF

You definitely want to establish ambitious goals when you negotiate for yourself. Too often, people approach these negotiations focused on what they feel they have to get, or they will quit and take another offer. Often, they do not focus on what they want, instead being obsessed by what they have to get. This is a critical, high-stakes negotiation that demands thorough preparation. Begin by thinking about your differentiators and how they address the employer's and hiring manager's pressing business needs. It is essential to differentiate yourself in employment negotiations so that you can demonstrate how the company can do something for you without establishing a precedent to do the same for everyone else.

Differentiating yourself also weakens the other side's BATNA. The more you differentiate yourself, the less likely the employer is to be able to hire someone else to do what you are uniquely positioned to accomplish. The more you highlight your unique competencies and capabilities, the weaker the employer's BATNA will be.

Once you have established your differentiators, analyze the weakness of the other party's BATNA using a BATNA Analysis Tool and develop your goal based on the weakness of their options. I have included an example of a BATNA Analysis Tool for personal negotiations in Figure 5.4; you may modify this based on your own skills and capabilities.

You will notice that your counterparty's BATNA is likely to be weaker when you are already in the company, when the employer has a very unique need that you fulfill, or when you have exceptionally unusual capabilities. The employer and hiring manager are likely to have stronger BATNA when you are in a cohort comprised of many similar other applicants, when they are hiring many people on a regular basis, and when they do not have an urgent need for your skills. Your goal should be based on the weakness of the other side's BATNA. Notice that sometimes the company may have relatively strong BATNA but the hiring manager or your current boss (if you are already employed) may have weak alternatives. This manager may need to do the work herself until she hires someone for the role, or she might not achieve her own objectives without your assistance. I would encourage you to complete the BATNA Analysis Tool for both the company and the manager separately and base your goal on the weaker score.

Many candidates encountering these types of negotiations have a tendency to focus on what people typically get or what is normally achieved. Instead, you should analyze the weakness of the other side's options to establish your goal.

Power Analysis

We have discussed the importance of assessing the weakness of the other party's BATNA to establish your goal for the negotiation. I recommend that you complete a BATNA Analysis Tool on a regular basis for ongoing customer, supplier, and partner relationships because their BATNAs will change over time. I also recommend that in developing your negotiation strategy, you consider how your counterparty's BATNA

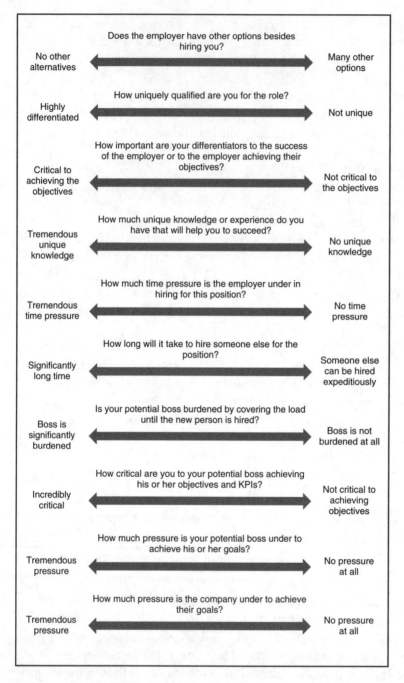

Figure 5.4: BATNA Analysis Tool: Negotiating for Yourself

will change. The other side's BATNA is dynamic, not static. Sometimes, their BATNA will improve after you begin to work with them, and sometimes their BATNA will become weaker as you work together. It is critical to analyze how your counterparty's BATNA will change over time. This *Power Analysis* should inform many components of your negotiation strategy, including your desired length of the agreement, pricing strategy, and your approach to phasing projects.

Length of an Agreement

For example, you would want to have a long-term agreement if the other side's BATNA would improve over time, because you would like to avoid the need to negotiate with them in the future when they have stronger alternatives. On the other hand, if the other party's BATNA would become weaker over time, you should actually prefer a short-term agreement, which would allow you to renegotiate when they would be more dependent on you. Many companies include terms allowing for contracts to renew automatically or "evergreen" without conducting a power analysis like this and mistakenly agree to a long-term agreement when a short-term one would give them an advantage. A careful power analysis will inform your strategy.

Pricing Strategy

This type of power analysis will also help you to establish pricing in a customer negotiation. Often, suppliers will try to employ a "foot in the door" strategy (Freedman & Fraser, 1966) going into a customer relationship with a very low price to try to win the work with the intent of raising the price once they have established the customer relationship. If the customer's BATNA goes down once the supplier begins to work with them, this strategy may work. On the other hand, if the customer's BATNA improves because the supplier solves some very challenging problem that only they could unravel, and now there are many alternative firms who can execute the resolved solution, then the low price "foot in the door" strategy may become a door in the face and will not work at all. If the customer's BATNA improves once the supplier begins the work, then the starting price is the highest price that may ever be received. This stresses why it is important to assess how power will change over time as you think about pricing.

Phasing a Project

Understanding how power will change over time is also essential if you are an engineering firm, construction company, or consulting firm considering phasing a project you are completing for a client. If the client's BATNA will improve after you begin the work, you would not want to phase a project because the client will have increasing options as the work is completed, and each subsequent phase might provide an opportunity for some other firm to take over the work. On the other hand, if the client's BATNA will decrease once you begin the work, you might want to phase the project. As the client's BATNA weakens, you would be able to negotiate from a position of strength for future phases of work. Often, when firms are phasing a project, they will provide estimates for the fees for later phases of the work up front. This analysis suggests, however, that you would not want to pre-price these future phases because you would want to negotiate them later when the client's BATNA is weaker. In fact, this power analysis would suggest that there would never be a case where you would want to phase a project and want to pre-price future phases of the work.

It is critical to consider how the other side's BATNA will change over time to determine how you want to structure an agreement. This is true when you are negotiating with a customer, supplier, or business partner. As we will discuss in the following section, this is also important to consider when you are negotiating for yourself

UNDERSTANDING HOW THE EMPLOYER'S BATNA WILL CHANGE OVER TIME WHEN NEGOTIATING FOR YOURSELF

Once you begin to work for a company, the employer's BATNA will change over time. If you are a top performer, the company may become more dependent on you as you work for them and their BATNA may decrease over time. If you become instrumental in many client or customer relationships, and your boss finds you indispensable, their BATNA may also decrease. As the company's BATNA weakens over time, your goal for what you can achieve should become more ambitious. This could translate into opportunities for you to seek increased compensation, additional development, and promotions.

As mentioned in Chapter 1, many people are afraid to negotiate for themselves. They often wait for their employer to initiate conversations about promotions, pay increases, and development opportunities rather than prompting these discussions. Women are more likely than men to fall into this trap, but many men do as well (Babcock & Laschever, 2003). I think that many people are afraid to ask for themselves because they think they will offend the other side and damage the relationship. People frequently tell me that they are also afraid to ask because they feel that in order to ask, they would have to be willing to walk away if the employer does not fulfill their request. I remind them that you do not walk away if you are not getting your goal; you should only walk away if you are not getting your reservation point. Your reservation point is based on your own BATNA (another job you might have) and has nothing to do with your goal, which is based on the weakness of the other side's options. If you consider that the employer's BATNA generally goes down over time, especially if you are a very strong performer, I recommend that as you work within a company over time, you establish more ambitious goals and have the courage to negotiate for yourself.

The analysis of how the employer's BATNA will change over time is also essential when you are recruiting for a new role. Each year, I advise many MBA students who are recruiting for their post-MBA roles. These students are very focused on what to negotiate with their new employers. As I advise them, I frequently find myself talking about how the employer's BATNA will change over time. For example, students may want to be transferred to Europe in their third year, secure a second rotation in the finance department in their fourth year, or be considered for an early review for a promotion two years after they begin. Often, they will want to negotiate for these things up front, before they accept their offer. Generally, I counsel students to consider that during this type of MBA recruiting, employers have strong BATNA because there are many other applicants who would like the position. However, the employer's BATNA will generally go down once a high-performing Kellogg MBA begins their role. Based on this analysis, it is typically more optimal to negotiate for these future opportunities later, when the company's BATNA has decreased, rather than up front when the company's BATNA is strong. There are exceptions to this, of course. For example, if a student is an extremely unique candidate with experience that the employer desperately wants, then the company may have weak BATNA in hiring and the student can negotiate future opportunities up front, but I have found that this is a more unusual situation.

It is important to analyze the employer's BATNA and to assess how it will change over time. Simultaneously, as discussed earlier, you should also consider the BATNA of your boss. Often the BATNA of your boss decreases over time even more markedly than the BATNA of your employer. Your boss may rely on you and need you to help him achieve his annual goals. He may recognize that it would be impossible to replace you quickly and that he would be overwhelmed with extra work if he did not have you on his team. You do not need to threaten to leave; you simply need to assess the weaknesses of the company's BATNA and your manager's BATNA and establish an ambitious goal.

Summary

If you have followed the steps recommended in all the preceding chapters, you have now completed the preparation phase of the negotiation. You thought hard about the issues that should be put on the table by first considering your objectives and allowing them to drive negotiable issues. You then analyzed the issues on the Issue Matrix to ensure that you had enough Storytelling Issues to allow the story to focus on the other side and to use these issues to capture what you want on Tradeoff and Contentious Issues. You built your best outside option (BATNA) to increase your power in the negotiation. Your BATNA will also be the single biggest determinant of your reservation point, or bottom line. Then, as a final step in your preparation phase, you analyzed the weakness of the other side's BATNA to establish an ambitious goal.

This ambitious goal is essential to maximize your outcome in the negotiation. Goals establish the ceiling in the negotiation. You will generally not do better than what you are trying to do, so it is essential to establish an ambitious goal.

This thorough preparation can help you reduce your fears as you approach a negotiation. Your fears of damaging the relationship, having a contentious discussion, losing the deal, and getting stuck with a poor agreement can all be reduced by putting the right issues on the table, building your BATNA, determining your bottom line, and analyzing the weakness of the other side's BATNA to establish an ambitious goal. Once you have completed this preparation, you can initiate the negotiation with a stronger sense of confidence and less fear.

6 Make the First Offer and Craft a Compelling Message

Now that you are well prepared, you are ready to begin the negotiation. This leads to a critical strategy question, though. Should you make the first offer, or should you let the other side go first? This is one of the most hotly debated questions in negotiations, even though there is very clear research indicating that the best strategy is to be well prepared and make the first offer. In this chapter, we will review the findings and provide clear evidence that you should make the first offer.

There is a lot of unfounded fear around making the first offer. People are afraid that they will offend the other side or cause the other party to walk away. This fear often causes negotiators to let the other side lead, and this saddles them with a tremendous disadvantage in the negotiation. This anxiety stems from a misunderstanding of what the first offer will include. As we discussed in Chapter 2, the offer should include many Storytelling and Tradeoff Issues, not just one single Contentious Issue.

In this chapter, we will discuss the importance of including a full package of issues in the first offer. The offer should also have a rationale that focuses on addressing the other side's needs or problems; the rationale should not focus on what *you* want but instead focus on the other side. When I go to the table with a package of issues focused on addressing the other side's needs and a story about how my differentiators will address those needs, I have nothing to fear. It is when I go to the table with a single Contentious Issue on the table—and my plan is to tell the other side what *I* want—that I have a reason to be afraid. The outcome of that sort of negotiation is likely to be poor and could damage the relationship. In this chapter, we will highlight why you want to make the first offer and how to do so in a way that can make you confident and successful. Starting negotiations with the right strategy will mitigate your fear and improve your outcomes.

Why You Should Lead

There is no topic I debate more vigorously with my clients than whether they should make the first offer or let the other side take the lead. The research on this is abundantly clear: People who make first offers get better outcomes in their negotiations than people who follow (Galinsky & Mussweiler, 2001). So, why do people argue that they should let the other side lead?

First of all, the research is relatively recent. The research findings on this have been uncovered in the last 20 years. Before this, many people thought that letting the other side take the lead was an advantage. Even some popular negotiation instructors stated that "He Who Speaks First Loses" (Karrass, 1992). On the contrary, the research clearly indicates that "Those Who Speak First Win," and that they win big (Galinsky & Mussweiler, 2001) as long as they are well prepared.

Advantages of Making the First Offer

There are numerous strategic advantages enabling negotiators who make the first offer to get better outcomes than those who follow. A significant advantage to making the first offer is that when you lead, you secure an *anchoring effect*. A great deal of research has demonstrated that people get anchored on numbers and ideas, and insufficiently adjust from these initial starting points (Tversky & Kahneman, 1974). Imagine that I invited two groups of people into two different rooms. I am standing at the front of each room with a big urn filled with balls with numbers on them. In one room, I pull out a ball and everyone in the room sees that the number 5,000 is on it. In the second room, I pull out a ball that has the number 50,000 on it. I then ask the people in each room to estimate the number of McDonald's restaurants in the world. Based on the research on anchoring, I would predict that the people who saw the 50,000 number will estimate that there are significantly more McDonald's restaurants than the people who saw the 5,000 ball. People get anchored on the number they see. When they are estimating the number of McDonald's restaurants, they know the number that they saw was irrelevant and they adjust, but they adjust insufficiently from the anchor point. This is referred to as an anchoring and insufficient adjustment bias (Tversky & Kahneman, 1974).

If anchoring impacts people's estimates of McDonald's locations, when people know there is absolutely no relationship between the number on the ball and the number of restaurants, consider what a strong effect anchoring can have in a negotiation when you put an offer on the table and build an entire rationale to show why it is relevant. Anchoring is a tremendous advantage that comes from making the first offer (Galinsky & Mussweiler, 2001; Magee, Galinsky, & Gruenfeld, 2007). When you lead, you create the starting point, and this gives you an advantage.

The second advantage of going first is that *you define the issues that are being discussed*. In essence, you set the table for the negotiation. If you let the other side lead, they may come in with just one Contentious Issue on the table, but when you lead, you can ensure you have plenty of Storytelling Issues on the table. This will allow you to focus the rationale on the other side and capture more on the Contentious and Tradeoff Issues also under discussion.

Imagine that you are negotiating with a customer. If you let them lead, they may ask for a price decrease. They have set the table, and the only issue being discussed is price. If you lead, you can start the conversation by highlighting how the COVID-19 pandemic has revealed the importance of having a very secure supply chain, and that many companies suffered who could not access their essential supplies. Because of this, you would like to talk to them about ways that you can help to increase the security of their supply chain. You want to discuss possibilities, such as holding emergency back stock for them at your location, allowing them to expedite orders when necessary, letting them increase orders when needed, generating the ability to create redundancy if desired by shipping the product from two different facilities, and enabling shipping alternatives to get them their supplies more quickly. You will also discuss the price for the coming year, but you are not only discussing price. You have set the table with many other issues that are critical to them and are discussing many Storytelling Issues in addition to the Contentious Issue of price.

A third related advantage of making the first offer is that *you frame the discussion*—because you have put the issues on the table. In the preceding example, you will not say that you want to discuss a price increase. Instead, you will frame the conversation around how COVID-19 really demonstrated the need for strong supply chains with redundancy and back stock built into them in case a crisis shut down the supply from one location, and how you would be willing to work to construct this type of situation in order to ensure that the customer always has timely delivery of essential supplies. You would then present three offers (a strategy we will learn about in Chapter 7) that would vary the level of redundancy, the amount of back stock held, the shipping locations, and the delivery times—along with prices that would be 20–30% higher than last year. Notice how this framing takes the focus away from the price increase and instead creates a focus on the customer's pressing need to maintain supply. When you go first, you get a tremendous advantage from defining the issues and framing the discussion.

In addition, when you lead, you are in the *relationship-enhancing position*, but when you follow, you are in the *relationship-damaging position*. When you make the first offer, you come to the table, frame what is being discussed, and make an offer that establishes a strong starting point. The other side then needs to respond to tell you what they do not like about your offer. If the other side leads, they make the offer, and you have to critique their offer. When I care about my relationship with the other side, I do not want to begin by criticizing their offer. I want to make the first offer and have them react instead.

Let me use a specific example to highlight the advantages of going first and the risks of letting the other side lead. One of my clients is a Big Four accounting firm; if they let a client lead in the negotiations, the client may begin by saying that they want a 20% fee reduction. The client has anchored the negotiation at 20% less than the current fee, has framed the conversation around a fee reduction, and has put only one Contentious Issue on the table. A partner from the firm who responds to this request is likely either to damage their economics (by just accepting the 20% reduction) or damage the relationship by critiquing this request and saying why this would not be possible. Letting the other side lead is likely to harm the firm's outcomes and damage their relationship with the client.

On the other hand, the partner could have come to the table and said that the firm was very focused on helping their client to survive during the challenging health crisis and economic crisis caused by COVID-19. Because the firm knows the company better than anyone, they can help them to identify redundancies, cut costs, and position themselves for future success. The partner could then negotiate a package of issues including: (1) an expanded scope of services; (2) the timeline for doing the work; (3) insight sessions with the CEO on how other companies are navigating the crisis; (4) the team who would be involved to incorporate team members who had worked on this client's account in the past; (5) the partner dedicated to the account who would be available to the client at any time and would be on Zoom every Wednesday at 2:00 p.m. for the next four months to provide support and guidance during the pandemic; (6) the fees for the various services; (7) a volume discount across the expanded service offerings; and (8) an additional discount if the client agreed to use only this firm for advisory work on cost-cutting areas. This would have allowed the partner to anchor a total increase in fees, expand their footprint with new service areas, build the relationship with the CEO, differentiate with a team who had worked for the client in the past, highlight the firm's expertise, and increase the client's dependency on the firm over time. In addition, the firm would look flexible, helpful, and concerned rather than looking stubborn when critiquing the client's request for a fee discount. Making the first offer has many advantages; when you let the other side go first, you put yourself at risk.

Why Do People Want to Let the Other Side Lead?

So, why do negotiators want the other side to make the first offer? Why do they fight the research highlighting the advantages of making the first offer? Why do they argue with such vigor when you suggest they should go first?

Experienced negotiators who have always gone second are likely to believe that their strategy is the right one because it has been reinforced over time. They have always let the other side go first and may have secured negotiation success. Of course, they have no idea how much more successful they would have been if they had led the negotiation instead. I recently encountered a client who had this perspective. He was in business development with a background in investment banking. He strongly believed in letting the other side lead because he had always let them lead and liked his past results. The challenge in the real world is that you never observe how much stronger your outcome might have been if you had used a different approach. The client asked me how certain I was that we should go first, and I said 100% certain, because I know that those who speak first win.

What do people fear that makes them want to have the other side lead? My client provided a rationale that I hear quite often. He argued that if we made the first offer, we might not ask for as much as what the other side would have offered if they had gone first. People may want the other side to lead because they are worried that they will undercut the bargaining zone and leave money on the table if they go first.

You do risk undercutting the bargaining zone with an ask that is not ambitious enough. This is why you need to prepare, analyze the weakness of the other side's BATNA, establish an ambitious goal, and then make the first offer. If you prepare well in this way, you can mitigate your risk of undercutting the bargaining zone and secure an anchoring advantage.

Another argument I hear from students and clients about why they would like the other side to go first is that they want to gain information about the other party's needs and preferences. They want to hear what their counterparty has to say, and they are convinced that they will learn from the other side's first offer. They do not see that they will be anchored by the other side's offer and that this will affect their outcome. Many negotiators I encounter contend they will be able to uncover information without getting anchored because they will ignore the anchor their counterparty is establishing.

Unfortunately, this is simply not true. Because anchoring happens at a subconscious level, we are not able to overcome it (Tversky & Kahneman, 1974; Galinsky & Mussweiler, 2001; Epley & Gilovich, 2005). Even after doing research on anchoring, I still find myself getting anchored by numbers every day (Galinsky, Mussweiler, & Medvec, 2002). Just as we cannot ignore the anchor established by the other side with their first offer, they will not be able to ignore the anchor we establish with our first offer. Thus, you gain a significant advantage by leading. But you need to be prepared to make the first offer; assessing the weakness of the other side's BATNA is a key element of this preparation and will allow you to go first confidently and reduce your risk of undercutting the bargaining zone.

An Information Asymmetry Between Buyers and Sellers

If we do not know anything about the other side, we may find it difficult to assess the weakness of their BATNA. There is actually a bit of an asymmetry between buyers and sellers in terms of what they tend to know about the other side's BATNA. Generally, sellers have much better insight into the other side's BATNA than buyers do because sellers know their customers and also know about their competitors. Even though this asymmetry exists, buyers would still want to make the first offer. The advantage of extending the first offer transcends roles; both buyers and sellers will get an advantage from leading. Clearly, there are some norms in particular industries about who generally leads, but norms should not replace understanding what the best strategy is and leveraging it to your advantage.

A buyer lacking information about the weakness of the seller's BATNA could mitigate the ensuing risk in two different ways. First, they could use an RFP to obtain information and learn more about the sellers in the market. By using an RFP as a BATNA generation tool, buyers can determine which sellers to advance to the negotiation phase and then go in and make the starting offer. Another way for buyers to reduce the likelihood of undercutting the bargaining zone is to make a very aggressive offer. This technique may work in one-shot negotiations (such as buying a car) where the relationship with the other side does not matter, but it is not an optimal approach when the relationship with the other side is important. Even in a one-shot deal, there are risks in doing this, which we will discuss in the next section. Because of these concerns, I suggest that you do your best to learn as much as you can about the other side, assess the weakness of the other side's BATNA, establish an ambitious goal, develop a first offer more aggressive than this goal, build a rationale for this offer that focuses on the other side's needs and then make the first offer in the negotiation.

In the next section, we will focus on the difference between an aggressive first offer and an outrageous offer.

How Aggressive Should My Offer Be?

There are two risks to making an offer that is perceived to be outrageous: (1) an extreme offer can provoke an extreme reaction from the other side, making it more likely to result in an impasse, and (2) you can lose credibility if your offer is perceived to be ridiculous.

Research has revealed that people are instinctively offended by asks that are well beyond a reasonable range and are more likely to respond to this type of offer with an aggressive counteroffer (Ames & Mason, 2015). Perhaps not surprisingly, first offers perceived as extreme are also more at risk of leading to an impasse in the negotiation (Galinsky et al., 2002; Schweinsberg, Ku, Wang, & Pillutla, 2012).

Your concern about credibility may relate to how much you value your relationship with the other party. If you care about your relationship, you want your first offer to be aggressive but not outrageous. The distinction between aggressive and outrageous rests on whether you can provide an appropriate rationale for your offer. If you cannot build a rationale it is likely that your offer is outrageous rather than ambitious. The divide between what is perceived as ambitious and what is viewed as outrageous may be different across cultures, so you need to adjust appropriately based on cultural norms. In this chapter, we will discuss how to build the rationale for your offer by crafting a compelling message that focuses on how your differentiators address the other side's pressing needs. We will also highlight the importance of focusing on the other party's interests and framing your message correctly.

Craft a Compelling Message

Many experienced negotiators fail to craft a compelling message when they negotiate. They go to the table focused on what they want to get, but they do not consider what they need to say.

TRAPS EXPERT NEGOTIATORS ENCOUNTER

Even expert negotiators get trapped.

1. Negotiating the wrong deal—negotiating what is standard or typical rather than putting the right issues on the table
2. Focusing primarily on highly quantified issues
3. Failing to establish an ambitious goal
4. **Telling no story or the wrong story in a negotiation**

Focus on How Your Differentiators Address the Other Side's Pressing Business Needs

When you build your rationale, you should ensure that it focuses on the other side and how your differentiators address the other side's pressing needs. In order to craft this message, you need to know what their needs are. What are their challenges? What do they need to accomplish? What problems are they having? If they are a publicly traded company, you may glean this information from the company's quarterly earnings calls, as we discussed in Chapter 2. If the other party is an individual, consider their goals and what they are trying to accomplish. Your differentiators may not meet all of your counterparty's needs, but you want to focus your message on how your differentiators address the specific needs that they have.

When building your rationale, you do not want to talk about yourself; you want to focus on the other side. I encourage my clients to be pronoun checkers and suggest that if they are using *I, me, we,* or *us* in their rationale, then they are talking about the wrong side. We have to be aware that our own egocentric bias (Ross & Sicoly, 1979) may cause us to focus on ourselves and we must overcome this tendency, focusing our rationale on the other side instead. When you build your rationale, make sure that your first sentence is about the other party, not yourself. This simple tactic helps you to ensure that you keep the focus on the other side.

If you are struggling to focus the rationale on the other side, it is likely that you do not have enough Storytelling Issues in your offer. This is an indication that you should go back to your list of Objectives and Negotiable Issues, ensure that you have objectives such as Addressing the Other Side's Pressing Needs, Differentiating Yourself, and Building the Relationship with the Other Side on your list and that you have negotiable issues connected to each of these objectives. It is likely that most of these issues will be Storytelling Issues when you categorize them on your Issue Matrix. When you have more Storytelling Issues on the table, it will be easier to focus your offer on the other party.

NEGOTIATING FOR YOURSELF IN EMPLOYMENT SITUATIONS

The tendency to focus on yourself rather than the other side seems to be even more pronounced when you are negotiating on your own behalf. One of my clients is a CEO who was based in Miami. He was being pursued for a different CEO role in New York, and the new job would require his family to move. The board was discussing his new role with him and wanted to give him a one-year contract.

He called me asking for assistance with the negotiation. He explained to me that he needed a long-term contract before he packed up his whole life to move to New York. His wife would be giving up her job and their children would be changing schools. It would be a chaotic year for them. In order to make the big move, he wanted at least a two-year contract. I asked him how he was going to ask for this, and he told me that he was planning to say exactly what he told me. I told him I was glad he called me before he spoke to his potential new employer, because he definitely needed my help. I advised him to shift the conversation away from his needs and toward the organization's needs. Why was the board hiring him? What did they want him to accomplish? He explained that the board was hiring him to come in and turn the company around; the company's margins had been declining for years and their reputation was severely damaged. The company needed a complete turnaround. We worked on an offer with a rationale that focused on the board's desire to implement a long-term plan for turning the business around within a five-year timeframe. His offer included metrics to measure the company's turnaround over a five-year period. His offer also included a five-year contract for him with a three-year review point, a performance-based bonus tied to the metrics for the turnaround, and a salary. The CEO ended the negotiation with a very attractive package and a five-year contract. I am confident that he would not have secured this if he had gone to the table talking about his family's challenges in moving rather than focusing on the company's needs for a turn-around plan.

A second example underscores that it is optimal to not only focus on the other side's pressing needs, but to highlight how your differentiators address these needs. This example comes from a woman who was enrolled in the Women's Senior Leadership Program offered through the Kellogg Center for Executive Women at the Kellogg School of Management, which I cofounded. I am passionate about helping women advance to senior roles in the corporate world. Given this, I was very concerned when I learned that one of our participants wanted to quit her job because she was traveling so much that her kids refused to call her mom—they would only call her by her first name. She was very upset by this and wanted to quit immediately. I urged her to try to negotiate with her employer before she quit to see if there was a way that she could travel less often. Research shows women are less likely to negotiate for themselves than are their male colleagues, and that women are very likely to leave a role when they are unhappy instead of trying to negotiate to change the situation (Babcock & Laschever, 2003). This tendency has very negative consequences for female executives, causing them to leave situations that might be able to be improved and often damaging relationships with their former employers. Companies generally like to have the opportunity to keep you and often are offended if you leave without discussing alternatives (Babcock & Laschever, 2003), so I always recommend that people negotiate before they depart.

This female executive worked for a biotech company in a role reporting directly to the CEO. She was on a fast track to a senior role, and her departure would definitely delay or derail this trajectory. I told her that quitting does not have an expiration date, and encouraged her to speak to her boss to try to adjust the situation before she quit. When we discussed her plan for this conversation, she initially wanted to go into the meeting and highlight that her kids needed her at home so she could not travel as much as she used to. It is natural to focus on yourself (Ross & Sicoly, 1979), and when you are negotiating for yourself, your own needs and desires are highly salient. It is critical, though, to take the time to do the translation and consider how what you want would help to meet the other side's needs and to add more Storytelling Issues to the table focused on the employer's and your manager's needs. I suggested that she consider why it would be good for the company if she was in the corporate office more often? It turned out that two of the company's drugs had been recently approved by the Food and Drug Administration.

The biotech had never been in the position before where multiple therapies had been approved at once. However, this executive came from a large pharmaceutical company and had a lot of experience commercializing multiple drugs at the same time, so she knew she could be uniquely helpful to the company as they brought these two products to market. She went into the discussion with her boss highlighting how the company's success would be tied to successfully delivering the two approved drugs to the market in rapid succession, that analysts were focused on the company's ability to accomplish this, and that nothing would impact the company's reputation more in the coming year than achieving this goal. She also explained that she was uniquely qualified to lead the company in delivering these two products to market but that she needed to be in the office every single day working with the team to achieve this goal. She highlighted that she knew that other people in the company could call on the customers in the field as well as she could, but that she was distinctively qualified to coordinate the various teams, provide strategic direction, and ensure that the two drugs were successfully positioned in the market to achieve commercial success. I am happy to report that her negotiation with her boss went incredibly well. Not only did she significantly cut down her travel time, she also got a promotion and a salary increase. I do not think she would have achieved these outcomes if she went into the meeting saying that she needed to travel less to have more time for her kids. This case is another demonstration that you will get more when you focus your first offer on how it addresses the other side's pressing business needs rather than when you talk about yourself.

Focus Your Rationale on the Other Side's Needs in Every Deal

Even in one-shot deals, you may secure an advantage from using a rationale that focuses on the other side's pressing needs rather than focusing on yourself. I mentioned earlier that when purchasing a car, I would be more inclined to use an outrageous offer than I would in a situation where I cared about an ongoing relationship with the other side. I guide a lot of friends and family members in car purchases. I always recommend that they ignore the sticker price, go into the dealership, and make the first offer. In fact, I suggest that if they want to look at the stickers on cars, they should visit dealerships in the evening or on a Sunday when the dealership is closed. If they pay attention to the sheet on the window, then the sticker price becomes the first offer. Instead, I encourage them to do their research in advance to uncover the invoice price, the holdback on the particular model, the advertising fee, and special incentives being offered in their zip code. Edmunds.com (https://www.edmunds.com/) is a great source for this information. Then, when they are well equipped with this research, I recommend going into the dealership to make the first offer. I suggest that if people are purchasing a new car from a dealership lot (not ordering a car and not having a dealer search for a car across the country and have it shipped to them), they start the negotiation at invoice minus holdback minus special incentives minus advertising fees minus $5,000–$12,000. It is not likely that you will be able to purchase a car at this price point, but I think it makes a good opening offer that anchors you well under invoice.

Even with this very aggressive starting point, though, I encourage people to make the rationale for the offer focus on the salesperson's interests and the dealership's needs, not on themselves. I encourage buyers to purchase their cars at the end of the month, at the end of the quarter, and if possible, when the weather is poor outside. When the weather is poor—think of the middle of winter in Chicago—fewer people may want to go out, walk the lot, and test drive new cars. If fewer people are shopping for cars, the dealership's BATNA is weaker, so you can establish a more ambitious goal. Most car salespeople want to close as many sales as possible by the end of the month to maximize their commissions. At the same time, many dealerships want to clear as many cars by the end of the quarter as possible to allow them to secure new inventory. So, when you are shopping at the end of the month, at the end of the quarter, in dreary weather, you can easily make the first offer with an ambitious goal and a rationale that focuses on the other side's needs to clear the car off the lot—rather than your need to get a good deal.

Focus on the Other Side's Interests

I want to build my rationale to focus on how my differentiators address the other side's pressing needs, and I want to ensure that I am focused on the other side's interests, rather than rights or power. When I open my mouth, I can speak at one of three levels: interests, rights, or power. William Ury, Jeanne Brett, and Stephen Goldberg (1988) identified these three levels of potential discussion and provided important advice about which level to focus on in your interactions. Interest-based comments focus on what the other side wants and why. Rights-based statements emphasize what the contract says, what we agreed to do, what our policy says, and whether something is fair or was promised to us. When we escalate to power-based remarks, we are generally delivering threats. These can be threats to remove business, suspend the shipment of products, escalate the conversation to a senior leader, sue the other side, or any other type of threat (Ury, Brett, & Goldberg, 1988). You can visualize these three levels of discussion as concentric circles, starting with interests in the middle, followed by rights, with the power circle around the outer edge, as shown in Figure 6.1.

The bull's-eye these concentric circles create is like a crystal ball. Ury, Brett, and Goldberg (1988) demonstrated that you can predict the other party's reaction before you even open your mouth. If you stay focused on interests, the other side is very likely to stay focused on interests as well. If you move off interests and highlight rights, the other side will at least escalate to rights, and they are even more likely to spiral to power. This escalation of conflict can be avoided by maintaining a focus on interests. In a later paper building on this initial research, Anne Lytle, Jeanne Brett, and Debra Shapiro recommend that negotiators stay focused on interests to keep the other side focused on interests, and that a focus on rights or power can often lead to one-sided outcomes that will favor the high-power party (Lytle, Brett, & Shapiro, 1999).

How do you know if you are focused on interests? If you are looking backward and talking about who said what, who did what, or who promised what, it is very unlikely you are focused on interests. I always say that if you are looking backward in the rearview mirror, you are probably not emphasizing the other side's interests. To maintain an interests focus, you want to stress the future—how can we move this ahead, how can we get this resolved to move forward, how can we work together again—this future orientation will keep you in the interests circle. If I am looking backward, it is likely that I have veered off interests and am focused on rights or even power. You want to stay

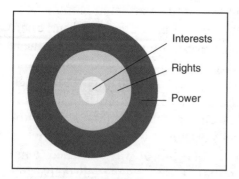

Figure 6.1: Three Levels of Discussion

focused on interests, and this is particularly critical when you are in the low-power position. If you have low power and escalate to rights, the discussion will likely advance to power and you will lose.

While it sounds easy to focus on interests, I find it relatively difficult to do this—especially when I know that I am right. Because I know that I have a natural tendency to escalate to rights and power and know that it is much more strategic for me to resist this temptation and remain focused on interests, I frequently draw the bull's-eye to remind myself to maintain an interests-focus. I remember when my oldest son Barrett (now a 24-year-old Stanford graduate) was a toddler and we were beginning to think about preschools. There was a preschool I really loved, but I knew they normally had a very long waiting list and that it was extremely difficult to get into the school unless you had an older child already attending the school, or you were on the board of directors. Barrett was my oldest, so there was no sibling connection to help him. Thus, I decided to volunteer for the board a year in advance to increase his chances to get into the school the following fall. Finally, the time for enrollment arrived and we applied. The school's policy was to first enroll siblings of current students and then to admit board members' children before the remaining slots were opened to others. I got a call from the board member responsible for admissions. She said there were many siblings in the class that year and that, unfortunately, after all of the siblings were admitted, there were only four slots remaining. Because there were five board members' children and only four slots, they resorted to a lottery, and unfortunately, Barrett did not get one of the four spots. He was placed on the waitlist—not at all the outcome I wanted.

At that point in time, I seem to have been convinced that my son going to the right preschool was the key to him getting into the right college. Despite feeling very disappointed as I listened to the admissions volunteer, I quickly realized that something seemed wrong. She was telling me that the school had a policy of keeping siblings together, and that one of the board members had twins, so when one got in, the other one automatically got in as well. I remember getting a tablet out of the drawer in the kitchen and drawing a bull's-eye on a piece of paper as I wrapped the telephone cord around the wall to sit in my dining room chair. I asked the volunteer exactly how they had done the lottery for the board members' children, and she told me that they had put the five children's names in the hat, pulled out one name, pulled out another name, and then pulled out one of the twins' names, so the other twin automatically took the fourth slot. I used to teach statistics when I was a graduate student at Cornell, so I knew what she had done was wrong. She had changed the probabilities, increasing the likelihood of the twins' admission over the other three children. I looked down at my bull's-eye—she had done the lottery wrong, and it was so tempting to point this out. However, this rights-based statement would have likely escalated to power, and I was in the low-power position—the school had the slots, and I had the child who needed one of them.

So, instead of pointing out the mathematical error, I asked if she had already called the other families. Of course, she had notified the families of the admitted children; everyone delivers good news before bad news. This meant that the lottery would clearly not be redone. I mentioned to the admissions volunteer that I loved the school's philosophy of keeping siblings together, but that in the future, we might want to consider how to operationalize this. I highlighted that the next year, a set of quadruplets might apply, and if so, we would need to consider how to handle this in the lottery. I suggested that in the future, we might want to include the names of the families rather than the names of the children. I said nothing else about the current error.

I then went to the director for the preschool, explained what had happened and how we needed to change our process going forward, but stressed that there was no reason to re-do the lottery this year. Instead, I asked her to look at the maximum numbers allowed for each class to see if there might be room in a class. Knowing that the director's interest would be to maintain harmony across all the board members, I emphasized that I did not want to cause any tension between board members this year. If I had highlighted the error to the volunteer responsible for admissions, I would have moved to the rights circle and violated the interests of the director. I am also quite confident that the volunteer in charge of admissions that year was not the one who developed the process, and that I probably would have heard that the process she used was the same way it had always been done. This escalation to rights would have created conflict, but I did not think that it would help to get my son into the school. In fact, I thought this escalation to rights would likely lead to an escalation to power that would decrease my son's chances for enrollment. Instead, I assessed that the chances of getting Barrett into the school were better served by focusing on the director's interest to avoid any board conflict and avoid discussing the problems of the past precedent. My conversation with the director was both positive and productive; she carefully reviewed the numbers for each of the classes and found that it was possible to increase the size in one of the classes so, happily, my son got into the preschool. While my strategy in this situation worked, I have to admit that I find it difficult in times like this to avoid a focus on rights. When I know I am right, I am tempted to highlight that I am right, but I know that it is more strategic to focus on the other side's interests so I draw my bull's-eye and try to maintain a focus on interests.

Framing Your Offer Correctly

When developing your offer, you want to build a rationale that focuses on the other side, highlights their interests, and frames the discussion correctly. Framing is one of the most powerful influence tools that exists, so you need to understand it well as you prepare to negotiate or resolve a dispute. Daniel Kahneman and Amos Tversky found that people are risk averse in the domain of gains and risk seeking in the domain of losses. They first explained this in Prospect Theory (Kahneman & Tversky, 1979), a theory so critical to describing human behavior that Danny Kahneman was awarded the 2002 Nobel Prize in Economics for his work developing this theory and his broader body of research. I had the privilege to meet Danny Kahneman, co-author a paper with him (Gilovich, Medvec, & Kahneman, 1998), and, when he invited me to present a paper at Princeton, I even got to have dinner at his home with him and his incredible wife, Anne Treisman. He is an amazing scholar who is an inspiration to social psychologists and economists across the globe.

Kahneman and Tversky (1979) explained that people are risk averse in the domain of gains, preferring a certain gain over the risky chance of getting more. On the other hand, people are risk seeking in the domain of losses and prefer the risk of a bigger loss over a certain loss. We like to hold on to our gains and prefer certain gains over the chance of a bigger gain. We do not like losses. We would prefer to take the risk of losing more to avoid having certain losses. I often use the analogy of an American soccer game (known as football in many other countries) to explain this idea. If you have ever played soccer or watched a professional soccer match or watched your children play soccer (as I have done for many years), you will notice that when a team is leading the match at the end of the game, they often become more risk averse and will pull back and play more defensively. On the other hand, when they are losing, they may become much more risk seeking and may even pull their goalie up on to the field to press forward with their attack, especially in the final minutes of the match.

Prospect theory (Kahneman & Tversky, 1979) explains that we are risk averse in the domain of gains, risk seeking in the domain of losses, and that losses loom larger than gains at a two-to-one ratio. That means that a loss is weighted two times more heavily in our minds than a gain of the same size.

How does this affect your strategy when you are building your rationale? You should first ask yourself what you want the other side to do. Do you want the other side to maintain the status quo and continue to do what they are currently doing or planning to do, or do you want them to move off the status quo and do something new or different? Doing what we are already doing is the risk averse course of action, so when you want to maintain the status quo, you want to highlight gains. Gain-frame words include benefit, advantage, increase, enhance, improve, value, revenue, expand, and value proposition. On the other hand, when you want to get the other side to do something new or different, you are asking them to take a risk, so you want to make them risk-seeking by highlighting loss. Loss-frame words include risk, competitive threat, cost, exposure, and vulnerability. I always remind my clients to highlight gain to *maintain* the status quo and highlight loss to *move off* the status quo.

We need to be very purposeful in selecting the frame in our rationale that drives people to do what we want them to do. To explain this concept, I often ask the executives with whom I work if they have ever tried leading change in their organizations. Almost all of them agree that it is incredibly difficult to drive change successfully. However, they also note that it is a lot easier to lead change in the middle of a crisis than trying to lead change proactively. A crisis creates a loss frame, making people more risk seeking and willing to do something different. We do not want to wait until a crisis occurs to lead change, though; we want to drive change proactively to avoid the crisis. The challenge is, however, that we often frame the change completely wrong; we often focus on the benefits, advantages, and improvements that the change will drive. We know from research, though, that people change to avoid losses, not to receive potential gains (Tversky & Kahneman, 1981; Kahneman,

Knetsch, & Thaler, 1991). If you want to drive change, you need to focus on the risk of not making the change.

We saw this in the recent COVID-19 pandemic. In the midst of this crisis, many organizations were able to drive changes in their business that would generally have taken a much longer time to implement. The often-quoted phrase that you "should never waste a crisis" stems from the fact that people are risk seeking in the domain of losses and willing to make changes. Consider how many companies were able to shift their businesses to virtual environments immediately. Companies adapted to new technology very quickly; the loss frame created by the crisis prompted quick movement that would never have been achieved prior to 2020 if companies were simply considering the benefits of enabling remote work.

Often in negotiations, you are trying to get the other side to do something new or different from what they are currently doing. You may be trying to get a customer to buy something new from you, motivate a supplier to improve their performance, encourage a potential acquirer to buy your business, or provoke a business partner to provide additional equity. Generally, when we are negotiating, we are trying to move the other side off the status quo, so we will often want to adopt a loss frame. Notice how the prompts that I have suggested for you to consider as you prepare for the negotiation are structured to lead you to a loss frame. I have advised you to think about the other side's pressing needs and challenges, analyze the weakness of the other side's alternatives, and structure a message to convey how your differentiators address the other side's pressing needs. All of these prompts are designed to provoke you to consider loss frames, because you will usually want to generate a loss frame as you approach your negotiations.

Highlight Loss to Create a Sense of Urgency

Imagine you are a sales executive for an equipment manufacturer and you are trying to get a customer to purchase equipment from you when they have always purchased their equipment from one of your competitors. It might be tempting to go to the customer and talk about the benefits of your equipment or how much faster it operates. But you have to remember that the customer will prefer the certain value they get from their current supplier over the risky chance that they might secure more value from your equipment. As Kahneman and Tversky

(1979) taught us, people prefer a certain gain over the chance of a bigger gain. Companies prefer certain value today from a current supplier over the potential for more value from switching to another provider. So, if you want a customer to switch to purchasing from you rather than your competitor, you need to highlight loss not gain. You would be more likely to get them to switch to your company's products if you discussed the risk of this type of equipment breaking down and the cost of it being out of service, and then explained how your equipment's unique ventilation system mitigates this risk. Without highlighting losses, you are less likely to get the potential customer to shift from the status quo.

I stress the importance of framing with my clients all the time. One of my Big 4 accounting clients was discussing options for their firm to expand their footprint with one of their global clients. At the time, there were a series of tax law changes in the United States, and the partner asked me for assistance in selling the firm's services to ensure that this client saved as much on their taxes as possible. He was planning to inform the client that they could potentially save $3 million in tax savings if they retrofitted their expat program to align with the new tax laws. I encouraged the partner to reframe his discussion, focusing on the loss his client would experience if they did not adjust their expat program. He shifted his language to a loss frame, explaining to his client that because of the new tax laws, there was now a significant disconnect between their existing expat program and the new tax laws, that this gap would cost them at least $3 million this year, and that if the program was not immediately adjusted, this gap would cost them $6 million within two years and $9 million over a three-year period. Given these extraordinary costs, he encouraged the client to make the changes immediately to their expat program. This loss framing worked and the client hired him to do the work.

Highlighting loss creates a sense of urgency that gains do not (De Martino, Kumaran, Seymour, & Dolan, 2006; Chou & Murnighan, 2013). Gains are nice to have; when I get around to it, I might like to have more gains. On the other hand, loss creates a sense of urgency; I do not like loss and I feel a sense of urgency to avoid the loss. In my client's example, the partner wanted the company to hire him that day, not sometime in the future. Highlighting loss created this sense of urgency.

When you are involved in selling a business, you want the other side to move off the status quo and purchase the company now—not someday in the future. Using gain words to discuss the benefits of owning the business, the value the company can provide, or the synergies the purchase will offer creates no sense of urgency. Synergies are often discussed in deals like this, but they do not drive the potential purchaser to want to acquire the business immediately. The gain frame around synergies lacks a sense of urgency and may lead the potential purchaser to think that they can do this deal sometime in the future. Instead, you want to use loss framing by highlighting the risks in the potential acquirer's business that will be mitigated by owning your company. Building your BATNA by generating other interested purchasers will also help you to create a strong loss frame because you can highlight the competitors' interest in acquiring your company and the risk to the potential acquirer if their competitor owns your business. I help many founders sell their companies, and I strongly believe that one of the most powerful motivators for companies to purchase a business is to keep their competitors from being able to make the purchase. A strong loss frame can be created in talking about the risk of a competitor doubling their footprint in the industry. Potential purchasers will not want to run the risk of another company swooping in to buy the business and will feel a sense of urgency to move the deal forward.

Highlight Loss—Do Not Create Fear

In my opinion, framing is one of the most powerful influence tools that exists, and I want to know how to frame my rationale effectively as I build my offer. I discussed the power of a loss frame to move the other side off the status quo, but I want to clarify that there is a critical distinction between loss and fear. We cannot drive change with fear. Fear often paralyzes people into a state of inaction and leads to the unintended consequence of freezing people into their current behavior (Job & Soames, 1988). This book focuses on taking the fear out of negotiation to eliminate the paralysis caused by this negative emotion. Psychological research has confirmed that fear has this effect: "When the fear is overwhelming, you experience fright: You neither fight nor flee; in fact, you do nothing. . . you obsess. . . ruminate, and complain, but you take no action" (Tsaousides, 2015). So, when you want to move the other side off the status quo, you want to highlight loss, not fear.

We can look at public service announcements to see the distinction between fear and loss. Many public service campaigns are highly ineffective because they utilize a gain frame to present the benefits of wearing a mask, the advantages of not smoking, or the value of cancer screening. These gain-frame messages are unlikely to move the other side off the status quo, so they are unlikely to yield the desired behavioral change. At some point in time, the individuals creating such public service campaigns started to harness loss language in their messages. One of the early attempts to do this was an anti-smoking campaign that featured a black lung. This ad failed because it crossed the line from a loss message to a fear message. People seeing the black lungs may have feared their lungs were already black—so they might as well continue to smoke. The anti-smoking campaign may have made smokers afraid but, unfortunately, did not change their behavior (Leshner, Bolls, & Wise, 2011). In fact, it may have even compounded the problem. According to Dr. R. F. Job, "High fear or anxiety provoking messages may be particularly ineffective in stopping behaviors which are themselves anxiety reducing since the message may elicit the unwanted behavior, e.g., reaching for a cigarette" (Job & Soames, 1988, p. 165).

In order to be effective, the message needs to highlight loss and tell people exactly how the loss can be avoided. An excellent example of a message that did this well was the "Back to Sleep" campaign to prevent SIDS by having babies sleep on their backs rather than on their stomachs (de Luca & Hinde, 2016). The message brought up a frightening event (the death of a child) but told people very clearly that they could avoid this event by flipping their babies over to sleep. The loss-framed campaign was a massive success with awareness among the general population that sleeping supine lowers the risk of SIDS rising from 50% to 80% from 2000 to 2010 (de Luca & Hinde, 2016) and deaths from SIDS steadily declining since the campaign's introduction (CDC, 2020). Loss messages effectively move people off the status quo whereas highlighting gains, such as benefits or advantages, or provoking fear do not.

Add a Story

Framing is a powerful influence tool that should be harnessed as you build the rationale for your offer. Sales executives often assume that the data they provide in their rationale will convince the other party to drop their existing supplier and purchase from them instead. Data is not an influence tool. Providing data is important, but you need to connect that data to an influence tool. The data alone is unlikely to bring about a change in suppliers, no matter how artfully it is presented.

Research has demonstrated that people remember data better when it is accompanied by a story. Experiments were run on individuals' retention of information with varying degrees of plot structure; comprehension and recall ability were found to increase as plot structure increased, regardless of the contents of the story (Thorndyke, 1977).

We know from research done by Amos Tversky and Danny Kahneman that events that are salient and easily come to mind are judged to be more likely to occur than events that are less salient (Tversky & Kahneman, 1973). One of the best ways to increase the salience of a message is to tell a story that reinforces your message. Imagine that I am a company selling cybersecurity services, and I am trying to convince a client to purchase these services. I would not want to discuss the advantage of having better cybersecurity because this gain-frame message will not cause the potential customer to move off the status quo and purchase my services. Instead, I would want to highlight the risk of cybersecurity attacks and discuss the need to monitor constantly for these ever-changing threats by purchasing my company's threat hunter services. This loss frame will be much more effective in moving the customer off the status quo. If I wanted to strengthen this message and make it more memorable, I would talk about the number of cyberattacks in the past year and give two vivid examples of huge data breaches with significant market consequences for the companies involved. The combination of the story and the correct framing will be a powerful one-two punch that will make my message more effective and much more memorable.

The Key Hallmarks of a Compelling Message

You want to ensure that you provide a compelling message before you make your first offer. This message should focus on how your differentiators address the other side's pressing needs. You also want to ensure that your message is focused on the other side's interests and that the offer is framed correctly. Remember that you want to highlight gain words when you want the other side to maintain the status quo, and that you want to highlight loss words when you want the other side to move off the status quo. This is critical in every negotiation you encounter, including times when you are negotiating for yourself.

MAKING THE OFFER AND CRAFTING A COMPELLING MESSAGE WHEN NEGOTIATING FOR YOURSELF

People often have a heightened sense of fear when negotiating for themselves. They are worried about whether they should lead and what they should say. I get many calls from clients, family, friends, and friends of friends seeking my advice on these personal negotiations.

Going First

Let's begin by discussing the desire to go first. As we discussed in this chapter, there is a tremendous advantage to making the first offer in any negotiation. When you go first, you can anchor the discussion at an attractive starting point, frame the conversation, set the table with the right issues, and secure the relationship-enhancing position. While I would like to go first in every negotiation, I cannot always go first when I am negotiating for myself. Why? Because I never want to begin to negotiate until I have an offer of employment in hand, and when I am young or am interviewing for a job with a large cohort (for example, an MBA student interviewing for a job with a consulting firm where the firm will make offers to many MBA students at the same time), the offer of employment is generally coupled with the terms of the offer. The potential employer is likely to say, "We would like to hire you and here is our offer." You do not want to begin the negotiation until you have the offer of employment because this may reduce the likelihood of getting that offer. So, you are obliged to wait for the employer to make the offer of employment, and it generally comes with the terms of the offer. In these situations, the employer goes first, even though you would like to lead.

As you advance in your career, however, you may have the chance to go first in employment negotiations. An employer may indicate that they would like to hire you and ask what it would take, providing you the chance to lead the conversation. Additionally, in situations where you are negotiating with your existing employer, you should always make the first offer. When you are asked to take on more responsibility, you should lead with an offer that discusses your new responsibilities, key metrics, transition plan, timeline, title, economics, and some bonus based on the performance that you are confident you will achieve in the role. Likewise, when you want a new role, you should ask for it by making the offer. When you make the first offer with your current employer, you get all of the advantages we have discussed.

The anchoring advantage is more pervasive in an employment negotiation because there will likely be fewer rounds of negotiation. When you are buying a car or purchasing a house, you may go back and forth many times with the other party making offers and counteroffers. This is not common in an employment negotiation, though; I often advise my clients and friends that they have three to four volleys in this situation (you make an offer, they respond, you finalize the deal or you make an offer, they respond, you counteroffer, they finalize the deal). So, if you already have the offer of employment, as you do when negotiating with your current employer, it is particularly important to go first and secure the starting point advantage.

Include Storytelling Issues

Your first offer needs to focus on a package of issues, not just salary. You need to include Storytelling Issues that highlight how your differentiators can address the employer's pressing business needs. Issues such as your responsibilities, the metrics for success, a timeline for achieving different metrics, a communication plan to announce progress being achieved, and a bet on the performance you can drive are excellent Storytelling Issues. The suggestion to include a bet on the performance you can achieve is a great way to communicate your confidence in what you can deliver. A contingency, such as a performance-based bonus where you will receive an additional 20% of your base salary if you achieve 10% growth in new customers while maintaining all profitable customers, can be an excellent Storytelling Issue because it allows you to communicate a clear message to the other side about what you are confident you can achieve. When you employ a contingency in your agreement, you want to include metrics that are objective, measurable, and known by both sides. For example, you would not want to bet on increasing profitability since you and your employer may have different access to information on the profitability of the business and varying levels of control over what this profitability is. Thus, a bet on new customers secured or revenue generated is a better bet. Revenue is objective, measurable, and known by both sides. If I were a company crafting a partnership agreement with another company, I might be worried that if the other company is booking the sales, they might know more about the revenue than I would, and if so, I might seek out a different metric that is objective, measurable, and known by both of us. We will discuss contingent agreements multiple times in the next few chapters, but I wanted to introduce them here because I tell everyone who is negotiating for themselves that they should include a contingency in their offer. As you will see in the next chapter, I also advise that they should include the contingency in one or two of their options but not all three of the options in their offer. You will learn more about this in the next chapter.

For now, I want you to see that a contingency like this is an incredible storytelling tool that emphasizes your confidence in what you can achieve for the employer. I would also encourage you to add a story that highlights how your differentiators have allowed you to achieve significant success in the past. People interviewing for jobs are often encouraged to be ready to tell a clear story that accentuates their capabilities, but I suggest that your storytelling should not cease at the interview stage. You should tell a story that stresses your differentiators when you are making an offer, and you should tell stories that highlight your performance on a regular basis as you work for your employer. As noted earlier, people remember data better when it is accompanied by a story. A story about your excellent performance will provoke the availability bias (Tversky & Kahneman,1973; Thorndyke, 1977) and make your excellent performance seem more frequent and likely to occur. Always remember that no one pays as much attention to your performance as you do (Heneman, 1974), so you want to tell compelling stories showing what you have accomplished and shape the way that others perceive your performance.

Do Not Focus on Rights or Power

Your offer should include a package of Storytelling Issues along with the normal Contentious Issues (salary and internal title) and Tradeoff Issues (timeline to begin, moving expenses, and external title). Your offer should also include a story that emphasizes how your differentiators can address the employer's pressing business needs. In addition, your offer should focus on the employer's interests rather than rights or power. When you are negotiating with your current employer, it may be tempting to say that you should get a raise because you know that Bob, who performs worse than you, is paid more than you. Avoid this statement, though, because it is problematic in numerous ways. First, it only focuses on the single issue of pay and will make your conversation more contentious. It is also risky because highlighting "unfairness" focuses on rights rather than on the other party's interests. We know that when we focus on rights, the other side will either focus on rights or escalate to power (Lytle et al.,1999). In this case, the employer may focus on rights, becoming defensive and providing evidence that Bob deserves to be paid more than you, or may escalate to power and say that if you do not like the current compensation system, you should find a new employer. In either case, this conversation will likely not go as well as it would if you focus on the employer's interests, stressing the challenges they are currently facing in achieving a few of their goals for the coming year and how your differentiators can help them to overcome these challenges and achieve their goals.

Frame Your Offer Correctly

I am suggesting that you discuss how your differentiators can help the employer to overcome specific challenges rather than simply discussing how your differentiators can help them to achieve their goals. This is because I am assuming that you are asking for a new role or a salary increase, so you want the employer to move off the status quo. Remember that when you want the other side to move off the status quo, you need to make them risk-seeking to do something new or different and that people are risk-seeking in the domain of losses, not in the domain of gains (Kahneman & Tversky, 1979). This is why I am encouraging you to include some loss words, such as the challenges they are facing, the competitive threat the business in encountering, or some risk to the business that you can help to mitigate. You want your offer to underscore how your differentiators can help the employer to overcome challenges, risks, or threats in their business. It may seem like you can only do these things if you are a very senior executive, but I would argue that these ideas can be deployed at any level of seniority.

The Plight of My Ice Cream Shop

To highlight this, I want to talk about my local ice cream store. My favorite ice cream store has two locations. One is downtown, just off a beautiful town square, and the other seasonal location is in a cabin in a small, nearby picturesque town, right beside a creek that is a favorite spot for locals to go tubing in the summer. This is an idyllic location for an ice cream shop because an afternoon of tubing is perfectly accompanied by a delicious ice cream cone afterward. The challenge for my favorite ice cream shop, and many other local businesses in the time of COVID-19, is that the pandemic limited the number of employees willing to work with the public, so many of the shops and restaurants struggled to have enough employees to deal with the high demand from the locals and the many summer tourists who visit our town. This challenge clearly affected my ice cream shop. I stopped by their cabin location for a cone on a Sunday afternoon and found them closed. Why would they be closed on a sunny, Sunday afternoon in the middle of summer? Probably because they did not have enough employees to staff their second location when their primary location had incredible demand.

Imagine I am an employee who scoops ice cream at the main location on the square, but I know I could assume a leadership role in running their second location. As I already have the job at the ice cream shop, I should feel comfortable going to the owner and making the first offer on how I can solve his dilemma of the sporadic schedule at the second location. My differentiators could be that I am incredibly reliable, I am a popular high school senior with many friends who would like to work with me, and I am so influential with these friends that I can get them to show up every day that they are scheduled, stay for their entire shift, pleasantly serve customers, and wear their face masks as they scoop the ice cream. I could go to my employer and discuss the losses he is encountering when the second location is closed and the competitive threat of having locals who desire ice cream visit another shop instead. I might even tell a story about the family of one of my friends who visited the location, found it closed, and then took his family of six to a competitor's location, stating how they had never tried the competitor's ice cream before but really liked it. I could then offer to become a supervisor at the second location and discuss that two of my responsibilities will be recruiting and retaining employees to scoop ice cream. Other responsibilities will be training the team to ensure that they are operating in a safe way during the COVID-19 pandemic, delivering good service to the customers, and overseeing the schedule for the second location so that it is consistently open every day. I might even suggest that I was so sure that I could achieve the goal of a consistently open, well-staffed shop that I would be willing to tie a portion of my pay to this commitment—with a performance bonus based on the shop being open for the posted hours every day.

This example highlights how it is important to put the right issues on the table and craft a compelling message whenever you are negotiating for yourself—at any level. In the next chapter, we will discuss how you can reinforce your message with a multiple offer and how to structure this offer.

Summary

Many negotiators are afraid to make the first offer and default to letting the other side lead. When they do this, however, they make a terrible mistake in allowing the other side to anchor the negotiation at an advantageous starting point, frame the discussion, set the table with only the issues that they want to discuss, and secure the relationship-enhancing position. Although you may be afraid to lead, you should really fear letting the other side go first.

Your fear in providing the opening offer will be reduced if you build the right rationale for your offer. You should go first and create a compelling message to go with your offer. Your message needs to focus on the other party, rather than yourself, highlight how your differentiators address the other side's pressing needs, focus on the other side's interests, and be framed correctly. You want to emphasize loss words when you want to move the other side off the status quo and gain words when you want the other side to maintain the status quo. You may also want to include a vivid story to increase the impact of the framing that you select.

Once you have your message, you need to create an offer that will reinforce your compelling message. In the next chapter, we will discuss how using three offers rather than one will help you to do this.

7

Reinforce Your Message with a Multiple Offer

Often, we are afraid to make the opening offer because we fear that we will offend the other side, or that they will walk away. You can reduce this fear and deliver an offer that reinforces your compelling message when you go to the table with three offers rather than one. This chapter focuses on the strategy of making a multiple equivalent simultaneous offers, known as a MESO. We will discuss why you should use multiple offers rather than a single offer, and how to construct your MESO most effectively to convey your compelling message.

Starting the negotiation with three offers delivered at the same time will engage the other side in the discussion and make you look flexible and cooperative—which will enhance your ability to build your relationship with your counterparty. Leading with multiple offers will take the fear out of negotiation and provide many strategic advantages that we will discuss in this chapter. These advantages will enable you to both build your relationship with the other side and maximize your outcome when you leverage MESOs, rather than single package offers, throughout the negotiation.

What Is a MESO?

When you deliver a *multiple equivalent simultaneous offer (MESO)*, you are providing multiple offers at the same time. I generally recommend that you deliver three offers. These three offers have relatively the same value to you, so they are considered "equivalent," but it is likely that the other side will value them quite differently. You will deliver the offers at the same time, side by side, in a simultaneous format. Table 7.1 shows you how the three offers would be structured.

Table 7.1: Your MESO Architecture

	Option A	Option B	Option C
Issue 1: Storytelling Issue	Vary	Vary	Vary
Issue 2: Storytelling Issue	Vary	Vary	Vary
Issue 3: Storytelling Issue	Vary	Vary	Vary
Issue 4: Storytelling Issue	Vary	Vary	Vary
Issue 5: Storytelling Issue	Vary	Vary	Vary
Issue 6: Tradeoff or Contentious Issue	Constant	Constant	Constant
Issue 7: Tradeoff or Contentious Issue	Constant	Constant	Constant
Issue 8: Tradeoff or Contentious Issue	Constant	Constant	Constant
Issue 9: Tradeoff or Contentious Issue	Constant	Constant	Constant
Issue 10: Contentious Issue	Vary or Constant	Vary or Constant	Vary or Constant
Issue 10: Tradeoff or Contentious Issue	Constant	Constant	Constant

I generally refer to the three offers as Option A, Option B, and Option C because I like to frame the discussion around choice rather than dealmaking. People love to have choice (Brehm, 1956; Brown, Read, & Summers, 2003). Though it is unlikely that your counterparty will simply pick one of the offers (you actually want to concede, as we will discuss in Chapter 9), providing them with a choice of three offers has been shown to have tremendous strategic advantages.

Why Three Offers Rather Than One?

When you use multiple offers, you secure a stronger anchoring effect. Three simultaneous offers will also allow you to gather more information about the other side's relative priorities and evaluate their preferences. In addition, multiple offers will enable you to be aggressive in your offer while signaling cooperation and flexibility. As this chapter will highlight, with MESOs you can persist longer on issues that are important to you while also highlighting your differentiators and communicating a compelling story to the other side. Most importantly, though, when you deploy a MESO instead of a single package offer, you can maximize your outcome and build your relationship with the other party.

While there are many advantages to delivering three offers instead

TRAPS EXPERT NEGOTIATORS ENCOUNTER

Even expert negotiators get trapped.

1. Negotiating the wrong deal—negotiating what is standard or typical rather than putting the right issues on the table
2. Focusing primarily on highly quantified issues
3. Failing to establish an ambitious goal
4. Telling no story or the wrong story in a negotiation
5. **Making single offers rather than employing a multiple-offer approach**

of one, many experienced negotiators continue to use a single-offer strategy. It may be the norm to make one offer, but this chapter will reveal that deploying a MESO is much more strategic.

Maximize Your Outcome

Research has demonstrated that people who deliver multiple offers secure better outcomes for themselves than people who make a single offer (Leonardelli, Gu, McRuer, Medvec, & Galinsky, 2019). You will get a better outcome because of the numerous tactical advantages defined in this chapter. Not only will you achieve a better outcome for yourself, but research reveals that this strategy is also likely to improve the outcome for the other side compared to the outcome attained with a single-offer strategy (Leonardelli et al., 2019).

Build Your Relationship

While you will maximize your outcome by using a MESO, the other side will also like you more than if you deliver a single offer. So, deploying a MESO allows you to maximize your outcome and build your relationship (Leonardelli et al., 2019).

Signal Flexibility and Cooperation

Why do you build your relationship when you deliver a MESO rather than a single offer? Research (Leonardelli et al., 2019) has demonstrated that when you provide a choice of multiple offers, you are perceived to be more flexible and cooperative. People like to have choice even when they do not select one of the choices (Brehm, 1956; Gilbert & Ebert, 2002). Using a multiple offer allows you to build your relationship with the other side while maximizing your own outcome; a key advantage of MESOs is that they simultaneously have a relationship and an outcome effect.

Establish a More Aggressive Starting Point

In addition to signaling your flexibility and cooperation, using a MESO allows you to make your first offer more ambitious than if you deliver a single offer. As mentioned in Chapter 6, when you care about your relationship with the other side, you want your offer to be ambitious but not outrageous; you want to develop a great rationale that focuses on the other side and how your differentiators address your counterparty's pressing needs. You do not want to make an offer that causes you to lose credibility. In addition, there is evidence that a very aggressive single offer may not only damage the relationship but might also have a negative impact on your outcome. This research reveals that an aggressive offer may provoke an aggressive counteroffer (Ames & Mason, 2015). However, research has also demonstrated that when you deliver a MESO, you look cooperative and flexible, so you can ask for more without provoking an aggressive counteroffer from the other side (Leonardelli et al., 2019).

Anchor the Starting Point

As discussed, one reason why you are likely to secure a better outcome for yourself when you deliver a MESO rather than a single offer is because you can start at a more aggressive point and are less likely to provoke an antagonistic response from the other side (Leonardelli et al., 2019; Jones & Nisbett, 1971). In addition, though, a multiple offer provides two other specific anchoring advantages. First, a multiple offer is more complex than a single offer, and we know from research that complexity prompts a stronger anchoring effect. Multiple offers are likely to produce a stronger starting point advantage than a single package offer. The higher the level of complexity, the stronger you would expect the anchoring effect to be (Tversky & Kahneman, 1974; Whyte & Sebenius, 1997; Galinsky, Ku, and Mussweiler, 2009).

In addition, recent research demonstrates that when you use a multiple offer, your opening offers are seen as more credible and people will spend more time considering them, further increasing the anchoring effect (Leonardelli et al., 2019). Specifically, this research revealed that MESOs are perceived as more sincere and are taken more seriously than a single package offer. This sincerity effect means your counterparty spends more time evaluating the offer, thus enhancing the anchoring effect and leading to a better outcome.

I experienced this effect when I was purchasing a house in the Chicago area. My husband and I had been looking at a lot of houses when our realtor showed us a home on a street that bordered Lake Michigan. The house was incredible, and it was also significantly outside of our price range. I am never deterred by a list price for a house, though, because I know that, depending on the weakness of the seller's BATNA, the list price may be significantly reduced during negotiation. I decided that we would try to secure this type of reduction on the house on Lake Road. I learned that the sellers who had built the home were retiring and moving to the city. I crafted our message to focus on making their move as simple as possible, and created three offers that varied which furniture would remain in the house at closing. I highlighted that we were a young family who would take excellent care of their beautiful home, where we planned to raise our two sons. I also conveyed that we wanted to make the move to their Chicago condo as easy as possible. In Option A, I said that we would be willing to purchase the house and all of its furniture to simplify their move. Option B noted that there might be some special pieces of furniture that they would like to keep but that we would take care of everything else they wanted to leave. On the other hand, if they wanted to take all of the furniture with them, this would be fine with us and we reflected this in Option C. We focused our message on how we wanted to make their transition to their new condo as easy as it could be. The prices for the house varied across Options A, B, and C, with A being the highest and C being the lowest, but all three of the offers were significantly lower than the asking price. How much lower, you might wonder? The offers started at about 40% off the asking price. The low range of the offers made our real estate agents very uncomfortable; they felt our offers were so low that we would lose credibility and not get a response at all. Although I acknowledged that the offers were ambitious, I believed we would get a response, because the MESO frames a story focused on the seller's needs.

One of the advantages of the Storytelling Issues in the negotiation is that you can focus your story on the needs of the other side. We were varying these Storytelling Issues across our three offers and had a very strong focus on addressing the sellers' needs. In my experience, when you focus your message on the other side, it is far less likely that they will not respond. Our agents resisted saying that they would damage their own reputations if they delivered such ridiculously low offers. I said I would be willing to meet with the seller directly to provide the three options so that their reputations would not be affected. The sellers preferred that I meet with their agent instead. I agreed and delivered my three offers to the sellers' agent; all of the offers focused on making the move as painless as possible for the sellers.

I was delighted when the sellers came back with a counteroffer that also contained three options. All three of their counteroffers were significantly lower than the original list price. The MESO we provided anchored the sellers, and they adjusted their price dramatically, shocking my agents, who had expected that we would get no more than 10% off the list price by the end of the negotiation. Instead, we had secured an extremely significant concession in the first counteroffer. I doubt we could have achieved this if we had not made three offers. If we went in with only one of our offers, we might have offended the sellers and could have elicited an aggressive counteroffer very close to their starting point. Instead, the MESO had the effect of anchoring while also making the first offer seem more credible and making us look flexible and cooperative. We were able to purchase the house at a price substantially lower than other offers the sellers had rejected in the past and well below the asking price. I am confident that the MESO we used was key to this success and to our ability to purchase the home we have loved for the past 16 years—although we never fell in love with the house during the negotiation!

Gather Information About the Other Side's Priorities

A MESO also allows you to gather better information about the other side's priorities and preferences than a single offer does. When you use a single offer, you often gather information by asking questions, but when you use a MESO, you learn from observing the other side's reactions. I would argue that this allows you to secure a much finer grade of information than questions alone. Questions allow you to uncover what the other side wants, but a multiple offer allows you to surface the value of different issues and learn what the other party is willing to give up in order to get what they say that they want.

Consider my negotiations with my nanny described in Chapter 4. If I had planned to make my nanny a single offer, I might have asked her a series of questions first. For example, I might have asked about her salary expectations. I am quite certain she would have said that she would rather make $21 an hour rather than $12 an hour. I am also certain that if I asked her whether she would prefer one week of vacation time or six weeks of vacation time, she would have said six weeks and that she would like to select the days. I think she would have also said that it would be great to have insurance and that the option of getting the master's degree was excellent for her. In essence, I would have learned what she wanted, and I expect that she would have wanted everything. Many negotiators ask a lot of questions because they want to uncover what the other side wants. I would argue, though, that it is not enough to know what the other side wants—what you really need to find out is what they are willing to give up to get what they say that they want. What is the value to the other side of each of the issues? It is unlikely that you will uncover this information through questions alone. You can unlock this information, however, by observing the other side's reactions to multiple offers.

I gave my nanny a MESO with three options rather than a single offer. These options were all equal in value to me but looked relatively different to her.

I thought that she was really excited about the health benefits. She told me that she had never had a position with health insurance included before, and she seemed delighted about this being a component of the offer.

Table 7.2: Offer to Nanny

	Option A	Option B	Option C
Opportunity to pursue master's degree in education	Employer will pay for one course per semester at (named) local college	Not included	Not included
Health insurance	Employer will provide health insurance with $100 annual deductible	Employer will provide health insurance with $500 annual deductible	Employer will provide health insurance with $1000 annual deductible
Number of vacation days	Six weeks of vacation time	Three weeks of vacation time	One week of vacation time
Selection of vacation days	Dates selected by employer but provided in full-week increments	Dates selected by employer but provided in full-week increments	4 days selected by employer; three days selected by employee
Hourly rate	$12/hour	$14/hour	$21/hour

Why would I want to include health benefits when this was not generally included in offers for in-home childcare workers at the time? The nanny was going to be with my two boys, so I needed her to be healthy and be able to see a doctor whenever needed. When my kids were little, I would often say that a sick nanny means a sick child → means a sick mommy → means a sick life, so I definitely wanted my nanny to be able to see a doctor when needed. When I delivered my three options, I had health insurance in each of the options. From her reactions to the offers, I could tell that she did not value the health benefits as much as the other items in the options; she clearly valued days off and dollars per hour much more than health insurance. I asked her if her husband had health insurance, and she informed me that he did. My health insurance would have been a secondary plan for her, and she did not really need it or value it that much. The cost of the health insurance was at least $3,500 a year to me, and I figured out that it was far less valuable than that to her. I ordinarily encourage my clients to modify one of their three options in their first concession and counteroffer, for example, with options A, B, and D. It is very rare to put all three initial offers aside, but it is exactly what you do if you learn that something is less valuable to the other side than it costs you to provide. So, I changed all three of the options and offered her options D, E, and F without health insurance. In D, I increased the hourly rate; in E, I increased the number of vacation days; and in F, I offered the combination of slightly more pay than the original three offers and slightly more vacation time. In each of the three new options, I offered an additional $1,700 in value between hourly wage and time off, but each of the three options was actually $1,800 better for me than my original three offers because the $3,500 health insurance benefit was not included. How did it look as I made three new offers that were all better for me than the original three? I think I looked flexible and cooperative. Based on what my nanny had told me she valued through her reactions to the original MESO, I provided two options that increased her pay, and two with more vacation days. One of the options provided the combination of more vacation time and slightly more pay. I used the MESO to identify what was important to her, and with this better information, I was able to "concede" by providing three options that were more valuable to her but cost me $1,800 less than my original three alternatives.

As this example reveals, a MESO allows you to uncover more information than a single-offer strategy, and most notably, to learn about the counterparty's relative preferences. When you ask a question about a single issue, you will only reveal the person's absolute preferences on that one issue and nothing deeper. If you asked my nanny if she wanted health insurance, she would have said yes; however, the MESO allowed us to uncover that she did not value health insurance as much as other issues that cost me less to provide. I encourage my clients to avoid single-issue questions. For example, I would avoid asking, "What geography do you want?" or "Can we be exclusive?" These types of single-issue questions reveal the other side's absolute preferences rather than their relative preferences. I encourage my clients to ask tradeoff questions instead, such as: what is more important to you, geography or exclusivity? Even better though, never believe what a counterparty tells you in response to any question and, instead, test it with an offer. It is not that the other side is intentionally deceiving you; it is simply that they may not be aware of their relative preferences, so a question will provoke feedback about their absolute preference. A multiple offer will allow you to uncover the other party's relative preferences and get a sense for how much your counterparty values each issue.

Make an Offer More Rapidly

Often, people ask many questions to uncover the information they feel they need from the other side in order to craft an offer. Of course, the risk is that every time you ask a question, you take a risk that your counterparty will answer with an offer and secure an anchoring advantage. Research has revealed that offers made early in the negotiation with a smaller amount of information yield less optimal outcomes than offers made later in the negotiation when more information has been exchanged (Sinaceur, Maddux, Vasiljevic, Nückel, & Galinsky, 2013). The risk, though, is that time you spend asking questions and exchanging information exposes you to the possibility that the other side makes a first offer.

Using a MESO can change the cadence of the negotiation by allowing you to make an offer much earlier in the exchange and leverage the MESO as an information collection tool. This allows you to uncover the information essential for optimal outcomes with an offer on the table to anchor the discussion.

Sometimes I observe my clients suffering from paralysis by analysis as they prepare to negotiate. As we discussed in the previous chapter, fear sparks this type of paralysis. They seem to have a desire to analyze every possible scenario before making their first offer. I encourage them to focus their analysis on the weakness of the other side's BATNA, establish an ambitious goal, ensure that they have considered all their objectives so they can put the right issues on the table, develop their message, and then craft their MESO and initiate the discussion with this first offer on the table. As we discussed earlier, you can learn from the other side's reactions to your offer and fuel your ongoing analysis with the information you are securing.

Maintain a Package Focus

Another significant advantage of MESOs is that they help you maintain focus on the whole package of issues rather than negotiating each issue separately. Many people believe it is easier to settle things one at a time as the discussion moves forward. If we do that, however, we are likely to end up with only Contentious Issues on the table, making the discussion much more heated. When you negotiate issue by issue, it is likely that the discussion will be more contentious and will take longer than if you have a package of issues on the table and can tradeoff on the differences in the two sides' preferences across the multiple items. When you negotiate issue by issue, you actually lose leverage because you cannot use an issue that is already settled to get what you want on something else. Issue-by-issue negotiations are also more likely to result in an impasse because you are left with only Contentious Issues on the table. Even if you secure an agreement in an issue-by-issue negotiation, it is more likely to be a suboptimal agreement than if you negotiate at the package level because when you settle things one at a time, you are not able to identify the right tradeoffs. When you negotiate at the package level, on the other hand, you have Storytelling Issues to use to capture more of what you want on the Contentious and Tradeoff Issues and the conversation is less contentious. When you are negotiating the full package of items, the negotiation also takes less time, and you are more likely to identify tradeoffs across the issues, resulting in a more optimal agreement.

People often tell me they like to settle easy issues early in the negotiation to create a sense of progress and build reciprocity. I believe that there are two significant challenges with this approach. First, just because something is easy for you to settle does not mean that the issue is not valuable to the other side. It could be an excellent Storytelling Issue that could be used to get more of what you want on a Contentious or Tradeoff Issue. Settling an issue in isolation weakens your ability to use it to get what you want on other issues.

I would also argue that reciprocity is a great thing, but that the other side's memory may become very short when you have made the last concession. You may try to remind them that you just gave them what they wanted on delivery time, but they may say, "We are not talking about the delivery anymore, we are discussing the customization of the product, and I need you to work with me on the fee for the customization." I encourage my clients to maintain leverage by keeping all of the issues on the table until everything is settled.

It is easy to talk about package deals, but it is hard to live by this rule. We tend to get absorbed in issue-by-issue negotiations all the time. One strategy to try to avoid being pulled into single-issue agreements is to watch your verb choice. Using the verb "will" pushes us into an issue-by-issue agreement, but the verb "could" opens us up to discussing a whole package. I encourage my clients to imagine that the other side has a gigantic vault sitting next to them, and every time they settle an issue, I like them to imagine it being locked away in the vault. When I say, "We will customize the product in this way," I have just put customization in the vault. If I say, "we will deliver the product to you by this date," I have just added delivery time to the vault as well. Imagine that I shut the vault door with these two commitments and hand the other side the vault and the key. We still need to discuss the price for the product, though, and I have nothing to use to secure a good price because the other side is already holding the other parts of the deal in the vault. I will be lucky if the other side does not take out a sledgehammer and pound me down on price because it is their fiduciary responsibility to get the best possible price, and I have not made anything at stake with the price. If, on the other hand, I said, "We could customize the product in this way, and we could deliver it by this date if this is a priority to you," I have left the vault door open and we can discuss everything as a package. I can maintain the leverage of using the other side's preferences on the customization and delivery time to get what I want on the price for the product. This example highlights why I always stress that when you negotiate issue by issue, you lose the leverage to get what you want on other elements; once you have settled something, you no longer have the issue that is settled to get what you want on anything else. The key is to keep the vault door open by avoiding commitments on single issues; remember, nothing is settled until the whole package is settled.

To settle at the package level, it is important to watch your verb choice and also to choose carefully the language you use in your discussion. Words such as "linked," "connected," "interdependent," "dependent," "integrated," and "full solution" make it easier to highlight the connectivity across the issues and focus on the package level.

In my opinion, though, the best way to maintain a package focus is to utilize a MESO rather than a single offer. When you use a single offer, the conversation will often fragment into issue-by-issue discussions. On the other hand, when you have a MESO on the table with three packages being presented, even if the conversation moves down a level, you are still focused on one of the three packages rather than on a single issue.

Many procurement departments will try to go issue by issue and then settle on a price at the end. In their words, they often like to "hold everything constant" so that they can compare the various suppliers on price. But if you are one of these suppliers, you do not want the comparison to be focused on price; you want to highlight how your company's differentiators best address the customer's pressing business needs. You want the full package to be discussed—not a single issue. You want the vault door open, and to ensure that everything—not just the price—is on the table as the customer selects their supplier. Using MESOs usually pushes the purchasing department to pull in the internal clients to clarify or discuss their preferences on the options that have been presented, which helps you maintain a focus on the whole package rather than on a single issue.

An example of keeping the vault door open comes from one of my consulting clients. Their firm does projects for integrated health care systems and hospitals. They were bidding on a project that focused on recapturing lost Medicare money for a large hospital. Their proposal was priced at $3 million. My client was informed that procurement could not approve the project because their competitor was willing to do the work for $1.5 million. The customer told my client they really liked their team, and they wanted to work with them, but they needed them to "match the competitor's price." How many times have you, or someone in your company, said, "We'll match it"? Be honest. If your answer is at least once, then I would encourage you and your team to practice the whole sentence that you are actually communicating to the other side. When you say, "We'll match it," you are conveying a full sentence, but you only hear yourself saying half of it. So, if you or someone on your team says, "We'll match it," then gather your team together and practice the full sentence out loud. "We'll match it . . . because we're no better than them." This is the clear message that you are conveying to the other side when you say these words. If you do not like the sound of that sentence, I would avoid saying the first half of it.

My client had sat in on my classes more than once, and he had become a savvy negotiator. My words sounded in his ears. He went back to the hospital group to apologize, saying that when he gave them the proposal, he had made the assumption that they were focused on getting back all of the Medicare money that they had lost. He reiterated that he had put together a team that had worked on projects like this 41 times in the past with exceptional recovery of Medicare dollars. He told the hospital that because he had assumed they wanted to get back all of their Medicare money, he had included this very experienced team in the proposal. He continued to explain that he was sure that his competitor has a fine team, but they could not be as experienced—because his firm was the first to do these types of projects and had completed many more of them than any other firm.

He suggested that perhaps the client was speaking to the competitor because they were trying to balance the cost of the project rather than being solely focused on the recovery of all of the Medicare money. He went on to say that if their goal was to balance the cost of the project against the likelihood of recovering all of the money, he was happy to work with them, explaining that he had many other teams doing this type of work. In fact, he had a team that looked more like the team he would expect the competitor to provide. He explained that this team had done this type of work five times for five hospitals with a nice recovery rate, but not the same type of recovery rate that the team achieved who had done it 41 times for 41 hospital systems. He said that this other team would look a lot more like the team the client would get from the competitor, so he would be willing to offer the team that had completed five of these projects for $1.5 million. On the other hand, if the client wanted the team that had completed 41 of these projects, he would offer that team for $3 million.

Not surprisingly, the hospital group chose the experienced team for $3 million and never looked back. In the world of Medicare funds, the $1.5 million difference in fees would be nothing compared to the value of getting all of the Medicare dollars refunded. It is very likely that if my client had made the mistake of negotiating issue by issue and settled on a specific team before he negotiated the fees, he would likely have ended up with the lower fee. By keeping the package of issues on the table and presenting a MESO, he maximized both his monetary outcome and his client's satisfaction with the completed work.

Multiple offers allow you to maintain a package focus and achieve more optimal outcomes. A key element to securing optimal agreements is to persist on issues that are important to you. As we will discuss in the next section, MESOs allow you to persist without frustrating the other side.

Persist Without Frustrating the Other Side

Often while negotiating, we will drop an issue as soon as the other side pushes back and says that something will not work for them. We may fear that we will offend the other party or lose the deal if we persist, so we quickly drop the issue. Dropping issues in this way leads to suboptimal agreements and causes us to leave an extraordinary amount of money on the table.

For example, let's say that you make a single offer to a potential Japanese business partner which includes your company booking the sales in North America. The other side responds that they want to book the sales in North America instead. You make a counteroffer with your firm booking North American sales, and they reiterate that they do not want this. It will then be very difficult to make another single offer that includes your company booking North American sales because it will look like you are not listening to the other side. You face the risk of either aggravating your counterparty or dropping the request for your company to book North American sales, an issue that is important to you. Neither solution is optimal—one option causes you to damage your outcome, and you fear that the other option may cause you to damage the relationship.

If you used a MESO instead, you could persist much longer and maximize your outcome while maintaining the relationship with the other side. Each of the three initial MESO packages would include your firm booking North American sales. Other elements of the offers would vary but this Tradeoff Issue would be constant across all three options. You now are positioned to persist on this issue. When your counterparty states that they want to book these sales instead, you can reveal that you hear them and are listening without dropping the issue from consideration. You would simply revise one of the options—turning Option C into Option D—and in this new option you might include a 50/50 split in booking North American sales, but you would show the other side what this change will do to the revenue share and other terms. So, now your counterparty is considering Options A, B, and D. Notice that your company booking all North American sales is still on the table in two of the three alternatives and that this issue is actively being discussed. Using a MESO allows you to signal that you are listening and being flexible by changing one of the alternatives, but you persist on the issue by maintaining it in the other two options. This type of persistence is critical to optimize your outcome and reduce the likelihood of leaving money on the table.

Communicate a Compelling Message

I always encourage my clients to leverage a MESO to reinforce the message that they want to communicate. A MESO provides a storyboard that can help you highlight how your differentiators address the other side's pressing business needs.

A MESO also prompts a discussion, whereas a single offer often results in a one-sided presentation. A MESO changes the framing of the discussion from "do you want to work with me?" to "how do you want to work with me?" pulling the other side into the conversation and increasing the likelihood of engaging them.

How to Structure Multiple Offers to Communicate the Strongest Message

When you are preparing the three options for your first offer, you want to vary the Storytelling Issues developed in your Issue Matrix, hold constant your Tradeoff Issues, and generally hold constant the Contentious Issues, although an issue like price might vary (Table 7.1 is repeated here for easy reference).

Since the story will focus on what you can do to address the other side's pressing needs, you want to list at the top of the offer the Storytelling Issues that highlight your differentiators that will address these needs. You would also want to vary what you are offering on these issues because people will pay more attention to the issues that vary than to those that are constant across the offer (Franconeri, Hollingworth, & Simons, 2005; Theeuwes, Kramer, Hahn, & Irwin, 1998).

Table 7.1: Your MESO Architecture

	Option A	Option B	Option C
Issue 1: Storytelling Issue	Vary	Vary	Vary
Issue 2: Storytelling Issue	Vary	Vary	Vary
Issue 3: Storytelling Issue	Vary	Vary	Vary
Issue 4: Storytelling Issue	Vary	Vary	Vary
Issue 5: Storytelling Issue	Vary	Vary	Vary
Issue 6: Tradeoff or Contentious Issue	Constant	Constant	Constant
Issue 7: Tradeoff or Contentious Issue	Constant	Constant	Constant
Issue 8: Tradeoff or Contentious Issue	Constant	Constant	Constant
Issue 9: Tradeoff or Contentious Issue	Constant	Constant	Constant
Issue 10: Contentious Issue	Vary or Constant	Vary or Constant	Vary or Constant
Issue 10: Tradeoff or Contentious Issue	Constant	Constant	Constant

There is no limit to the number of issues that you can include in an offer, but there is a limit to how many issues you can vary. People generally can remember five to nine things (Miller, 1956). If you want your message to be clear and unambiguous, never vary more than nine issues in your initial offer. You can vary fewer issues across your three options, but do not vary more than nine. Select the critical Storytelling Issues that will help to reinforce your message and vary these in your initial options; you will vary some of your Tradeoff and Contentious Issues in later offers to show how you are responding to the other side. In your initial offer, however, you want to vary the Storytelling Issues that highlight how your differentiators address the other side's pressing business needs, hold constant your Tradeoff Issues, and generally hold constant the Contentious Issues (although a quantified issue like price might vary).

An Example of Varying the Right Issues in Your MESO to Communicate Your Message

I believe an example will provide clarity to the design of the initial MESO. Let's review an example from one of my clients who manufactures corrugated packaging material—essentially, boxes. You may think that boxes are a commodity, but my client had three big differentiators that they wanted to stress: (1) they made boxes in different shapes because they had a unique die cut; (2) they made very high quality boxes that did not rip, tear, or have the bottom fall out, so their boxes reduced breakage; and (3) they were the only company in the industry to offer a 24-hour call center. Potentially, customers could contact the call center and order more boxes if required, reducing the need to either hold more packaging material inventory than desirable or risk running out of boxes and needing to shut down their manufacturing lines.

My client would highlight these differentiators all the time, but their customers would sometimes say, "How much is your box? If you match the competitor's price, we will buy your box." Of course, they did not want to match another company's price (which would communicate they were no better than the competitor), so they decided that they needed to use a MESO to highlight their differentiators.

This client's differentiation chart is shown in Figure 7.1. Notice how effectively this client translated their differentiators into negotiable issues.

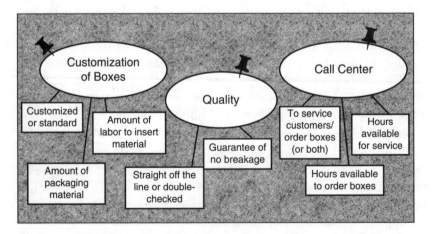

Figure 7.1: The Box Company Differentiators

These issues then populate their Issue Matrix, as shown in Figure 7.2. The issues that connect to their differentiators fill the Storytelling quadrant, giving them many issues to use to get more of what they want on the Contentious and Tradeoff Issues.

My client wanted to communicate a message about how their differentiators address their customers' pressing business needs, so they constructed the MESO detailed in Table 7.3 to do this.

Notice how the first issue is whether the customer would like a standard square box or a customized shape using my client's unique die cut. The competitor can only deliver a square box, but my client is uniquely positioned to offer the customized one. The shape of the box affects the amount of packaging material required, the cost of this material, the

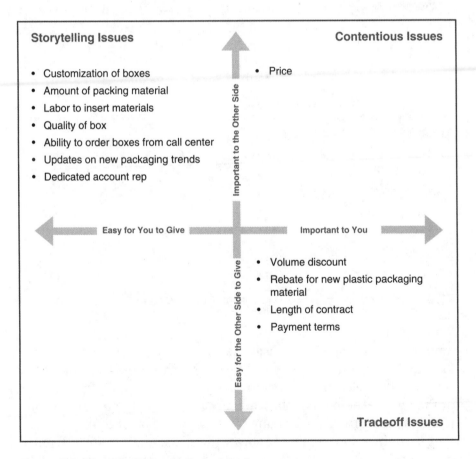

Figure 7.2: The Box Company Issue Matrix

Table 7.3: The Box Company MESO

	Option A	Option B	Option C
Customization	Standard square box	Customized die-cut box	Customized die-cut box
Amount of packing material	XXXXXXX	X	X
Cost of packing material	$$$$$	$	$
Labor to insert packing material	XXXXXXX	X	X
Cost of labor to insert packing material	$$$$$	$	$
Quality of box	Straight off the line	Straight off the line	Hand-check each box
Order new boxes	Once a month (industry standard)	Using call center (8 a.m.–10 a.m. EST)	Using call center (24/7)
Updates on new packaging trends	Once a year	Twice a year	Twice a year
Volume discount	Constant	Constant	Constant
Rebate for new plastic packaging material	Constant	Constant	Constant
Dedicated account rep	On-site one day a week	On-site one day a week	On-site one day a week
Price	$	$$	$$$
Payment terms	Constant	Constant	Constant
Length of contract	Constant	Constant	Constant

amount of labor needed to insert it, and the cost of this labor. Notice how the offer emphasized the differences on these issues based on whether they select a standard box that the competitor can also deliver or the unique die-cut box that only my client offers. Interestingly, my client did not provide packaging material or the labor to insert it, but they used these four issues to educate their customer on the difference between what they were offering and what the competitor offered. In a single-offer scenario, highlighting that the competitor's box required costly packaging material and the labor to insert that material would sound disparaging. By using a multiple offer, my client was simply educating the customer about the implications of the different options that they could provide.

The next issue involves the quality of the boxes. My client can ship the box straight off the production line, which provides better quality than the competitor's box. This is included in Options A and B. Option C, however, included a double-check of the box quality by hand before every box is shipped. This offered an even higher quality level that would reduce the chance of any breakage when the customer shipped their product in the box, which was a critical issue to this particular customer.

Next, the offer focused on how the customer would order boxes. The industry standard is to order monthly, and this was in the first option. In the second option, my client offered to allow the customer to order boxes via their call center any morning between 8:00 and 10:00 a.m. EST, and have boxes on site by the next day. This may not be enough coverage for this customer, though, given the global footprint of their plants, so in the third option, the customer could order boxes via the call center 24 hours a day 7 days a week. With this alternative, if they needed boxes at any time, they could reach out to the call center and have boxes by the next morning.

As the industry leader in packaging material, my client wanted to highlight their expertise. To do this, they varied the idea of providing updates on packaging trends once or twice a year. You want to vary your Storytelling Issues in your offer because they will become a focal point for the discussion.

At the same time, you want to hold constant your Tradeoff Issues. In this case, the volume incentive (a Tradeoff Issue) was held constant across the three options with much room to concede on this issue. Likewise, another Tradeoff Issue was the rebate dollars that my client offered their customer that would be earned based on the corrugated purchase amount and could be applied toward a new plastic packaging material that my client offered. This issue was also held constant with a lot of room to concede. All of these issues flowed into the Contentious Issue of price, which was varied across the three options.

The MESO we created allowed my client to highlight a message about how their differentiators (customization of the box, quality of the box, and their customer-centric unique call center that can be used to order boxes) addressed their customer's pressing business needs. Allowing the customer to purchase a customized box that fit well around the item they were shipping would reduce the amount of packaging material that would be required, and the labor needed to insert this packaging material, saving the customer money in two areas. In addition, the quality of the box would reduce the possibility of breakage, which was critical to this customer, who stated that "their brand depended on nothing ever arriving broken." Moreover, the ability to order boxes as needed using the call center to place these unexpected orders would mean that the customer would never run out of boxes and have to shut down their manufacturing line because they were out of packaging material. At the same time though, the flexibility to order boxes on demand would limit the customer's need to hold a huge inventory of boxes in the limited space in their plants.

The Elbow Issue

In the next chapter, we will discuss how to deliver this multiple offer along with your message to convey your story most effectively. Notice how the structure of the multiple offer focuses the recipient's attention on the issues that vary across the three options rather than those that are constant. The Tradeoff and Contentious Issues may vary in the next round of the negotiation as concessions are made, but the initial offer communicates a clear message by varying the Storytelling Issues.

You want your MESO to reinforce your message and serve as a storyboard so it is essential that you consider the order of the issues in your offer. The first issue is what I like to call the "elbow" issue because it connects your offer to your message. In the case of the box manufacturer, the "elbow" issue was whether the box being provided was a standard shape or a unique die-cut shape because this is what distinguished the box my client could offer from those offered by a competitor. You need the first issue to provide a direct connection to your message. I always encourage my clients to practice delivering their offer so that they can assess if they have the issues in the right order. You want the order of the issues to reinforce the message you want to convey.

You may have more than nine Storytelling Issues; if so, you will want to be selective about which ones you vary versus those that you hold constant. Vary the ones that connect to your key message. Notice in the example with the box manufacturer that we held constant the dedicated account representative. This is a Storytelling Issue, but it is not a key differentiator that relates to the message about the difference between a standard box and a customized box. Because of this, it is held constant in the first offer and may be varied in later rounds as concessions are made.

The Differentiation Chart and the Issue Matrix Are the Ingredients for Your MESO Recipe

Let's discuss another example to highlight how the Differentiation Chart and the Issue Matrix provide the ingredients for a MESO that will reinforce your message about how your differentiators address the other side's pressing needs. I teach these concepts to clients all the time, and I use them myself with my clients at Medvec & Associates. If you look at the Differentiation Chart for Medvec & Associates presented in Chapter 2, you will see that our differentiators are experience advising on deals, award-winning teaching capability, subject-matter expertise, and confidence that strategies will improve outcomes.

Each of these differentiators translates into negotiable issues that allow us to reinforce our differentiators. On the Differentiation Chart shown in Figure 7.3, I have specified the ways that these issues could be varied across my multiple offers. I then lay out these issues on my Issue Matrix, shown in Figure 7.4, and I know that for my first offer, I want to vary my Storytelling Issues in my MESO.

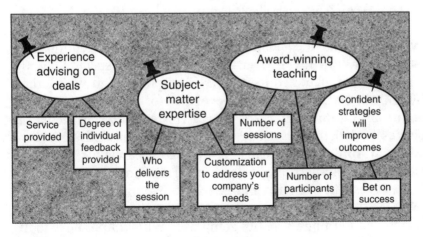

Figure 7.3: Medvec & Associates Differentiators

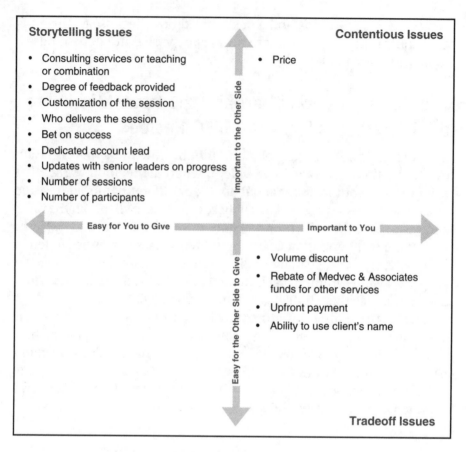

Figure 7.4: Medvec & Associates Issue Matrix

My MESO needs to be customized for each client to reinforce the message about how my differentiators address the specific client's pressing business needs so every MESO will look slightly different. The MESO shown in Table 7.4 was developed for a client who was new to Medvec & Associates and who was interested in having Medvec & Associates teach their sales team negotiation strategies. This client contacted me in April of 2020 during the COVID-19 pandemic, so instead of offering a live, in-person one-day session, I offered four 2-hour live virtual sessions. The client recognized the need for the training because they were in the midst of a very significant negotiation with their largest customer and things were not going well. When I first spoke to the company's CEO, he said they might be interested in some consulting on this specific deal as well as general training for the team.

Table 7.4: Medvec & Associates MESO

	Option A	Option B	Option C
Services Provided	Teaching 4 Advanced Negotiation sessions to sales team	Teaching 4 Advanced Negotiation sessions to sales team and consulting on specific deal	Teaching 4 Advanced Negotiation sessions to sales team and consulting on specific deal
Provider of Expertise	The session content will be developed by Dr. Victoria Medvec. Content delivered by one of Medvec & Associates' Senior Associates.	The session content will be developed by Dr. Victoria Medvec. Content delivered by one of Medvec & Associates' Senior Associates. Consulting will be personally provided by Dr. Medvec with support from the dedicated Senior Associate who is working with your team.	The session content will be developed and delivered by Dr. Victoria Medvec. Consulting will be personally provided by Dr. Medvec with support from a dedicated Senior Associate.
Leadership Input and Coaching Sessions	Dr. Medvec will meet with your senior leaders to uncover your negotiation challenges and design the course. She will also meet with the senior leaders at the end of the workshop to discuss coaching strategies to secure maximum pull-through and impact.	Dr. Medvec will meet with your senior leaders to uncover your negotiation challenges and design the course. In addition, Dr. Medvec and your dedicated Senior Associate will meet with your senior leaders between each session to update on the progress of the team and secure feedback to make course adjustments. In each of these meetings and in an additional meeting following the fourth session, Dr. Medvec will discuss coaching strategies to secure maximum pull-through and impact.	Dr. Medvec will meet with your senior leaders to uncover your negotiation challenges and design the course. In addition, Dr. Medvec and your dedicated Senior Associate will meet with your senior leaders between each session to update on the progress of the team and secure feedback to make course adjustments. In each of these meetings and in an additional meeting following the fourth session, Dr. Medvec will discuss coaching strategies to secure maximum pull-through and impact.

(Continued)

Table 7.4: (*Continued*)

Participant Feedback Provided	Provide verbal feedback on participant's negotiation plans in the curated, customized sessions	Review of participants' negotiation plans between each session with individual, written feedback provided to each participant on their own negotiation plan. In addition, curated, customized sessions including participant examples with verbal feedback on negotiation plans in the session.	Review of participants' negotiation plans between each session with individual, written feedback provided to each participant on their own negotiation plan. In addition, curated, customized sessions including participant examples with verbal feedback on negotiation plans in the session.
Updates with Company's Senior Leaders to Address Emerging Negotiation Challenges	Once per year following the completion of the training	Once per year following the completion of the training	Twice per year following the completion of the training
Bet on Success for the Consulting Provided on the Specified Deal	Not included	Not included	Dr. Medvec is very confident that the advice she provides will yield success in your negotiation and is happy to tie her compensation to this success in the following way (include unique specified contingency).
Number of Sessions per Workshop	4	4	4

Number of Participants per Workshop	40	40	40
Fee Per Session	$	$$	$$$
Fee for Consulting Services	Not included	YY	Y (less than the base fee in Option B but the total will be more than this with the contingency included)
Volume Discount	First 8 sessions at stated fee Next 8 sessions at 5% discount Next 16 sessions at 10% discount All additional sessions at 15% discount	First 8 sessions at stated fee Next 8 sessions at 5% discount Next 16 sessions at 10% discount All additional sessions at 15% discount	First 8 sessions at stated fee Next 8 sessions at 5% discount Next 16 sessions at 10% discount All additional sessions at 15% discount
Rebate of Medvec & Associates Dollars to Apply Toward Future Consulting Services and Executive Decision-Making Sessions	$5,000 per workshop	$5,000 per workshop	$5,000 per workshop

I designed the MESO to reinforce the message that I was delivering to my prospective client about how Medvec & Associates was uniquely positioned to teach his team negotiation strategies, advise on many ongoing negotiations, and provide specific, targeted consulting on the company's current negotiation with their largest customer. Notice how the offer varies the services provided (*teaching* or *teaching and consulting*) and also varies who provides the services. The intent is to highlight the extensive expertise of the team and discuss whether the client would like me to develop and deliver the content or if they would prefer that I develop the content and one of my Senior Associates delivers the course. I also want to emphasize that the courses are highly customized for each client, so I vary whether I meet with the senior leaders to uncover the company's challenges and design the course content only before the course begins, or whether I meet with the senior leaders before the course and between each of the four sessions. The coaching sessions are intended to highlight the impact that the training will have on the company's results, and the frequency of these is also varied across the options to draw attention to this point.

In order to stress that we are different from training companies because we are negotiation experts uniquely qualified to advise on their ongoing negotiations and impact their outcomes, we include an issue that relates to the feedback that we will provide during the sessions on the participants' negotiation plans. Every participant in our programs builds a plan for one of their own negotiations in one of our proprietary Playbooks. Notice that in the first option, we review all of the negotiation plans to curate the content for the sessions, include specific participant examples in the class, and provide verbal feedback on the participants' examples. In the second and third options, we do all of this and also provide each participant with personalized, written feedback on their negotiation plan between each session.

You will see that consulting on the negotiation with their largest customer is included in Options B and C. I stress that all consulting services will be provided by me to reinforce that I will personally be involved in solving the problem they are facing in this very high stakes situation. I want to express my confidence that I can help them to achieve success in this negotiation, so I include a bet on the outcome in Option C, where my fee for the consulting will be tied to their success, whereas Option B includes a flat rate for consulting services. I like to include this bet on success to demonstrate my confidence in the service I am providing. Often, one of your differentiators hinges on something that you are confident you can deliver or achieve. When you have a differentiator like this, betting on your success to achieve these goals conveys a compelling message.

Enhancing Your Story with a Contingent Agreement

Bets are a great way to show your confidence and highlight your differentiators, but you need to know how to craft these contingencies. First, you want to ensure that you are betting on metrics that are objective, measurable, and known by both sides. For example, you might bet with the other side on the achievement of a specified outcome when you both will have information on whether the goal was achieved. In the case of my client, I would be willing to bet on whether they retained their customer, or I would be willing to bet on the revenue that was agreed to in the contract with their client, but I would not bet on the margin they would secure. I only want to bet on things that are objective, measurable, and known by both sides; whether or not they secure an agreement is objective, measurable, and can be known by both sides (because I trust this client to tell me this information). The revenue that is agreed upon is also objective, measurable, and can be known by both sides (because I trust this client to show me the contract). Even though I trust the client, I would not bet on margin because information on margin is known by one side, but not the other, and it can be measured in many different ways. This creates risk in the agreement and the potential for us to be arguing over this in the future.

If you are using a contingency, you want to ensure that you are not being overconfident when you bet. Contingent offers do not expand the size of the pie. Instead of adding value, they transfer value, because one side pays and the other side collects. However, contingencies add the perception of value because each side believes that they have correctly predicted the future. If you are being overconfident in your ability to deliver on the metrics defined, though, you will end up paying a lot of bets.

Contingencies to Overcome a Negative Bargaining Zone

Contingent contracts can also help to overcome negative bargaining zones. Often, negotiations have a positive bargaining zone (where the buyer's Reservation Point is higher than the seller's Reservation Point), but sometimes we find ourselves in a situation where we have a negative bargaining zone (the seller's Reservation Point is higher than the buyer's Reservation Point). This can happen when a buyer is not confident that a seller can deliver what is being promised. Imagine that a supplier of a piece of mechanical equipment is selling to a large manufacturing company for the first time, claiming that this equipment will reduce the downtime on the company's manufacturing line. The seller thinks they are selling an exceptional piece of equipment which will be incredibly valuable to the buyer, but the buyer, who is unfamiliar with the equipment, thinks the price seems very high. This case is likely to result in a negative bargaining zone. A contingent agreement is the best way to overcome a negative bargaining zone. In this example, there could be a small base price for the equipment, and the buyer could pay an additional premium at the end of the year if the equipment kept their manufacturing line running without failure for an entire year. Another way to construct this contingency would be for the buyer to pay the higher price up front and then get money back if their manufacturing line shut down. It is likely that the buyer would prefer the first structure and the seller would prefer the second arrangement. In either case, though, the contingent agreement would make a deal possible that would not otherwise be attainable if the seller's Reservation Point was higher than the buyer's.

Whenever you find yourself arguing with the other side about something that will happen in the future, you should consider whether it might be possible to bet on it rather than argue about it. A contingent agreement is a useful tool to stop the argument. Be certain to bet on metrics that are objective, measurable, and known by both sides, though, so you do not stop the argument today only to find yourself litigating over it in the future.

Contingencies to Test What the Other Side Is Telling You

Contingent agreements can also be used to detect whether what the other side is telling you is an overstatement, or even if they are lying to you. As I explained in Chapter 3, I used a contingency for this purpose when I negotiated with the contractor who installed the in-ground pool in my backyard. In that chapter, I discussed how we used a contingency to test what the suppliers were telling us about their ability to complete the project by May 1. While all of them said that they could meet the deadline, only one of them was willing to bet in a significant way on achieving this timeframe.

When one of the contractors confidently stated that he would guarantee the deadline with a $500 per day penalty, I knew he believed he could complete the job on time. A contingency can be used as a storytelling tool to highlight the confidence you have in what you can achieve, and it can be used as a risk mitigation tool to assess the confidence the other side has in what they are telling you.

When you use a contingency to communicate your confidence in something you can deliver, it is a Storytelling Issue so you should vary whether you include it or not across your three options. You might include it in one of the options and leave it out of the other two. On the other hand, when you use a contingency to mitigate risk, the contingency is a Tradeoff Issue, so you should hold it constant across all three options.

Deploying MESOs to Win in Competitive Bidding Situations

MESOs are powerful storytelling tools, and a MESO with a performance-based contingency in one or two of the offers communicates an even more compelling message. Given this, MESOs are an excellent tool to use in competitive bidding situations. For example, I recommend that all my clients use a MESO when they are responding to a customer's Request for Proposal (RFP).

Multiple Offers in RFP Responses

I highlight to my clients that if they submit a single offer in an RFP situation, they may be trying to win on price but they will never do so. If you have the best price but the buyer does not want to select you, then the buyer will simply take your low price and use it to lower the price of the supplier that they prefer. I believe that you can lose on price, but you will never win on price. The key in an RFP is to differentiate yourself. If you respond to the RFP with one single offer, then you have answered the same questions as everyone else and have probably made yourself look like everyone else. Harnessing a multiple offer, on the other hand, allows you to differentiate yourself because you can vary your differentiators across the three options to draw attention to them.

One of my clients was responding to a consulting RFP to assist a company in creating risk mitigation strategies. My client had a sponsor on the inside who told him that the company was going to select a different firm and that they were only including my client in the process to fulfill a procurement requirement. The sponsor also said that the project was expected to be priced at $5M. The partner with whom I was working thought his firm was going to lose the project, so he decided to try a MESO, even though he had never used one before. He asked me to assist him in designing the offer.

When I started digging deeper into the project, I learned that the company was located in the United States but was owned by an Australian holding company that intended to sell the business in the next year. I asked the partner whether having the risk mitigation strategies in place would enhance the selling price of the business. I know nothing about these types of projects, but I know a lot about transactions, and I knew that if the completion of this project would impact the multiple in the transaction, then the project would be very valuable to the company. The partner said that if the company's auditor signed off on the risk mitigation strategies before the transaction, it would be incredibly valuable, but that he did not think this timing was possible because such projects generally took much longer than the six month window before the sales process would begin. I asked him if his team could complete the project very quickly, and he explained that they do not typically do such projects that way. I pushed to find out if it would be possible to complete the project quickly. He responded that technically they could complete the project in a shorter timeframe, but that it would require a lot more senior partner time and that they would need to pull experienced consultants off other projects to do this. He said he would want to charge something closer to $15M rather than $5M to complete the project in a shorter time. I recommended that we make this the C option in our MESO and focus this entire option around positioning the company for sale.

When completing an RFP, Option A should always be exactly what the other side asks for. You do not want someone in procurement to throw out your bid because you did not respond directly to their request, so I always suggest that my clients indicate that Option A is "in response to your bid" or "as you requested." I also suggest that my clients highlight that Options B and C are designed to address something the client asked for or something that they have indicated was a priority in the past. You want the client to feel as though the additional two options were, in some way, requested by them.

So, my client's Option A contained exactly what was requested in the RFP with no extra bells or whistles. The RFP indicated that the project should be completed in 12 months and this was the timeline included in Option A, which was priced at $5.3M. Option C, which focused on positioning the company for sale by completing the project very quickly and having the company's auditor sign off on the risk mitigation strategies before a transaction took place, was priced at $15M. The partner decided to include a two-year proposal in the B option because he thought the best way to conduct the project was to put the risk mitigation strategies in place the first year and then test them during the second year. He could include the two-year option that he thought was optimal, even though the RFP stated a one-year timeline, because his other two options would be completed in the specified one-year window. He priced this option at $13M.

The RFP process specified that my client was restricted to speak only to procurement about the bid. The partner asked the procurement team if they would be interested in an option to get the project completed very quickly and whether this might increase the multiple in the potential sale of the business. The procurement executive suggested that the partner speak to the CFO to inquire about this. When the partner asked the CFO the same question, the CFO suggested that he speak to the CEO. Remember, my client was initially not allowed to speak to anyone other than procurement and now he was on his way to the CEO's office for a meeting. When he asked the same question to the CEO, the CEO said, "I think you thought harder about this project than we did." At that moment, my client recognized that his chances of winning the project were definitely improving.

He ended up selling the two-year deal (Option B) with a few modifications for $12M. The most interesting part, though, is that over the next 18 months, he grew the work his firm was doing for this client to more than $70M. The additional $58M of work was all focused on positioning the company for sale, something the customer probably would not have considered my client to do until he responded to this RFP. The partner very effectively differentiated his firm by focusing not on the work requested, but rather on why the client needed this work to be completed and how his firm was uniquely positioned to help the company prepare for the future sale of the business. This differentiation resulted in my client winning the project and a lot of future work as well.

My clients often ask how they can deliver an offer that highlights their differentiators without speaking poorly about their competitors. I agree that you never want to sell negatively by speaking badly about your competitors. I encourage my clients to focus their message and offer on the fact that they are uniquely positioned to address a specific problem, or how they are the only one who can provide a certain service or product that addresses a particular need. Presenting their offer in this way does not say anything negative about a competitor but instead, highlights the risks in the customers' business that my client is inimitably positioned to address.

Using a MESO to respond to an RFP has many advantages, including the fact that it generally prompts the procurement department to go back to the economic buyers to understand more about what they want and to pull them into the discussion. Procurement executives often construct RFPs so that they can "hold everything constant" and compare the alternatives on price alone. While procurement may want to commoditize potential suppliers so that they can be compared only on price, a supplier definitely does not want to engage in this. Suppliers need to focus the purchaser on their differentiators and how these distinctive capabilities address the customer's pressing business needs. When the supplier responds with a multiple offer, it weakens procurement's ability to hold everything constant because issues are moving across the three options, and this is likely to secure the attention and involvement of the economic buyer.

Multiple Offers in Competitive Situations in Your Personal Life

Competitive bidding situations that require the use of a multiple offer do not only occur at work. I was assisting a friend in purchasing a house that became a competitive situation, and we found that MESOs performed well and allowed my friend to highlight her family's differentiators very effectively.

Let me begin by stressing that you would prefer not to purchase a home in a competitive situation. It is far better to buy a house when the seller's BATNA is low rather than when the seller's BATNA is high. My friend wanted to purchase a house in Hawaii, however, in a resort area where homes sell very quickly. Consequently, she was extremely excited when she found a home that had been on the market for more than a year without any activity. She thought this was a tremendous opportunity where the seller's BATNA would be weak and she could get a great deal on the house. As she was completing her analysis to make her first offer, she got a call from her realtor who said that the seller was going to be getting two other offers. By this time, she had consulted with me and I was assisting her in the negotiation. She and I were both skeptical of the realtor's information as it seemed suspicious that a house that had languished on the market without any activity suddenly was expecting two simultaneous offers just when my friend was about to make an offer. She advised her realtor that she did not believe there were really two other offers and asked for proof of them. The realtor said that one of the offers had been in the background as a verbal offer for quite a while, but now that there was activity, the seller asked that buyer to submit a formal offer to be considered. The realtor explained that this potential purchaser had to sell a house in another, less desirable geography before they could purchase the new house, and that was why the seller had initially had no interest in this verbal offer. I told my friend I did not think this buyer would be a competitor because the seller would still not want to take the risk that the buyer could not sell the other house, nor would the seller want to wait for this to happen.

The second potential buyer, however, was a completely different situation and was clearly a threat. This buyer was an investor who had become interested in the house because it had been on the market for so long and, with its recent price reduction, now seemed to be a good deal. The neighborhood was a gated community with a wide range of homes. There were smaller homes, like the one my friend was interested in purchasing, as well as large estate homes with ocean views, and gigantic estates directly on the ocean. The span in value from the smallest homes to the oceanfront homes was enormous, and the home my friend wanted was probably the smallest and least expensive one in the neighborhood. My clients in real estate always say that location matters the most, and this house had an excellent location.

As I explained to my friend, an investor is generally a competitive buyer because they usually bring cash and a quick close. You often hear people in real estate say that "cash is king." I think what they mean is that cash brings certainty of closure and speed in getting the deal done—two things that are often incredibly attractive to a seller. My friend became discouraged when she learned about the investor's interest, especially when she learned that the price the investor was offering was higher than she could spend. She was about to pull out of the entire process, but I encouraged her to get out her differentiation chart and evaluate what distinguished her from the investor. Remember that a differentiator is only a differentiator if the other side cares about it. To identify my friend's differentiators, we did some research on the seller. We learned that the seller had purchased this small home while his family was building a spectacular oceanfront property in the same neighborhood. We drove by that new house and were impressed by its beauty. It would definitely be one of the best houses in the neighborhood, and the small house that my friend was trying to purchase could be seen from some of the windows in the gigantic new home. As we considered this, we realized that a potentially important differentiator between my friend and the investor would focus on what each potential purchaser would do with the house. The investor would most likely rent the house. The neighborhood is zoned for rental, but no one really rents, so this would become one of the first rental properties in the neighborhood. On the other hand, my friend would live in the home for much of the year and be active in the community; she had no interest in renting because she is a complete germaphobe with no desire to have strangers staying in her home.

I suggested to my friend that this could differentiate her in a significant way from the investor. We scripted her message and her MESO to focus on highlighting what she would do with the home. She could have easily just told the seller that she would not be renting the house, but this would not suffice. She needed to differentiate herself actively as a buyer and frame the conversation around the future use of the home rather than the price or terms. She learned that the investor had made a cash offer that would close in two weeks for a purchase price that was higher than she was capable of paying. At first glance, it may have appeared that she did not have a chance to win. She would need to secure a mortgage, so she needed a financing contingency, and she wanted more time to complete her diligence on the area, so she really wanted a four-month close (the longest period of time she could hold her mortgage commitment), and the price she was offering was lower than the investor's. I told her not to be discouraged. I said that although the seller wanted to get as much as possible for his small home, I was certain that he cared far more about protecting the asset value of his beautiful new oceanfront estate and that we could make this the focal point for the discussion. I told her that it would not be enough simply to state that she would not rent the house, because this point might fade into the background when the offers were being considered. Instead, I suggested that she turn this differentiator into a number of negotiable issues that would be on the table at the same moment that the price and the closing date were being evaluated.

She and I generated a number of issues that would highlight her differentiator, such as whether she would rent or not, how many times a year she could rent the house, and what the minimal amount of rental time could be since the seller might perceive that there was a difference between a renter coming into the house for one night versus renting it for a month. As we constructed the MESO, our goal was to frame the conversation around the potential risks of having the property rented.

When my friend delivered the offer to the seller, she said that she imagined that the seller would like to get a good price for his small house, but that since he was building such a beautiful oceanfront estate in the neighborhood, she thought he might be concerned not only about how much he would get paid for the house but also how the potential buyer would use the home. She said that she could certainly pay the most for the home if she could rent it, because the rental income would easily pay for her mortgage—and Hawaiian rentals were so popular with tourists. However, she said she was concerned that he might not want to have a rental property in the neighborhood. Renters could cause damage to the home, and could also cause damage to other homes in the neighborhood, to the golf course, to the clubhouse, to the beach-front, and maybe even to his beautiful new estate. Perhaps he would prefer not to have the home rented to avoid this potential damage. She also highlighted that she understood that having rental property in the neighborhood might decimate the property values of the other homes, especially the most expensive homes, and that this might concern him and the other neighbors. She offered to restrict what she could do with the property if this was important to him. In Option A, she could rent the house 365 days a year with a minimum of a one-night rental. This option had the highest purchase price. In Option B, she offered to limit the rentals to 12 times a year with a seven-night minimum stay; this option had a price that was lower than Option A, but higher than Option C. Option C stated that my friend would never rent the house. Of course, the purchase price for this option was much lower than the price in Options A or B. All three of the prices listed were significantly lower than what the investor had offered, and all included a finance contingency, an inspection contingency, and a four-month close.

Happily, my friend got the house and I now have a great place to stay in Hawaii. None of her first offers were accepted, but she had left room to concede and ended up with the house for less than the investor was offering with a finance contingency and a four-month close. How did she do this? Because she differentiated herself and used a MESO to reinforce the message about how her unique qualities addressed the seller's needs. It is critical to differentiate yourself in competitive situations, and using a MESO allows you to reinforce the message about your differentiators in a very compelling way.

HARNESSING MESOS IN YOUR PERSONAL NEGOTIATIONS

While it is critical to distinguish yourself in competitive situations, it is also critical to differentiate yourself when you are negotiating for yourself. As we discussed in the last chapter, you must make yourself distinctive in employment situations so that you can highlight how the employer can do something for you without establishing a precedent that will force them to do the same thing for everyone else. In essence, your differentiators provide the employer with the ability to give you more than everyone else. Once you have identified your differentiators, translated them into negotiable issues, and developed a message to highlight how your unique capabilities address the employer's pressing business needs, you should develop a MESO to reinforce your message.

I recommend that people use a MESO in all employment negotiations, whether they are discussing a role with a new employer, a new role with an existing employer, new responsibility with an existing employer, or returning to a former employer. As this chapter has demonstrated, a MESO allows you to look flexible, build the relationship, and maximize your own outcome. It is critical in employment negotiations that you focus on building and maintaining your relationship with the other side. You do not want to end up with $5,000 more and a poor relationship where you are sent to a faraway office and never promoted again. It is essential to protect your relationships in employment situations, so you want to negotiate in a manner that builds the relationship while optimizing your outcome. MESOs allow you to do this.

Remember that in an employment situation, if you are discussing a potential opportunity with a new company, you cannot begin to negotiate until you have the offer of employment. You do not want to start to negotiate during the interview phase or you may not secure the offer. This means that in new employment situations, especially when you are young, you will often not get to make the first offer. The employer will often secure the anchoring advantage of the first offer because the offer of employment is linked to the actual offer. When this occurs, you gain a tremendous advantage if you counter with a multiple offer rather than a single offer. The multiple offer makes you look flexible and cooperative, but it also re-anchors the starting point because it is generally more complex than the employer's first offer. In addition, the multiple offer enables you to be more aggressive in what you ask for and helps you reinforce your message about how your differentiators address the employer's pressing business needs.

When you are negotiating with your current employer, you can initiate the discussion about a promotion or new responsibility and use a MESO to make your offer. This strategy will allow you to frame the discussion around the responsibilities that you will take on to address the employer's needs and how you are uniquely qualified to do this.

Many people ask for my advice on their salary negotiation, and I always say that there is no such thing as a salary negotiation. You want to discuss your employment engagement as an entire package and never simply discuss salary. I often use the analogy of a train when offering advice in these situations. The engine is never your salary; the engine is the employer's pressing business needs. The next car back has your responsibilities that will address the company's needs and goals. The next car back is filled with your differentiators that address the employer's pressing business needs. The next car back might be a bet on how your unique capabilities will address the company's needs and the performance that you will achieve. The next car back is filled with other differentiators and additional Storytelling Issues. The caboose is your salary and annual bonus. The caboose is always attached to the train and rides along, but it comes at the end of the discussion, not the beginning of the conversation. You want to lead with the engine and keep the message focused on the company and their needs.

How would you structure a MESO in this type of situation? I have helped many MBA students, friends, and clients create offers for their employment situations. I have helped people negotiate on their way in, up, and out of companies. The offers are all unique, but they follow a few simple rules. First, learn as much as you can about the company's most pressing business needs. What public commitments has the CEO made? If it is a public company, what concerns are analysts expressing? If it is a start-up that is raising money, what are potential investors asking at investor conferences (transcripts from investor conferences and earnings calls are generally available on a company's website under the Investor Relations tab).

Next, consider your role relative to the company's needs. No single individual will solve all of a company's needs, but how does one or more of your differentiators relate directly to the company's needs and objectives? You will generally want to vary the responsibilities in some way across your three options based on these differentiators and demonstrate more impact on the company's objectives in one or two of the offers than in the third. Including responsibilities as the elbow issue listed first provides an excellent link between your message and your offer. The next issues should be focused on how other differentiators will meet the company's needs. Perhaps you have unique skills that are valuable to the company that would allow you to expand your role or complete particular tasks. Again, you want to vary these issues to draw attention to your differentiators.

The next issue should be a bet on what you can achieve; this is a performance-based bonus that would be included in one or two of the options. You do not want to include this in all three options because you want to draw attention to your confidence that you can achieve specific goals. Remember that you should only bet on things that are objective, measurable, and known by both sides. Other differentiators and Storytelling Issues would follow, and you would vary the ones that relate to addressing the company's pressing business needs. You would hold constant all Tradeoff Issues, such as your title. You would also hold constant most Contentious Issues, although the base salary would likely vary because it would be higher in the options without the performance-based bonus and would be lower in the option with the performance-based bonus, although the total compensation would be higher with the bonus than without it. This structure draws attention to your confidence in what you can achieve, and it also generates a powerful contrast effect; the higher total compensation in the option with the bet seems reasonable because it is contingent on the company's goal being achieved but it also makes the compensation requested in the other two offers (with the higher base) seem more reasonable. Again, individual offers vary, but this pattern is fairly constant for the MESO in an employment situation.

For example, imagine that a company has a need for rapid growth in its customer base and is considering expanding into South America to achieve growth. You are an excellent sales executive with a history of success in securing new customers and expanding business with existing customers. You worked in multiple South American cities over a nine-year period before moving to Boston and are fluent in

Spanish. You are currently working in the company in a marketing role, but you know that you could be a valuable resource in driving revenue growth because you worked in sales for your prior two companies when you were located in South America. There are tremendous growth opportunities for your current company's business in the South American market, but few people in the company in Boston speak Spanish, and most have never done business in South America, or even traveled there, so the company has significant hurdles to overcome to achieve the growth it desires in South America. The senior leadership team lacks an understanding of the South American market and does not know which cities to target for expansion. You are confident that you can drive the revenue in South America that the company seeks if you are able to hire a team on the ground who understands each of the local markets. You would like to move into a sales role and be promoted to a vice president level when you make this change; you are currently a director, which is one level lower in your organization than a VP. Your salary is currently $135,000 and your goal is to get your total compensation elevated to $165,000. Table 7.5 shows a MESO that could be used for this negotiation.

Notice how the offer highlights the challenges the company is facing and varies which of these challenges you will focus on in your new role. The responsibilities and role vary across the three options. Notice how the "elbow issue" of responsibilities connects directly to the message about the company's need for revenue growth. The first and second options focus on the company developing business in the South American market immediately or within a year, while in the third option, you would help the company generate immediate revenue in North America with a longer-term plan to expand into South America. Also notice how the differentiators of experience in the South American market, fluency in Spanish, and ability to grow customer revenue are highlighted by varying how you would help the company to achieve its goals across the three alternatives. Note that promotion to the VP level is held constant across all three options. The pay is constant in the second two options but the base pay in the first option is lower because there is a $100,000 performance-based bonus included in this alternative; although the base is lower, the total compensation is higher if you achieve the company's goal for growth in South America. Notice that the bet is on

Table 7.5: Employment Negotiation MESO

	Option A: Drive immediate revenue growth in the South American market	Option B: Drive revenue growth in the South American market within one year	Option C: Drive immediate revenue growth in North America with a two-year plan to expand to South America
Responsibilities	■ Focus on growing new business in South America ■ Team with Executive Leadership to select target markets leveraging extensive experience in South America ■ Utilize fluency in Spanish to conduct interviews with potential sales team members to secure sales team on the ground in South America ■ Handle key customer accounts in South America and U.S. accounts with large presence in South America	■ Focus on growing new business in South America ■ Team with Executive Leadership to select target markets leveraging extensive experience in South America ■ Utilize fluency in Spanish to hire Spanish-speaking sales executives in the Boston area to begin to serve the South American market ■ Handle key customer accounts in South America and U.S. accounts with large presence in South America	■ Focus on growing new business and retaining existing business from customers in the United States ■ Particular focus on expanding business from existing U.S. customers ■ Prepare team for expansion into South America within two years
Role	VP of Sales for the South American Region	VP of Sales for the South American Region	VP of Sales

(Continued)

Table 7.5: (Continued)

Speed to generate revenue in South America	Very rapidly—within 6 months	Rapidly—within 1 year	Within 18 months—2 years
Briefings on doing business in South America and South American culture	Meetings every 2 weeks with Senior Leadership Team and Sales Team	Monthly meetings with Senior Leadership Team	Quarterly meetings with Senior Leadership Team
Strategic selection of South American markets to target	Weekly meetings with EVP of Sales to select locations and briefings for the Executive Leadership Team	Monthly meetings with EVP of Sales to select locations and briefings for the Executive Leadership Team	Quarterly meetings with EVP of Sales to select locations and briefings for the Executive Leadership Team
Bet on expansion of business into South America	Bonus of $100,000 if sales originated in South America exceed $5M within 12 months	Not included	Not included
Transition to new role	Within 1 month	Within one month	Within one month
Reporting structure	Report to EVP of Sales	Report to EVP of Sales	Report to EVP of Sales
Base pay	$165,000	$180,000	$180,000

revenue—something objective, measurable, and known by both you and the employer. Also note that you are placing the bet when you are following the plan that you would recommend, which is to hire the team on the ground in the local markets.

The offer is designed to pull the employer into a conversation about how you will help the company to overcome their challenges and achieve revenue growth rather than a discussion about a promotion and a salary increase. A MESO allows you to communicate a compelling message about how your differentiators address the company's pressing business needs, and it is a great tool to use when you are negotiating for yourself.

Summary

There are many advantages to delivering a multiple offer rather than a single offer. A MESO allows you to effectively anchor the starting point with an ambitious offer, uncover information about your counterparty's preferences, and persist on things that are important to you while also signaling flexibility and cooperation. At the same time, a MESO helps you communicate a compelling message and change the frame of the discussion from "do you want to work together?" to "how do you want to work together?" This reframing is critical to pulling the other side into the discussion. Using a MESO allows you to secure a better outcome while also building the relationship with the other party.

A MESO can be used in all types of negotiations—with customers, suppliers, potential acquirers, partners, employers, home sellers, and others. In all these cases, you can use the MESO to highlight how your differentiators address the other side's pressing needs. A MESO also allows you to test your assumptions about the other party's preferences and priorities and to learn not just what the other side wants, but also how important each issue is to them. Additionally, a MESO allows you to change the cadence of the negotiation. Traditionally, you ask a question and learn something. Ask another and learn more. Ask more questions, and then make an offer. The risk though is that every time you ask a question, your counterparty can respond with an offer and secure the anchoring advantage that we discussed in Chapter 6. A MESO allows you to make an offer much earlier in the discussion, allowing you to anchor the conversation and learn from the other party's reaction to the offer. You will learn more about the dimensions that are important to the other side and what tradeoffs you can make.

This chapter also highlighted how to structure the MESO to communicate a clear message. The Differentiation Chart and the Issue Matrix, discussed in Chapter 2, provide essential ingredients for the MESO recipe we reviewed. In your first offer, you want to vary the Storytelling Issues, hold constant the Tradeoff Issues, and generally hold constant the Contentious Issues, although some of these, such as price, may vary because everything factors into them. In order to keep your message clear, you should vary no more than nine of the issues across your three options. In the next chapter, we will discuss how to deliver this offer in the most effective manner.

Using a MESO eliminates many of the fears negotiators experience. It emboldens a negotiator to make the first offer and reduces the fears of losing the deal, offending the other side, damaging the relationship, and leaving money on the table. MESOs help negotiators optimize their outcomes while building relationships with the other side and are a critical tool to Negotiate Without Fear.

8

Say It, Don't Send It

One of the biggest sources of fear in a negotiation is that the other side will walk away. People fear that if this happens, they will lose the ability to secure a deal and end with an impasse rather than an agreement. As we said in Chapter 6, this fear often causes people to make the mistake of allowing the other side to make the first offer, but you know that you want to make the first offer. Chapter 7 highlighted how you can lead the negotiation and reduce your fear of losing the deal by providing multiple offers instead of a single offer.

In this chapter, I will underscore the importance of selecting the right channel of communication to convey your multiple offer. You will learn why I always encourage my clients to "say it, don't send it," and why seeking synchronicity in a negotiation allows you to take the fear out of the interaction by reducing the likelihood that the other side will walk away.

Negotiate in a Synchronous Channel

You should strive to negotiate in a synchronous channel, not an asynchronous channel. *Synchronous channels* for communication include face-to-face meetings, speaking on the telephone, and meeting together on a virtual channel such as Zoom, Microsoft Teams, Webex, Google-Meet, or your other favorite platform that lets you see the other side as you speak. On the other hand, *asynchronous communication* takes place through channels such as e-mail, voicemail, text messages, and sending a proposal.

Take the Fear Out of Making an Offer

If I engage in synchronous communication, I can speak and immediately get feedback and a reaction from the other side. If I make an offer in a synchronous channel, I can hear the other party's reaction, adjust the frame of my message, react, and concede (Swaab & Galinsky, 2007). Synchronous communication takes the fear out of the exchange.

On the other hand, if I send an offer in an asynchronous channel, such as e-mail, voicemail, text, or by responding to an RFP, I cannot immediately respond. I will not be present when the recipient reacts, and I cannot control the interaction. I am much more afraid to send my offer than to say it; I want to be able to walk the other side through my offer in a synchronous channel.

I often highlight the importance of "saying it, not sending it" with my clients. I will frequently propose that if I am in an office across the desk from the customer, I am not going to lose the deal because of my starting offer. I am in the room. I can see the customer's reaction, reframe my offer, adjust, modify, and concede. I may lose the deal if the customer does not like where we are by the time I leave the room, but I will not lose the deal because of my starting point. The same is true if I am on a virtual video platform such as Zoom, Google Meet, Teams, or Webex where I can control the conversation around the offer. In these synchronous channels, I do not need to fear that my first offer will cause the other side to walk away.

When I am on a telephone call, it is also true that I can immediately react, if needed. It may be easier for the customer just to hang up on me over the phone than to walk out of the meeting when I am sitting at the customer's desk, but the customer is not likely simply to hang up. I will generally have the opportunity to respond in this synchronous channel.

On the other hand, if I e-mail the offer to the customer, I lose all control over the interaction and the customer's reaction. The customer could get angry and I am not there to immediately reframe the conversation. The exchange is much riskier in an asynchronous channel.

People should not be afraid to make the first offer, but they should be afraid to send the other side their offer. There is no need to be afraid to lead the negotiation if you seek synchronicity when you negotiate. Synchronicity takes the fear out of negotiation.

Asking for More

When you are in a synchronous communication channel, you can make a more ambitious ask without the fear of losing the deal. You know that you will be able to adjust based on the other side's reaction, so you can lead with a more ambitious starting offer. If you were sending an e-mail, you might fear that your offer would offend the other side, that they might refuse to meet with you again, or that they might walk away. These fears might lead you to begin to negotiate against yourself, by walking your offer back toward a less aggressive starting point because you are worried about the inability to manage the other side's reaction. When you seek synchronicity, you are likely to both get more and maintain a stronger relationship.

Maintaining the Relationship

Research demonstrates that we are more likely to damage the relationship when we communicate in asynchronous channels that do not allow us to see and hear the other side simultaneously (Kiesler & Sproull, 1992; Swaab & Galinsky, 2007; Swaab, Kern, Diermeier, & Medvec, 2009). This is because we tend to say things in these channels that we would never say to the other side if we were face-to-face and because there is an increased likelihood that we will be misunderstood (Swaab et al., 2009; Swaab & Galinsky, 2007).

Negotiating in a synchronous channel also helps to reduce the *Illusion of Transparency*, a phenomenon that my research colleagues and I originally identified (Gilovich, Savitsky, & Medvec, 1998). We tend to overestimate how much others can read or pick up on our internal thoughts or feelings. The Illusion of Transparency is a form of an anchoring and insufficient adjustment bias. We get anchored on how clear our own thoughts are to ourselves. We know that they cannot possibly be as clear to others as they are to us, and we adjust our estimates of what we convey—but we insufficiently adjust off our own perceptions. The

Illusion of Transparency affects us in both synchronous and asynchronous communication, but in synchronous channels, we are able to update based on the other party's feedback that is absent in asynchronous communication. When we are in a synchronous channel, we say something and then see or hear the other side's reactions. The other side may look confused or angry, or sound upset. All this information helps us to adjust off the anchor we have of how clear the message is to ourselves and to get a better sense of how clear it is to the other side.

The lack of this adjustment may result in more misunderstanding and misperception in an asynchronous negotiation than in a synchronous one. I always tell my clients that if you have to communicate something critical to others or something that may cause conflict (as in a negotiation), you always want to be in a synchronous channel. Asynchronous communication increases the likelihood that I might unintentionally offend the other side or irritate them. Research further demonstrates that direct, synchronous communication heavily reduces the chance of misunderstanding in potentially contentious interactions such as negotiation (Schaerer, Kern, Berger, & Medvec, 2018). In a synchronous communication channel, you can immediately assess the other side's reaction and clarify your point to ensure that a dangerous misunderstanding does not impede the progress of the negotiation.

Saving Time

Synchronicity also reduces the time it takes to complete a negotiation. I tell my clients that the fastest way to get a deal done is to get in front of the other side. Multiple studies have shown that communications via asynchronous electronic formats, such as e-mail, are slower and less efficient than those through face-to-face channels (Baltes, Dickson, Sherman, & Bauer, 2002; Purdy, Nye, & Balakrishnan, 2000; Straus & McGrath, 1994).

People often believe they save time by using e-mail in negotiations because they can begin the communication at any time. They can start at 3:00 a.m., 6:00 a.m., 2:00 p.m., or midnight; they can literally begin the negotiation at any time, so they think they are saving time by using this asynchronous channel. However, as I always tell my clients, beginning the negotiation is not the goal. In negotiation, closing is the goal—and the distance between starting and closing is much greater when I choose e-mail over speaking face-to-face. Seeking synchronicity saves time.

How to Be Synchronous in a World Where We Cannot Be in Person

COVID-19 limited our ability to be face-to-face in person with customers, suppliers, partners, potential acquirers, and others. We were forced into remote interaction instead. However, technology emerged to help us navigate these exchanges. While Zoom, Teams, Webex, and Google Meet (in its earlier Google Hangouts format) may have existed in pre-pandemic times, these platforms improved and became a commonplace form for interaction in the midst of the lockdown. We celebrated birthdays and cocktail parties on these platforms, had many team meetings, and connected with friends and family members whom we could not see in person. These platforms also provided a vehicle for negotiations to carry on in a synchronous, face-to-face channel when we could not be together.

I have been encouraging my clients to use these platforms for their negotiations rather than telephone calls or conference calls when they cannot physically meet with the other side. I was advising a client on a very large deal in March, 2020, and was pushing my client to get in person with their counterparty. My client used a private plane to get to a meeting in mid-March when their company limited commercial travel, but then offices started to lock down, making it impossible to meet in person to continue the negotiation. I was very skeptical that my client could be as effective in the negotiation if they were not in front of the other side. The first meeting after the face-to-face meeting was done via telephone. Although this channel was synchronous, it lacked the connection that we achieved when we were in the room with the other side. We could not see the counterparty's reactions to the offers we were discussing. For the next meeting, I encouraged my client to use their corporate platform, which happened to be Zoom, and turn on their cameras. I observed a dramatic difference in the interaction. This was the first time I had conducted a negotiation on Zoom, and I was shocked by how clearly we could see the faces of each of the members of the other party and how much information we secured from watching their reactions. Many months have passed since then, and now with thousands of Zoom sessions, Teams meetings, Webex interactions, and Google Meet events under my belt, I have emerged with a very strong opinion that when we cannot be face-to-face in person, we should be face-to-face on one of these platforms with our video on and encourage the other side to turn on their cameras as well. I have become a master at getting people to turn on their cameras. I have found that the key to doing this is to turn your video on 100% of the time and then, if the other side does not have their video on, say immediately, "I am sorry, I cannot see you. Can you restart your video?" I have also asked parties that are at a large conference room table if they would mind all joining the video platform from their individual offices so that I can see each of their faces.

Research shows that people are more creative when they can look the other side in the eye (Colvin, 2020). I strongly believe that negotiations require creativity and that this ingenuity and a sense of connection are enhanced when you can see the other party.

I also believe that it is incredibly helpful to see the other side's reactions rather than simply hearing them reply over the telephone line. I have been in many negotiations where I carefully watched the other side to ascertain whether I needed to make an additional concession to close the deal and how large my adjustment needed to be. If I had been on the phone rather than in person or on a video screen, I would have made unnecessary concessions. Negotiating face-to-face, whether in person or on video, has saved me a lot of unwarranted concessions and a great deal of money over the years. So, I now stress to my clients that they should "say it, don't send it, and see them when you say it."

What to Do When You Are Forced into an Asynchronous Channel

Sometimes you are forced into an asynchronous negotiation. For example, when you are a supplier responding to an RFP for a customer, you may feel trapped into having an asynchronous negotiation. My advice to clients is that you should always try to get a conversation before you submit the RFP response. In an optimal situation, you would like to get the customer on a video meeting, walk them through your options, and revise your offer before you submit your proposal. You would also want to highlight the changes you made before you submitted your response to create a sense that the other side's "fingerprints" are on the offer.

Sometimes the rules surrounding the RFP preclude this type of inter-action, and you are forced to engage in an asynchronous negotiation. I am not saying that this will never happen; but I am advising that you do not want it to happen. Avoid turning conversations with the other side into this type of RFP situation. At the end of a meeting with a customer, if you are not ready to deliver an offer, ask for another meeting; do not say, "I will send you a proposal." When you are on a Zoom meeting with a customer and they say send me a proposal, either say immediately, "Of course, let me walk you through what that proposal will look like," or say that you would be happy to send them something after your next quick chat because you want to be certain you are sending them exactly what they want to avoid wasting any of their time. Think of sending a proposal as turning the interaction into the asynchronous RFP-like interaction that you want to avoid and always remember to try to "say it, don't send it."

What to Say

We know that we want to "say it, don't send it, and see them when we say it" by conveying our offer in a synchronous, face-to-face channel. The question of what to say remains, though, and this is the focal point for the rest of this chapter. We understand that we want to deliver a message highlighting how our differentiators address the other side's pressing business needs and that we want our multiple offer to reinforce this message.

How to Convey the Multiple Offer

When delivering your offer, think about your message being shaped like an hourglass. You want to start broadly with your elevator pitch of a message, then narrow in on the details of the offer, and end by broadly reinforcing the key points of your message.

For example, if I were delivering the offer to the customer on behalf of the box company, I would begin by highlighting how pleased I am to be discussing their need for packaging. I would note that I know they wanted to discuss price, and I would be happy to do this, but first I want to be certain that we are providing them with exactly the packaging they need. Specifically, I want to be sure that we are providing them with the box shape they desire, the quality they need, and with the ability to order new boxes when they want. I would state that I know they are talking to my competitor about a square box, and that we can certainly provide a simple square box if this is what they would like, but I would point out that we are the only packaging company that offers a very unique die cut that allows us to provide a shaped box, like the octagonal box that they have ordered in the past.

I would say that we are certainly happy to supply a square box if this is what they would like, but we want to be sure because a square box will require a lot of packaging material that will come at a cost and labor to insert the packaging material that will also be costly. The total cost of shipping may be lower with the octagonal box because it will not require much packaging material at all. I would acknowledge that they might have a great new source for packaging material and really do desire the square box, but that I would not want them to be disappointed receiving the square box if they wanted the octagonal box.

I would indicate that I also wanted to discuss the quality of the box that they desire because they always told me that their brand relied on nothing ever arriving broken. I would emphasize that the quality of our boxes shipped straight off the line are better than our competitors' boxes, but that we have always done an extra check by hand of every single box we shipped to them because we knew that quality was essential.

Finally, I would ask how they wanted to order boxes. Of course, we could ship the boxes to them once per month, which is the industry norm and what you would get with any of our competitors. My concern with this, though, is that I know that they frequently receive expedited orders that require immediate and unexpected shipping. I know that their plants are somewhat small, making it difficult to store a lot of excess packaging material. I would remind them that they told me a story once about an experience before we started to work together when they ran out of boxes for a week and had to shut down their manufacturing line completely because they could not ship any product at all. They told me that they lost customers that week that they never recovered and this was why they switched from their former packaging company to us. I would never want this type of situation to happen to them again; consequently, if they would like, we could provide them with access to order boxes for emergency orders through our very unique 24-hour customer service center. I would say that I want to understand their preferences on the shape of the box, the quality of the box, and how they want to order boxes, and have developed three potential options regarding these issues.

I would then show them the written MESO, shown in Table 8.1, with Option A, Option B, and Option C side by side. Notice that the "elbow issue" is the shape of the box; this issue effectively connects the message to the rest of the offer. As I review the offer with them, I would work my way across the issues that are varying on the top of the options. I would not go down Option A and then down Option B. Instead, I would go across, first discussing the shape of the box they desired, highlighting that Option A was for the square box while Options B and C were for the inimitable, die-cut octagonal box that they had been receiving. I would then discuss the implications of the shape on the packaging material and the cost of this as well as the labor to insert the packaging material and the cost of this.

I would then highlight that we could ship the box straight off of our manufacturing line as indicated in Option A and Option B, and I would remind them that the quality of boxes straight off our line is better than our competitors' quality, but that we would also be happy to continue to hand-check every box if they desired, as we indicated in Option C.

In terms of ordering boxes, they could order them once a month as they would with our competitors, or they could access our unique customer service center to order boxes between 8:00 a.m. EST and 10:00 a.m. EST in Option B. If they are running short on boxes, they can call in the morning and have them by the next day. I would stress, though, that this might not be sufficient for them since they have plants around the globe, and in Option C we are offering them an alternative to order boxes 24/7 via our customer service center, providing the ability to restock boxes by the following morning and never run the risk of having to shut down their manufacturing line.

I would declare that as the industry leader in packaging, we would love to keep them updated on new packaging trends once or twice a year, or as often as they would like. I would then say that, of course, if they want customized boxes that are hand-checked to ensure exceptional quality and have the ability to order boxes 24/7, that comes at a higher price than if they want a standard square box, shipped straight off the line, which is ordered once a month. I would emphasize that I really want to understand their preferences on the shape of the box, the quality of the box, and how they want to order their boxes so that we can deliver them the exact packaging option they desire.

Notice how I go across the MESO highlighting the Storytelling Issues that I am varying across the three options. Often, I do not even mention the Tradeoff and Contentious Issues that are constant across the three options. They are in front of the other side in the written offer, but I am not drawing any attention to these issues.

Table 8.1: The Box Company MESO

	Option A	Option B	Option C
Customization	Standard square box	Customized die-cut box	Customized die-cut box
Amount of packing material	XXXXXXX	X	X
Cost of packing material	$$$$$	$	$
Labor to insert packing material	XXXXXXX	X	X
Cost of labor to insert packing material	$$$$$	$	$
Quality of box	Straight off the line	Straight off the line	Hand-check each box
Order new boxes	Once a month (industry standard)	Using call center (8 a.m.–10 a.m. EST)	Using call center (24/7)
Updates on new packaging trends	Once a year	Twice a year	Twice a year
Volume discount	Constant	Constant	Constant
Rebate for new plastic packaging material	Constant	Constant	Constant
Dedicated account rep	On-site one day a week	On-site one day a week	On-site one day a week
Price	$	$$	$$$
Payment terms	Constant	Constant	Constant

Note also how I blend some stories into the presentation and incorporate loss framing, because I want the other side to move off their status quo assumption that they are going to switch to the competitor if we do not match the competitor's price. I would never say that I will match the competitor' price because this would communicate that I am no better than the competitor. Instead, I want to use the multiple offer to highlight my differentiators and convey how my differentiators address the customer's pressing business needs. My offer starts with my elevator pitch message, narrows in on the details across the three options, and then returns to the key message highlighting my differentiators.

How to Deliver the Offer

If you are delivering a complex offer, the three options should be written down to provide a visual cue as you are reviewing them. In an in-person meeting, I like to have the offer printed and provided to each person. I may also have the offer projected on a screen, but I like to have it printed because this allows me to make changes to it with my red pen as I make concessions, a topic we will address in the next chapter. I do not hand out the offer or project it until I have finished the elevator pitch of my message, though. I want all attention on the message before I dig into the details of the offer.

In a virtual meeting, I will still start with the message and will not project the MESO until I finish the message and refer to the offer. I will then project the offer on the screen and, if possible on the platform, annotate changes to this projected offer as I make concessions throughout our discussion. I will then send the other party the version with the changes in red via e-mail at the end of the meeting. All of this advice is consistent with the "say it, don't send it" philosophy because you are not sending the other side anything until after you have discussed it with them.

If the offer is very simple, you can deliver the options verbally. For example, if I wanted to meet with a client, I might say to them that I know that they had wanted to meet to discuss an issue that was urgent to them. Would they rather meet on Monday at 2:00 p.m., Tuesday at 3:00 p.m., or Friday at noon? I have offered a very simple MESO that frames the conversation around when we are going to meet rather than discussing if we are going to meet. Of course, this simple MESO could be verbally presented. As the MESO becomes more complex, it is important to write it down in addition to saying it so that the other side can follow the visual cues while they are listening to you.

There are times when you want the offer to appear to emerge more spontaneously from the conversation rather than being written in advance. In these cases, you could practice writing the offer many times in advance, so you can memorize what is in each option and then write the offer "spontaneously" as you discuss it with the other side. Even though you practiced writing the options, it seems extemporaneous if you are writing it down in front of the other side as you are providing your rationale. Often, when you are negotiating for yourself, you want to achieve this spontaneous sense, as we will discuss in the next section.

SEEKING SYNCHRONICITY IN YOUR PERSONAL NEGOTIATIONS

It is critical to seek synchronicity when you want to maintain the relationship with the other side. This is essential in your employment negotiations. You should never e-mail, text, or leave a voicemail for an employer about an offer, something you do not like about your job, a promotion opportunity, or anything else consequential to your career. I always tell my students that they need to remember to "say it, don't send it" when they are communicating with employers. E-mail can be an excellent coordination tool to organize a meeting with the employer, but you do not want to begin to negotiate in this asynchronous channel.

I say this every year in my MBA classes, and I often tell my students about one particular student who did not follow this advice. One of my students had offers from different employers but was most interested in one particular offer. She e-mailed the employer and said that she was very excited about their offer, but that she had an offer with Company X which was higher, and she wanted to speak to them to see if they would match this offer. The company wrote a very nice e-mail back saying that they hoped she enjoyed her career at Company X. She was shocked and horrified by their response. When I share this story with my students, I stress the need to "say it, don't send it"; highlighting that it is absolutely essential to seek synchronicity in employment negotiations.

I find that my students can never hear this advice too often. In today's world, asynchronous communication is so common that it is easy to default to this option without considering the risk. I see this even with my own children. When my oldest son, Barrett, was a student at Stanford, he did an internship each summer. I remember that early in his academic career, he had been interviewing with a firm for an internship that he really wanted. The first and second round interviews had gone quite well, and he thought he might get an offer. I told him to call me as soon as he received it so we could discuss what to do next. When he received the offer, he immediately texted me. I was in a session with a client but texted him back that I would call him during one of our breaks. When I called him to congratulate him on the offer, he told me that they wanted him to start the job on June 12, but that he could not start on June 12 because he had exams until June 14. I told him this was not a problem at all, and that he would just call them to explain this and get the start date moved to July 1, reminding him that we were going on a family vacation to Europe as soon as he was finished with his exams. He said that the employer said this wasn't possible and that he needed to start earlier. I explained this was just the employer's first offer and I was confident that he would be able to get a later start date since he would be available to work for the employer for the first three weeks of September because Stanford's fall quarter would begin much later than most other schools. He said, "No, Mom, I e-mailed them about my exams lasting until June 14, and they said I could start on June 16 then." I said, "You did what?" and he repeated that he had e-mailed them. I said "Barrett, what does Mom always say—never ever, never ever, ever e-mail an employer." He missed that family trip to Europe that year but learned a valuable life lesson early in his professional career—"say it, don't send it."

You want to seek synchronicity in all employment negotiations, whether you are speaking with a potential new employer or with your current employer. Do not send e-mails to your boss about a new role or a situation that you do not like. You want to lead with a synchronous conversation. You may follow your discussion with an e-mail to thank the person for the discussion and create a record of the conversation, but you want to start out with synchronous communication.

Summary

This chapter highlighted that you can reduce your fear in the negotiation by delivering your offer in a synchronous channel. There are many advantages to delivering the offer in person, but if you cannot be face-to-face in person, you want to be face-to-face on a virtual platform like Zoom, Webex, Google Meet, or Teams. These are all examples of synchronous communication where you can deliver your offer, hear and see the other side's reaction, and immediately frame, shape, modify, and concede. When you are in a synchronous channel, you can better control the discussion, ask for more, and protect the relationship at the same time. Asynchronous negotiation generates much more risk of offending the other side and losing the deal. Because we fear these risks, we often do not ask for as much when we are negotiating in asynchronous channels. We sacrifice our outcome and the relationship when we negotiate over e-mail, mail, text, voicemail, or other asynchronous ways. We can remove fear and maximize our outcomes when we seek synchronicity in the negotiation.

This chapter also explained how to deliver the offer in the most compelling way by focusing the story on how your differentiators address the other side's pressing business needs. A multiple offer is an excellent tool to reinforce this message, and we reviewed how to deliver the multiple offer in the most effective way as well.

When I make my first offer, I know that it is unlikely to be accepted. In fact, as we will discuss in the next chapter, I may not want it to be accepted. In Chapter 9, we will discuss the need to leave yourself room to concede and how to do this well to close the deal and build the relationship with the other side.

9

Leave Yourself Room to Concede to Close the Deal

Leaving yourself room to concede is a great way to alleviate your fear in negotiating. The very act of conceding makes you look flexible and cooperative, and it increases the likelihood that you will settle an agreement (Pruitt, 1981). As you make your first offer, you should plan to concede. In fact, I would suggest that you want to make adjustments to your starting point. When you concede, the other side thinks they are winning; they become more satisfied with the deal, are more likely to settle, and are more inclined to want to do a deal with you again in the future (Hughes & Ertel, 2020). Research also reveals that people are actually happier to pay more when the other side is seen to concede than they are paying less in a negotiation that concludes with no concessions (Galinksy, Mussweiler, & Medvec, 2002). In order to give the other side the feeling of winning, you need to plan and purposely give yourself ample room to adjust. You want your counterparty to feel like they won while you got everything you wanted, so you should plan to concede.

I recommend that you develop your concession plan before you make your first offer. It is not that you will concede if you have to or concede if they make you; but rather, I encourage my clients to recognize that they want to concede. If you make a first offer that is immediately accepted, you should consider it a very bad day; if it was that easy for the other side to accept, you probably could have secured a much better deal. You want to concede, and in this chapter, we will discuss how to do this effectively.

The Importance of Concessions

I am often asked how ambitious a first offer should be. I always say your first offer should be more ambitious than your goal, so that you have room to concede and still get to your goal. In Chapter 6, we talked about the need to build a rationale for that aggressive, but not outrageous, first offer. A first offer is rarely immediately accepted (Galinsky, Mussweiler, & Medvec, 2002) and, as noted earlier, if your first offer is immediately accepted, it is probably the case that you made a poor first offer and could have asked for more.

If we deliver our first offer too close to our own reservation point, we do not give ourselves enough room to move. This inability to move makes an impasse and damaged relationships more likely (Babcock & Loewenstein, 1997). The interesting thing is that negotiators often start close to their own reservation point when they are very worried about the relationship and do not want to offend the other side with an ambitious ask. This is when people will often start to "negotiate with themselves" before making the offer.

I watched a consulting firm do this once. Three partners were on the phone discussing an offer they wanted to make to a client; one suggested that the offer should be for $2 million. Another partner said he thought this seemed too high, stressed that the firm's relationship with this client was critically important, and suggested they go in at $1.8 million. The other partner said that he felt other firms would come in at $1.7 million. The three considered $1.7 million and said perhaps they should make their offer for $1.6 million, so that they would stand out from their competitors. I pointed out to the three of them that their costs for the project were at $1.5 million, so the $1.6 million offer would leave them little room to concede. I reminded them that their BATNA Analysis score for the client was a relatively low 3.2, suggesting that the client needed them to do the project. I proposed that they go in at $2.5 million, leaving room to concede so that they could demonstrate their interest in working with the client. I told them that a concession made before you start the negotiation counts for zero in the relationship bank. People like to see you concede during the negotiation—not before the negotiation begins. The other side never knows about concessions you made before you started the negotiation, so they cannot appreciate this movement. When we start close to our reservation point and do not leave ourselves room to concede, we look stubborn and may damage the relationship, even though our intent was to look reasonable and concerned about the relationship.

You need to concede while you are in discussion with the other side, and you need to highlight these concessions. You also need to rationalize the concessions that you make. If you ask for $100 million, and when the other side pushes back, you immediately drop your request to $80 million, it looks like you were just trying to assess if the other side was an idiot who would pay $100 million because you seem to have been perfectly willing to settle at $80 million. To avoid this impression, you need to ensure that you build a rationale for the concessions you are making and that you never negotiate a single issue. When you have a package of issues on the table all being negotiated at the same time, you can craft a rationale for your concessions.

Package Deals

In the situation I was describing above, the partners were worried about how they would rationalize making a concession on the fee if they needed to do so to win the business. I reminded them that they should want to concede but that they would not concede on the fee in isolation. Instead, they would make the concession as a part of the package for the agreement regarding the overall engagement. When you negotiate, you do not want to settle issues one at a time. As we discussed in Chapter 7, you almost always want to settle at the package level. When you settle things issue by issue, the negotiation will likely become more heated because you are not identifying tradeoffs, so you are essentially making every issue into a Contentious Issue. Because of this, the negotiation will be more contentious and may take longer. If the negotiation is more contentious and takes longer, you are more likely to reach an impasse when you settle things issue by issue. Even if you reach an agreement, though, it is more likely that your settlement will leave money on the table.

Howard Raiffa famously discussed the importance of Pareto Optimal outcomes, which leave no money on the table (Raiffa, 1982). What this means is that one party cannot do any better without hurting the other party. If the outcome is not Pareto Efficient, it means that one party could do better at no expense at all to the other party or perhaps both parties could actually do better. I do not want to accept an agreement where I could have done better at no cost at all to the other side, or the other side could have done better at no cost at all to me, or perhaps both of us could have done better. I do not want to leave money on the table and agree to a suboptimal outcome. In order to push toward a Pareto Efficient outcome, we have to identify tradeoffs between the issues, so we need to negotiate at the package level. I encourage my clients to remember that nothing should be settled until everything is settled.

In order to maintain a package focus, you would like to establish your goal and your reservation point across the whole package rather than on an issue-by-issue basis. This means that when you are developing a scoring tool, as described in Chapter 4, you should avoid setting a reservation point for each specific issue and instead establish your reservation point across the whole package based on your BATNA. In certain negotiations, you cannot avoid specific, individual reservation points, but in general, you should try to establish your goal and reservation point at the package level. For example, in pharmaceutical sales, "best price" is a situation where there may be a reservation point on a singular issue. The current "best price" across all formulary agreements impacts a pharmaceutical company's Medicaid contracts; a negative change to this price would cause tremendous harm across the company, so price cannot be compromised for one individual formulary agreement. Notice, though, that when you establish a reservation point on a single issue, you may lose power. If the other side figures out that you cannot move on this one issue, they may try to extract what they want on all of the other issues. For this reason, it is best to establish your reservation point and goal across the package of issues rather than on a single issue. You want to maintain as much flexibility as possible in the negotiation by having different ways to achieve your goal.

Do You Ever Want to Negotiate on a Single Issue?

Notice that I said you generally want to negotiate at the package level. There are two exceptions to this rule that need to be discussed. First, if you are confident that you can grab your most important issue from the other side in a negotiation, you may want to do this and then package together the rest of the issues. There is an inherent drawback to this high-risk, high-reward strategy, though. If it works, you may be able to get what you want on your most important issue and secure a huge advantage in the negotiation. The challenge, though, is that when it does not work, you are left in a very difficult position when you go back to try to bundle the issues together. I generally recommend that people not pursue this strategy unless they are absolutely confident that they can out-negotiate the other side. I am not saying that I never use this strategy. I will deploy this strategy occasionally, but very infrequently.

In general, I contend that all of the issues that you really care about need to be in a package, including the Contentious Issues and Tradeoff Issues, and the Storytelling Issues that highlight how your differentiators address the other side's pressing business needs.

I do recommend, though, that you keep some issues out of your original package offer. In particular, I suggest that you have some less important Storytelling Issues in a bucket of issues that you keep on the side.

A Bucket of Issues on the Side

I suggest that even when you are pursuing a package deal approach, you should always have a few less important Storytelling Issues in a bucket ready to go. Why do you need this bucket of issues? You need to have something to add into the negotiation in case the other side puts themselves in a corner by saying, "Take it or leave it" or "This is my final offer." Whenever they do this, you have to help them out of the corner in a face-saving way so that you can settle the deal. The best way to help your counterparty out of the corner is to throw in a new issue.

Of course, you want to be certain that you never put yourself in a corner, so you should avoid saying anything like "Take it or leave it" or "This is my final offer." You also want to avoid shoving the other side into a corner, so never ask them for a "best and final offer." You want the other party to maintain flexibility, just as you want to remain flexible to get the best agreement.

I always try to fill up my extra bucket of issues when I am first analyzing my Issue Matrix and developing my first offer. Sometimes, however, I have been in a situation where I felt like my bucket of extra issues was empty. For example, when the Kellogg School of Management approached me to work at Northwestern University, my husband and I moved to Chicago from upstate New York. I had been on the faculty at Cornell University, and my husband and I were looking at homes in Ithaca, on the shores of the spectacular Cayuga Lake. For the same price as a brand-new, beautiful four-bedroom home with a view of the lake in Ithaca, I could purchase a dilapidated three-bedroom ranch in a northern suburb of Chicago. My husband and I both suffered an incredible shock when we saw the home prices in Chicago. This shock was complicated by the fact that I have a rule on house buying which is that you need to have three houses toward which you are indifferent before you make an offer on one house. Given the sticker shock we were suffering due to our lack of knowledge about the Chicago market, we had to look at a lot of homes—precisely 152—to find our set of three houses to pursue the first time we purchased a home in the Chicago area. One of the three houses was a new home that was under construction. The house was being built by a small, custom builder on speculation (remember the days when homes were built on spec?). The home was partially constructed, but there was still the opportunity to make numerous changes in the design and finishes.

I needed to use all of my negotiation strategies as we bid on this house because it was slightly above our price range and well beyond what we had expected to pay in Ithaca. The builder wanted to talk about the price of the home and the add-ons separately, but I packaged them together and started with aggressive multiple offers. We went back and forth many times with offers and counteroffers, and I could tell that the builder was losing patience with me. I suspected that at any moment he was going to say "take it or leave it," with a few colorful words added. I was concerned because I had no issues in my bucket. I had been using a bunch of Storytelling Issues in the negotiation package to try to get more on the Contentious and Tradeoff Issues, but I had no new issues to add to the discussion. Then one day the builder asked if he could take photos of the house if we purchased it. I asked him what he was going to do with the photographs, and he explained that as a custom builder he sells everything he builds, and he would like the photographs to show off the quality of his work. This gave me an idea. The next day I asked him if he might have some homes he built that we could walk through. I explained that I thought we were far apart because he knew the quality of his work, but I had not seen this quality and that if I saw his work, I thought that we might bridge the significant gap between us. He asked me if I had driven by the addresses that he had provided. I said I had driven by the homes and seen the outside of each of them, but I wanted to walk through one of his houses, see the crown moldings, walk on his stairs, feel the banisters, open the cupboards, and really see the quality of his work. He told me that unfortunately he had nothing to show me because he was a custom builder and sold everything that he built; he said that he wished he had something to show me, though, because he believed his work was exceptional and it would be very valuable to him to be able to show off the quality of his work.

I now had an issue in my bucket. It was not the time to use it yet because the builder had not put himself in a corner. I suspected that it would happen very soon though, because I knew he was growing incredibly frustrated with me. Two days later, he said, "Take it or leave it" with a lot of emotion. At that moment, I pulled my issue out of the bucket. I said that I had been thinking about how valuable he said it would be to show off the quality of his work and suggested that our home could be a model home for him to show. I highlighted that this would allow him to show off the quality of his workmanship and convince prospective buyers to purchase a home from him.

Adding this new issue allowed the builder to save face as we discussed four different options, with three of the alternatives including price points lower than his "take it or leave it" offer. In the first option, he could show his quality work in our house to prospective buyers 12 times over the next two years with two hours of notice. In the second option, he could show the house eight times over the next two years, and in the third option, he could show the house four times over the next two years. The fourth option was at his "take it or leave it" price, but it included no opportunity to show the house. I was adding a new issue that the builder had said was very valuable to him into a multiple offer to test whether we were really at his reservation point or whether it was possible to get more off the price of the home.

At the end of a negotiation, you can add a new Storytelling Issue into a MESO to see if there are more potential trades to be made; this is a great technique to try to optimize the deal by pushing toward the Pareto Efficient frontier. Notice that in this case I used four options, whereas I almost always offer three. I would say that 98% of the time when I develop a MESO, I provide three alternatives. I used four options in this situation because I had no idea how valuable it would be to a custom builder to have a model house to show, and I had no sense of how many potential customers he would want to try to close in a year. I was willing to let him show off the house for anything over $10,000, so I wanted to signal flexibility and decided to offer four alternatives. My husband was horrified by the MESO; he said, "You are going to let strangers come into our house and see all of our valuables?" I pointed out to him, though, that we had no valuables and given how much we were pushing our budget if we purchased this house, we would have no valuables for a very long time. I think my husband was relieved when the builder chose the fourth option of not showing the house. This signaled to me that we were at or very close to his reservation point because he had explicitly said that the issue would be very valuable to him, yet he was not willing to trade anything to get it.

While this builder did not choose an option to show the house, I have used the strategy of offering contractors the chance to show off the quality of their work many times over the past 25 years. Most have taken this alternative, so keep this option in mind the next time you are hiring a contractor (as long as you have no valuables!). One of my favorite examples of the advantage of this approach actually came from one of my former students, Daniel. He had a lot of success in his life post-Kellogg, and he was at a point in his career when he and his wife, Susan, were purchasing a home in an upscale neighborhood that was being developed by a developer and a few custom builders. The homes were selling at high price points and, given the initial cost of the land to build the homes, the builders were not holding any houses as "model homes." Daniel negotiated with the builder of the home that he and Susan were purchasing to allow the builder to show their house as a model home. In return for this, Daniel and Susan got a significant amount off the purchase price.

However, Daniel and Susan got so much more than this with this agreement. For example, the builder finished the entire punch list for the new home within one week. If you have built or purchased a new home in the past, you know that the punch list often takes a year to be completed. Their punch list was finished in one week because the builder was very motivated to have everything look perfect when other people saw the house. Daniel and Susan were moving into the house in October and planned to wait until the following spring to have all of the landscaping installed. However, the builder wanted the house to show well, so he installed basic landscaping, plus a driveway and sidewalk constructed of stone pavers at his own expense. Daniel and Susan would change these items in the future, but now there was no time pressure to have this done. They were able to wait to do this work for three years while enjoying the paved driveway, sidewalk, and land-scaping the builder had provided.

Like me, Daniel used this issue at the end of the negotiation with his builder, throwing it into a multiple offer from his bucket on the side. Adding a new issue into the negotiation in this way allows you to see if there is additional value to be captured in trades, and Daniel and Susan definitely generated and captured additional value. It is likely that the builder captured a great deal of additional value as well. Daniel and Susan's home was spectacular and probably convinced many potential buyers to purchase homes from the wise builder who agreed to the package. Identifying optimal tradeoffs often allows both sides to secure better outcomes, and I think this was the case for Daniel, Susan, and their builder.

What If the Other Side Goes First?

You know from Chapter 6 that you want to make the first offer, but let us assume that the other side sat in one of my classes, too, and they race to go first. You planned to make the first offer, but they get their offer on the table before you. What should you do? There are many possible ways to respond, but only a few of these options are actually strategic. You could ask questions about the other party's offer, point out what is wrong with their offer, say that their offer is ridiculous, be silent, ignore their offer, or give an immediate counteroffer. The two most strategic responses are ignoring their offer and giving them a counteroffer. Both of these strategies allow you to avoid increasing the anchoring advantage the other side secured by going first. If you ask questions, discuss the offer, or tell them what is wrong with the offer, you are discussing their offer, and this allows their offer to become further entrenched. Any time that you spend on the starting point allows the anchor to grow deeper roots and become the key point of discussion. Even being silent is dangerous because silence provokes the other side to offer up more information and possibly counteroffer, but if the other party provides a counteroffer, it will likely be close to their starting point and further embed their initial offer.

The best move for you is to counteroffer with three options. A MESO is more complex than a single offer, and this complexity leads to a strong anchoring effect. The MESO will allow you to take back some of the anchoring advantage the other side secured by going first.

Conceding When You Have Multiple Offers on the Table

Whether you are delivering options A, B, and C as a first offer, or as a first counteroffer if the other side was able to make the first offer, you should have a plan to concede. You want to have a plan prepared to make concessions to give options D, E, and F. You should not just pull these offers out already printed, however. You need to make it feel like the concessions are in response to the other side's reactions, objections, and concerns. If it looks like you had the offers prepared in advance of the negotiation, it shows you were always willing to make these adjustments and that the other side is not driving them. Instead of pulling the offers out, you should modify one or more of the offers in front of the other side. If you are in an in-person meeting, I recommend that you handwrite changes to the offers on the original MESO in a red pen. When you cross out the C option and create the D alternative, you will really emphasize the concessions that you are making for the other side.

If you are in a virtual meeting, you may be able to annotate the offer to modify it in red. If not, though, you could type Option D beside the other three options. You want to make sure you are always highlighting your concessions, both verbally and visually. For instance, if you make concessions in one meeting and then return for another meeting, do not clean up the offer and present the other side with a clean sheet in the next meeting. Instead, show them the same sheet with the changes noted to highlight your concessions.

Many fear using multiple offers because they are afraid the other side will "cherry-pick" by taking the best from each of the alternatives. They worry that the other side will take the best of A, the best of B, and the best of C and pull all of this together as their counteroffer. Many negotiators worry about cherry-picking, but I do not see it as a bad thing. I think you glean valuable information from listening to what the other side selects. The risk in cherry-picking is that you will get anchored on the other side's cherry-picked offer, so you should never discuss it. Instead, you should anticipate what your counterparty is likely to push on and make a counteroffer of D or E that addresses some of the objections that you expect them to raise. I generally do not go from Options A, B, and C to options D, E, and F. That is, I generally do not replace all three of my initial offers with new offers, unless I uncover a piece of critical information that suggests something in A, B, and C is not as valuable to the other side as it costs me to provide it (as I did when negotiating with my nanny, described in Chapters 4 and 7, when I realized that she did not value the health insurance that I would be paying a lot to provide). Instead of replacing all of the offers, I will generally make a change to two issues in one of the options and make it into Option

D and then later move some other issues to generate Option E. I try to anticipate the objections that the other side will raise and create Option D and Option E in advance to address these concerns but I will update based on our conversation and make it appear that these offers emerge from our discussion. I might say something such as, "I hear what you are saying, and as I listen to you, it sounds like what is important to you is X. Perhaps we can best address your concern about X in this way," and then write out Option D in front of them.

Overcoming Objections

As we have just discussed, you want to try to anticipate the objections that you believe the other side will raise and generate options that will address these concerns. This is a part of your concession plan. People often fear that the other side will say "no" and worry that this will be the end of the negotiation. I always tell my clients that "no" is not the ending but the beginning of the negotiation. You should not view "no" as a wall you run into that stops the negotiation but rather as the window you climb through to begin negotiating. Negotiation starts with "no." When you hear "no," you can be confident that you have tested the boundary conditions; you know at what point the other side will push back.

When you are preparing for the negotiation, you should consider your script for the entire negotiation, anticipating the objections the other side will raise. I always encourage my clients not only to plan how they will start the negotiation but also how they will end it. Many people do not prepare to negotiate, and even those who do often only consider how they will begin. You want to start strong, but the end is often where people start to make the biggest mistakes. It is at the end that they say, "Take it or leave it" or "That is my final offer," two statements that should be avoided, as we previously discussed. I encourage my clients to consider how the negotiation might end "from a dream to a nightmare," suggesting that they consider all of the possible ways that the negotiation could go and how they will end in a way that allows them to have a chance to maintain the relationship with the other party and to re-engage while keeping their credibility intact.

Many large professional negotiations take place over multiple meetings. I recommend to my clients that they always make at least one concession in the first meeting and draw a lot of attention to it. This makes you look flexible and signals that you want to work with the other side. Remember that you do not want to agree to anything in isolation but instead should change one or two components in one of the options you are proposing.

I also suggest that my clients ensure that their modified MESO is the one on the table at the end of a meeting so that it gains the anchoring advantage of being what people are considering between two meetings. Remember, the longer people spend on a topic, the more deeply rooted the anchor becomes, so having your offer as the "holding offer" between meetings is definitely an advantage.

Harnessing a Trigger Strategy

One strategy that you might want to deploy when the other side says "no" is a *trigger strategy*, which is a great tool to move the other side off the status quo. I created the term "trigger strategy" because I think that often in a negotiation you feel like you have convinced the other side to agree to something, but you just cannot get them to commit. They do not want to sign on the dotted line. You want them to "pull the trigger" and agree. Your challenge in this situation is to get your counterparty to move off the status quo, agree to something new, and allow this preferred, new state to gain traction as the new status quo.

The status quo is like rubber cement. It is very sticky, and it is the most likely future state of affairs (Kahneman, Knetsch, & Thaler, 1991). The easiest way to move the other side off the status quo is by highlighting losses (as discussed in Chapter 6) and coupling this loss frame with what I refer to as a trigger strategy; that is, giving the other party the feeling that they have the opportunity to change their minds. I often suggest that this is like flashing the "exit" sign. Highlighting how the other side can revert back to the original status quo if they desire actually causes them to be willing to try what you want. Of course, as soon as they try it, a new status quo emerges, and it is likely that this new status quo will again be very sticky and likely to be maintained. Let me provide a few examples to illustrate this concept and the psychology underlying it.

My first example will highlight how we overestimate the value of being able to change our minds. Imagine that you have two retirement packages in front of you: one has no administrative fees, but once the money is in the fund you cannot move it around. The other one has administrative fees, but you can move your money whenever you want. If I ask people which one they might choose, most would select the second fund that has a fee because they want the freedom to move their money around. We know, however, that many Americans do not move around the money in their accounts (Malito, 2019), but they value the idea that they could do this. We overestimate the value we place on being able to change our minds, even when we are not likely to change them. We underestimate how sticky the status quo is.

This idea of overvaluing the ability to change our mind provides the foundation for a trigger strategy. Giving people an out makes it more likely that you can get them to try something new. For example, info-mercials on TV almost always include money-back guarantees. These money-back guarantees are trigger strategies. If you were simply watching the commercial for a new product, you might be reluctant to move off the status quo and purchase the product. You might think that before you buy it, you should look around and evaluate your options. By giving you the opportunity to change your mind and simply send the product back for a full refund, the company reduces the barrier for you to make the decision to try the product. Of course, once you have the product, it is unlikely that you will send it back because a new status quo is established where you have the product, and this status quo is very sticky. Notice, too, that if you are offered a 30-day money-back guarantee, no one calls you on Day 29 to warn you that your time is up, and you need to send back the product immediately or keep it forever. A key element of a trigger strategy is that it should be structured so that the other side must take action to move off the newly established status quo.

I once purchased a Total Gym from an infomercial like this. I was very impressed that Chuck Norris at 75 used a Total Gym and was in such great shape, so I decided to purchase one too. The money-back guarantee made the decision easy for me because I could return it if I was not satisfied. I had not planned on purchasing a piece of gym equipment that day—I had not looked around or considered other alternatives—but I thought I might as well try it. I knew this was a trigger strategy lulling me into the purchase, but I also knew that Chuck Norris looked like he was in really awesome shape. Of course, once the Total Gym was delivered, unboxed, and sitting in my gym, there was a new status quo established, and I knew that this status quo would be maintained. I liked the Total Gym and was excited to keep it, but even if I wanted to send it back, how would I have returned it? Where was the box? How would I get this gigantic piece of equipment back into the box? Who would carry it upstairs? Returning it would be a challenge, and the new status quo of me having the equipment had a very firm stickiness to it. This is the essence of a trigger strategy.

In the midst of a recession when manufacturers were struggling to sell cars to a population worried about job security, Hyundai utilized a brilliant trigger strategy. Hyundai overcame buyers' hesitation by creating their Buyer Assurance Plan. Customers could buy a Hyundai, and if they lost their job, Hyundai would simply take the car back (Valdes-Dapena, 2009). This is an excellent use of a trigger strategy. The ability to send the car back reduces the barrier to purchase the car. Once a person purchases a new Hyundai though, a new status quo of owning the car is established. Imagine that these buyers lose their jobs. Are they really going to return the cars? How are they going to get new jobs without the convenience of cars? The trigger strategy worked, and Hyundai sold a lot of cars while others in the automobile industry suffered. In 2009, Hyundai's sales were up 47% from the prior year, when the overall automotive industry's sales were only up 1% (Bunkley, 2009).

I find that the tactic of giving the other side an out with the ability to change their mind frequently helps clients close deals by encouraging the other party to commit. For example, imagine that you are leasing commercial real estate. A potential corporate tenant is very interested but reluctant to sign the deal. If you wanted to use a trigger strategy, you would need to start with a loss frame. You could highlight that it is the last available space with a view of the water, a number of others are interested in the space, and you want to ensure that the potential tenant does not lose the space. You offer that they can sign the lease, and you will give them two weeks to change their mind. At any time over the next two weeks, they can change their mind and get out of the lease. This ability to get out of the lease may make them more likely to sign. As they sign, the tenant may think that they are going to look around, investigate other options, and visit other spaces. However, once the tenant signs the lease, they may never visit another spot. The ability to change their minds may make the tenant more likely to sign, but once they have signed, they are less likely to change their minds because the new status quo has staying power.

You can use this to close an agreement with a customer as well. Imagine that you want the customer to purchase a new service that your company offers. You would highlight a loss frame, such as the customer's current exposure or risk, to increase their willingness to try the service. Then you would note that although they are signing a two-year service agreement, there is a two-month trial period during which they can cancel at any time. The customer is more likely to sign because they have a clear opportunity to get out of the agreement. Once the agreement begins, however, a new status quo is created. Having the service becomes the new norm. By saying that there is a trial period, you are giving the customer a way out, but the customer fails to recognize that having the service will become a sticky, new status quo.

It is critical to understand the difference between a trigger strategy with a trial period and a pilot. A pilot generally has a review point with a time period associated with it. When you use a trigger strategy, there is no scheduled review point. The other side must take an action to move off the newly established status quo. With a pilot, you will often assess whether you should progress, whereas with a trigger strategy, you are planning to progress unless the other side takes an action to stop it. Trigger strategies are a powerful tool to get the other side to commit and close the deal.

Harnessing a Contingency to Close

We discussed contingent agreements in Chapter 3 and Chapter 7. A contingency that highlights your confidence in how your differentiator will solve the other side's pressing needs should be included in one or two options in your initial offer.

However, a contingency that is less tied to your differentiators could also be a bucket issue. Adding in some type of "guarantee" might make the other side more comfortable proceeding with the agreement and allow you to close the deal. For example, if you are selling a piece of equipment to a manufacturing company and the negotiation is stalling, you might add a guarantee that you will have the equipment installed within three weeks or they will receive a significant refund. You would still want the contingency to be based on metrics that are objective, measurable, and known by both sides, but this type of guarantee might reduce the other side's fears about delays in getting the equipment installed and allow you to close the deal.

Using Ratification

Imagine that you are trying to close the deal and the other side keeps pushing for more. You are tempted to say that this is your final offer, but you recognize that this is dangerous because you are not at your reservation point. Saying "take it or leave it" or "this is my final offer' are commitment tactics to try to secure closure. Both of these are very dangerous tactics to use, though, because if the other side does not accept the settlement you are proposing, you have no credible way to re-engage them. A better commitment tactic is to use ratification (Narayanan, Buche, McTeague, Joshi, & Lavanchy, 2018). *Ratification* is an end-game tactic that can be used to secure agreement. You literally tie your hands to increase your power. You could say something like "the board has only approved this" or "I am only authorized to go this far," These ratification statements will provide a stickiness to the settlement that you are discussing but still allow you a back door to resume the conversation if the other side walks away. Once you say "this is my final offer," it is nearly impossible to credibly re-engage, but when you use ratification, you can always say that the board reconsidered or that they asked you to reconvene.

If the other side is using ratification against you, your best defense is to use ratification as well. Whenever I am purchasing a car, I expect the salesperson to say that they have to check with their manager. This is a ratification technique, and I know they are likely going to the restroom, not to their manager's office. To neutralize the power this ratification tactic has provided, I ensure that I can use ratification as well by having someone to check with, too.

Knowing Your Reservation Point

This chapter has highlighted that you should be planning to concede and that you want to appear flexible and cooperative as you negotiate. Your desire is to maximize your outcome and build your relationship with the other side as well. Ideally, you have established an aggressive goal, started at a point beyond your goal, and left yourself plenty of room to concede. You want to be negotiating around your goal—not around your reservation point.

You need to know your reservation point, though, because you have to know at what point it is better to walk away than continue conceding. There is a pressure in negotiations to get an agreement (Carnevale, O'Connor, &McCuscker, 1993) and this can sometimes lead you to keep pushing for a settlement when it would be better for you to exit with an impasse.

If you follow all of the suggestions we have discussed throughout these nine chapters, I doubt that you will negotiate near your reservation point too often or that you will have to walk away, but it is critical to know your bottom line. This is true in every negotiation, but one of the most difficult times to maintain this discipline is when you are negotiating for yourself.

LEAVING ROOM TO CONCEDE WHEN NEGOTIATING FOR YOURSELF

Often when we are negotiating for ourselves, we negotiate against ourselves before we begin. We are so worried that we will be too aggressive that we often make many concessions before we initiate the discussion with our employer. Remember, though, that concessions made before we begin count for zero in the relationship bank. You should plan to concede during the discussion, not before you start.

For example, imagine that you feel like your workload has grown so much that you absolutely need an assistant who will work for you full-time, five days a week. You know that it will be difficult to get your boss to agree to this because there is a hiring freeze in place and all hiring requests must go through the CFO. You really need the help, though. The company has a huge revenue target, and you and your team need to be focused on capturing more customers and securing renewals. You know that you want to ask for the assistant but think maybe you could get by if the assistant worked for you four days a week rather than five. As you consider this more, you think maybe a request for an assistant who works for you three days a week would be better because it might be more palatable to the CFO if the person being hired is part-time. You then think that what might really help with your request is to make it for an assistant three days a week who works for you and one of your peers. This way, it is not just meeting your needs, but helping another department as well. You then wonder if perhaps you should include one more peer in your request. The three of you are all at the same level and perhaps it will look the best if the request is for someone to support you and two of your peers three days a week. This is the bare minimum, though; you feel like you need this level of support or your role will be intolerable.

So, you go to your boss and say that you need to hire an assistant who will work for you and two of your peers three days a week. Your boss responds by saying this will be very difficult to achieve because there is a hiring freeze. Your voice raises as you say, "I have to have this support." Your boss reminds you that all hiring requests must be approved by the CFO. Of course, you know that it has to be approved, this is why you backed down from having the person five days a week to three days a week and added support for two of your peers to your request. You find yourself losing patience as you firmly state, even more loudly, that "I must have this support." You fear that you are looking like a crazy person, but you really need the help.

Imagine an alternative scenario where you started by highlighting the need for your team to be focused on attracting more new business and securing renewals to help the company achieve its revenue targets. To do this, you need to hire two assistants to support the team five days a week: one that would be supporting you and one to help the rest of the team be able to maintain their focus on the field. When your boss raised the hiring freeze, you could have negotiated all of the way down to just one assistant who would support you. In this case, you would have looked flexible, cooperative, and focused on the company. In the alternative situation, where you conceded before you started, it is likely that you would look aggressive and stubborn.

When we concede before we start, we often begin too close to our own reservation point. This makes us look inflexible and demanding in the negotiation. You want to leave yourself room to concede, and you want to remember that you will only get credit for concessions you make in the negotiation, not those that you make before you start the negotiation.

In this case, you would also be far better served to go to the table talking about the company's revenue target, the various approaches that you are planning to use to attract new customers, the timeline to get the renewals completed, and how often you would update your boss on the counts for new customers and renewals at the same time that you raise the issue of two new assistants. It is optimal to negotiate at the package level and leave yourself room to concede.

Summary

In this chapter, we discussed how to close the deal. You want to end the negotiation with the best possible outcome for yourself, but you also want to build and maintain your relationship with the other side. This chapter highlighted how you can achieve these two goals simultaneously.

In particular, this chapter reminded you to have a plan to concede and an intent to concede. When you concede, the other side feels like they are winning, and they are happier with the deal. Moreover, if your first offer is immediately accepted, it is likely that you did not ask for enough. So, you should go into each negotiation expecting to concede, wanting to concede, and planning what concessions you will make.

If you are only negotiating a single issue, though, you lose the ability to concede credibly. For example, if you are only negotiating price and you make a concession on price, it looks like you were always willing to make that concession. If I ask for $15,000, you push back, and then I change my offer to $12,000 and this is the only issue we are discussing, it looks like I was trying to assess if you would be foolish and pay the $15,000 price because it seems like I was always willing to offer $12,000. You need to ensure that you have a full package of issues on the table and negotiate at the package level. This allows you to create a rationale for every concession and leave yourself room to concede.

This chapter also presented some specific tactics to overcome objections and close the deal. In addition to your concession plan, consider how your "bucket issues" and contingent offers can be used to allow the other side a face-saving way to concede so that you can close the deal. Trigger strategies are also a great tool to use to secure closure. By giving the other party the opportunity to change their mind, you make it easier for them to commit.

Your desire to close the deal may tempt you into some poor moves, such as saying, "Take it or leave it" or "This is my final offer." You should avoid those statements and deploy a safer commitment tactic, such as ratification, to create a stickiness around an attractive settlement point while still maintaining a credible way to re-engage the other side, if needed. Also remember that you never want to shove the other party into a corner by asking for their "best and final offer"—rather, you want them to maintain flexibility to get the deal done. If the other side puts themselves in a corner accidentally by saying "take it or leave it" or "this is my final offer," you know how to get them out of that situation by adding a new issue out of your bucket to the discussion.

While you need to have a plan to concede, you also need to know at what point you would walk away. It is important to know your reservation point because there is often a lot of pressure on you to "do the deal," and it is better to walk away than to do a deal that is worse than your reservation point. By deploying all of the strategies we have been discussing in the book, you should be negotiating around your goal, not around your reservation point, and reducing the need to walk away.

The strategies presented in this chapter will reduce your fears of losing the deal, ending with an impasse, or taking an agreement when it would have been better for you to walk away. You now have all of the tools you need to close the deal, maximize your outcome, and build the relationship with the other side.

10

The Five F's to Ensure You Are a Fearless Negotiator

In the early chapters of this book, we focused on getting prepared for the negotiation. We discussed how you could reduce your fear when facing a negotiation by thoroughly preparing. We highlighted the importance of putting the right issues on the table, including a lot of Storytelling Issues in the discussion, understanding how your differentiators address the other side's pressing needs, and establishing an ambitious goal based on the weakness of the other side's options to leave you a lot of room to concede. We also focused on building your power to reduce your fear. We talked about multiple sources of power and highlighted that you could build your biggest source of power by improving your BATNA. We also discussed the importance of establishing your reservation point based on your BATNA and always recognizing the difference between your ambitious goal and your bottom line.

The preparation strategies we discussed should reduce your fears of having a contentious discussion, having the other side walk away, losing the deal, accepting a poor outcome, offending the other side, diminishing your credibility, and damaging the relationship. Being well prepared clearly takes the fear out of negotiation, and Chapters 1–5 taught you how to do this.

In later chapters, we focused on what you could do at the table, during the actual negotiation, to eliminate your fear. These chapters highlighted five essential strategies to make you fearless in a negotiation.

The following list highlights these strategies, which I like to refer to as the Five F's to Ensure You Are a Fearless Negotiator:

Five F's to Ensure You Are a Fearless Negotiator

1. **Go FIRST:** You want to make the first offer.
2. **FOCUS on them:** Craft a rationale that focuses on the other side rather than on yourself and, in particular, deliver a message

that highlights how your differentiators address the other party's pressing needs.

3. **FRAME your offer correctly:** Highlight loss words to move your counterparty off the status quo and highlight gain words to maintain the status quo.

4. **Be FLEXIBLE:** Leave yourself room to concede and leverage multiple equivalent simultaneous offers (MESOs).

5. **No FEEBLE offers**.

While the preceding chapters have covered the first four of these points, the last one has not yet been discussed. You want to ensure that you are making a clear, specific offer. Too often, we go to the table and make feeble requests that are not specific asks. For example, you might walk into a store where you see a shirt on the rack that has a tear and ask the cashier, "Can you take something off?" This is a feeble offer that does not make a specific request. Instead, you might say, "Wow, I cannot believe that tear. That's too bad because you probably will not be able to sell it. I will take it off your hands for a 35% discount." That is a clear, specific offer that focuses on the other side, not on yourself. People often make feeble offers. Even experienced negotiators will say, "Could you take something off?" or "Is it possible to give us better shelf space?" or "Can you give us a better price?" All of these are feeble requests because they do not make a clear, specific ask. Always keep in mind that you want to go *first*, *focus* on the other side, *frame* your offer correctly, be *flexible*, and do not make a *feeble* offer.

I want to share one last story to demonstrate the Five F's. If you have teenage boys, you will relate to it when I say that as my boys became preteens, they stopped communicating with me in expansive ways. They would frequently respond with monosyllabic answers, which made conversation challenging. They were always very communicative with their friends, however, and I figured out early on that I would learn a lot when I was around them with their friends. When they were young, I would frequently suggest inviting their friends to dinner or to a movie because I would overhear a lot while in the car. As they grew older, though, going to dinner and a movie with their friends and Mom and Dad was not at the top of their entertainment list. So, I became more creative with activities. When my older son entered high school, I suggested that we go on a ski weekend with five of his best friends. The weekend was really fun and a great chance to source a lot of information about what was happening in his life.

The following year, I put together a similar trip. We headed to a resort in the mountains that had both hotel rooms and condominiums in the same building. We were scheduled to stay in a brand-new condo that had just been finished. In fact, the owners had not stayed there yet. They were coming for the first time over the holidays. We always went on this trip the week before the holiday rush when the rooms were much less expensive, so we were the first guests to stay in this spectacular condo. Of course, since it was brand new, there were a number of "punch list" items that needed to be addressed. The biggest problem was that the TV in the living room did not work. If the TV was not working, my fantasy of sitting around after dinner, eating popcorn, watching movies with the boys, and chatting would never happen. As soon as we knew that there was a problem with the TV when we arrived on Thursday evening, I called the front desk and asked them to send up someone to fix it. A bellman arrived, spent about 30 minutes trying to fix the TV but could not get it to operate. The front desk manager then came up and tried his best, but the TV just would not work. It appeared that this was not a simple TV problem but a much more complicated problem with the wiring of the room. The building engineer, who was off on Thursday evening, came to our room as soon as he arrived for work on Friday morning. He spent a long time in the room but could not get the TV to function. After skiing on Friday, I was notified that the TV would not be fixed until Monday, when the company that installed the entertainment system was available. I was told that, unfortunately, this company did not work on weekends.

I immediately headed to the front desk. I asked to speak to the front desk manager. I said that I was very concerned that they could not get anyone to fix the TV because I was not going to be able to pay for the unit until the TV was fixed and I would feel guilty staying for four entire nights without paying anything. The next morning at 7:00 a.m., the company who installed the entertainment system was at the door. The installer worked on the system all day, and by 2:00 p.m., the TV was finally fixed.

That day when I returned from skiing, the general manager of the hotel called me. He said that he had heard there was a problem with the unit. I said that it was a spectacular unit and that I was so pleased that we were able to be the "punch list family" to ensure that everything was perfect before the new owners arrived the following week. I said that I knew that his highest priority was to make sure that the new owners were thrilled with their new home, and since we had found all of the glitches and were having them fixed, I was confident that it would be perfect for them. He indicated that he had heard that I did not want to pay for the unit because the TV was broken. I assured him that I was absolutely happy to pay now that the TV was fixed but that, of course, I did not want to pay for the days when there had been a problem with the room. He said he could not give me two nights free because the TV had been broken. I said that it had actually been 2.5 days. He noted he would be willing to provide one night free of charge, but that he could not provide more. After all, there were TVs in each of the four bedrooms, so even though the TV in the living room was broken, there were four others to watch. I replied that the four other TVs were exactly the problem and the reason I was so happy that we had been available to be their "punch list family." I said that I could only imagine how angry the owners would be if they arrived for their first night in their new home, arranged for a chef to make dinner in the beautiful new kitchen, set the table in the great room, lit the fire in the stunning fireplace, and then tried to turn on the TV only to find out it was broken. If there were no other TVs, then perhaps the children would have stayed at the table and played games, but with four other TVs, the kids would immediately scatter, and the special family dinner would be destroyed. I said I was so glad that this disaster was averted and that I was really happy we were able to be the "punch list family" to ensure that the owners were thrilled with their new home. The general manager said that he would give me one night free immediately and one night free the next time we returned. I said we would certainly prefer to have the two nights free immediately, but that I understood that he had limits on what he could do. I said that we really liked the unit and that his team was wonderful, so we would be willing to agree to the one night free immediately and the other night when we returned for President's Day weekend. I reiterated that I was really happy that we were available to be the "punch list family," and that I was certain the owners would love their new home.

If you have ever gone skiing over President's Day weekend in the United States, you probably know that the rates for the rooms are extremely high—often double the typical room rate. This meant that we ended up getting the equivalent of three nights free. Why do I share this story? Because I think it highlights the Five F's, and particularly demonstrates the principle of no feeble offers. I might have called down to the front desk and said, "My TV is broken. Can you do something for me?" This would have been a feeble request. I might have felt like I was making the first offer, but it was a weak and ambiguous request. A feeble offer like this does not give you an advantage, and in fact, it often generates a weakness because you have asked for something vague and the other side has responded, leaving you in a more vulnerable position to react to their offer. For example, in the hotel situation, if I had said, "Can you do something for me?" I think the hotel would have sent up chocolate covered strawberries, the amenity this particular hotel uses to address minor guest issues. I think they probably would have sent six chocolate covered strawberries rather than three, but that they would have left out the bottle of champagne because I was with a group of kids. Once the hotel defined this as a six-chocolate-covered-strawberry problem, it would have been very challenging for me to redefine it as a multiple thousand-dollar level problem. This is why it is critical to go first with a clear, specific ask.

You also want to focus on the other side, not on yourself. I used the term "punch list family" 16 times in the actual call with the GM. Clearly, I was frustrated by a unit with a TV that did not work, but I knew the GM's interests would focus on ensuring that the new condominium was perfect for the owners who would arrive the following week.

While you need to focus on the other side, you also need to frame the offer correctly. In this case, I was purposefully highlighting loss words because I wanted to get the GM to move off the status quo and adjust my billing. I was in a low power position in this negotiation. The hotel had my credit card, and I had six boys that needed a place to stay. I was not going to switch hotels, so I had weak BATNA and my reservation point was not attractive. I had an ambitious goal though, because I thought the GM's BATNA was also quite weak. He would not want a guest who frequented his hotel to be dissatisfied, and he would not want to fail to learn about anything in the unit that needed to be repaired before the new owners arrived the following week. My goal was ambitious but my BATNA was weak, so there was a large spread between my goal and my reservation point. It was essential in this situation to use the right strategy to try to move the other side off the status quo, and framing was key to this strategy. I framed the discussion around the strong need to please the condo owners who had spent a lot of money on their new home, how they would be upset if they arrived to problems in the unit, how angry they would have been if the TV did not work, how their first family dinner in their new home would have been destroyed if they tried to use the TV for the first time and found that it did not work, and how happy I was that we could be the "punch list family" to find all of the problems in the unit and have them resolved before the new owners arrived. I was using heavy loss framing in the rationale.

I was also flexible and left myself room to concede. When I first returned to the unit on Friday evening after speaking to the front desk manager, the boys asked me what I had requested. I told them that I had said that I would not be paying for the unit until the TV was fixed. Their mouths dropped open in disbelief. I said, "It is my first offer and I have room to concede." You want to go into the negotiation with an intent to concede and a plan about the concessions you are likely to make. The second element of being flexible is to use multiple offers. I did not actively deploy this strategy in this negotiation, although I generally do, especially when the stakes in the negotiation are high.

Notice too, though, that I made a clear, specific ask in this negotiation, not a feeble request. When you prepare well, as this book has described, and deploy the Five F's at the table, you will be a fearless negotiator. Probably the most important part of the story is that I was willing to ask. I think that many of us are discontented in different situations and become quite frustrated. I always tell people that you should never be dissatisfied; instead, you should negotiate to try to change the situation. Do not let your fear regarding the negotiation impede your willingness to ask. When you use the strategies we discussed in this book, you can be fearless, secure great outcomes for yourself, and build the relationship with the other side.

When people hear my hotel story, they often suggest that the GM probably hoped that I would never return to the hotel. This is actually not true at all, as I continued to go to the hotel every year for many years afterward, and if I failed to book for the holidays by July, the GM would always call and remind me to book my dates. One of the greatest fears people have as they approach a negotiation is that they will damage their relationship with the other side. This fear may hold them back from even starting the negotiation at all. In my opinion, the most successful negotiation is one where I both maximize my outcome and build the relationship with the other side. The strategies presented in this book will help you to achieve these simultaneous goals.

Since most negotiations we encounter take place in ongoing relationships where we care about our rapport with the other side, we must negotiate in ways that allow us to protect and build these connections while maximizing our outcomes. Putting Storytelling Issues on the table so that we can build a rationale that focuses on the other side, establishing ambitious goals that lead us to make first offers that leave us a lot of room to concede, providing multiple offers that allow us to look flexible and cooperative, and highlighting the concessions we make are all strategies that will eliminate the fear of damaging the relationship.

We can negotiate well and build our connection with the other side at the same time. We do not need to fear that we will damage the relationship or lose the deal. When we deploy the right strategies and tools, we can be fearless negotiators and enjoy spectacular success. Good luck in all of your future negotiations, and please keep me informed about your success at www.medvecandassociates.com/contact.

Bibliography

Chapter 1

Babcock, Linda, and Sara Laschever (2007). *Women Don't Ask: The High Cost of Avoiding Negotiation—and Positive Strategies for Change.* New York: Bantam.

Chapter 2

Franconeri, Steven, Andrew Hollingworth, and Daniel J. Simons. (2005). "Do New Objects Capture Attention?" *Psychological Science 16*(4): 275–281.

Harnett, Donald and Larry Cummings. (1980). *Bargaining Behavior: An International Study.* Houston, TX: Dane Publications.

Kahneman, Daniel, Jack L. Knetsch, and Richard H. Thaler. (1990). "Experimental Tests of the Endowment Effect and the Coase Theorem." *Journal of Political Economy, 98*(6): 1325–1348.

Kerr, Steven. (2008) *Reward Systems: Does Yours Measure Up?* Boston: Harvard Business School Press.

Newcomb, Theodore M. (1960). "Varieties of Interpersonal Attraction." In D. Cartwright & A. Zander (Eds.), *Group Dynamics: Research and Theory* (2nd ed., pp. 104–119). Row, Peterson.

Raiffa, Howard. (1982). *The Art and Science of Negotiation.* Cambridge, MA: Belknap Press.

Ross, Michael, and Fiore Sicoly. (1979). "Egocentric Biases in Availability and Attribution." *Journal of Personality and Social Psychology, 37*(3): 322–336.

Theeuwes J., Kramer A.F., Hahn S., Irwin D.E. Our Eyes do Not Always Go Where we Want Them to Go: Capture of the Eyes by New Objects (1998). Psychological Science. 1998; 9(5):379-385. doi:10.1111/1467-9280.00071

Chapter 3

Fisher, Roger, William Ury, and Bruce Patton. (1981). *Getting to Yes: Negotiating Agreement Without Giving In.* New York: Penguin.

Gallo, Amy. (2016). "Setting the Record Straight: Using an Outside Offer to Get a Raise." *Harvard Business Review,* July 5, 2016. hbr.org/2016/07/setting-the-record-straight-using-an-outside-offer-to-get-a-raise

Chapter 4

Raiffa, Howard. (1982). *The Art and Science of Negotiation.* Cambridge, MA: Belknap Press.

Chapter 5

Babcock, Linda, and Sara Laschever. (2003). *Women Don't Ask: Negotiation and the Gender Divide.* Princeton, NJ: Princeton University Press.

Freedman, Jonathan L., and Scott C. Fraser. (1966). "Compliance Without Pressure: The Foot-in-the-Door Technique." *Journal of Personality and Social Psychology, 4*(2): 195–202. https://doi.org/10.1037/h0023552

Galinsky, Adam D., and Thomas Mussweiler. (2001). "First Offers as Anchors: The Role of Perspective-Taking and Negotiator Focus." *Journal of Personality and Social Psychology, 81*(4), 2001: 657–669.

Galinsky, Adam D., Thomas Mussweiler, and Victoria Medvec. (2002). "Disconnecting Outcomes and Evaluations: The Role of Negotiator Focus." *Journal of Personality and Social Psychology 83*(5), March 22, 2002: 1131–1140.

Lewicki, Roy J., Bruce Barry, and David M. Saunders. (2015) [1985]. "Zone of Potential Agreement." *Negotiation* (7th ed.). New York: McGraw-Hill Education.

Ross, Michael, and Fiore Sicoly. (1979). "Egocentric Biases in Availability and Attribution." *Journal of Personality and Social Psychology, 37*(3): 322–336.

Chapter 6

Ames, Daniel. R., and Mason, Malia. F. (2015). "Tandem Anchoring: Informational and Politeness Effects of Range Offers in Social Exchange." *Journal of Personality and Social Psychology, 108*(2): 254–274. https://doi.org/10.1037/pspi0000016

Babcock, Linda, and Sara Laschever. (2003). *Women Don't Ask: Negotiation and the Gender Divide*. Princeton, NJ: Princeton University Press.

CDC. (2020). "Data and Statistics for SIDS and SUID." Centers for Disease Control and Prevention, Apr. 21, 2020. www.cdc.gov/sids/data.htm#graph

Chou, E. Y., and J. K. Murnighan. (2013). "Life or Death Decisions: Framing the Call for Help." *PLoS ONE 8*(3): e57351. doi:10.1371/journal.pone.0057351

de Luca, Federico, and Andrew Hinde. (2016). "Effectiveness of the 'Back-to-Sleep' Campaigns Among Healthcare Professionals in the Past 20 Years: A Systematic Review." *BMJ Open 6*(9): e011435, Sep. 30, 2016. doi:10.1136/bmjopen-2016-011435

De Martino, Benedetto, Dharshan Kumaran, Ben Seymour, and Raymond J. Dolan. (2006). "Frames, Biases, and Rational Decision-Making in the Human Brain." *Science 313*(5787), Aug. 4, 2006: 684–687.

Epley, Nicholas, and Thomas Gilovich. (2005). "When Effortful Thinking Influences Judgmental Anchoring: Differential Effects of Forewarning and Incentives on Self-Generated and Externally-Provided Anchors." *Journal of Behavioral Decision Making 18*: 199–212. http://dx.doi.org/10.1002/bdm.495

Galinsky, Adam D., and Thomas Mussweiler. (2001). "First Offers as Anchors: The Role of Perspective-Taking and Negotiator Focus." *Journal of Personality and Social Psychology 81*(4): 657–669.

Galinsky, Adam D., Thomas Mussweiler, and Victoria Medvec. (2002). "Disconnecting Outcomes and Evaluations: The Role of Negotiator Focus." *Journal of Personality and Social Psychology 83*(5), March 22, 2002: 1131–1140.

Gilovich, Thomas, Victoria Medvec, and Daniel Kahneman. (1998). "Varieties of Regret: A Debate and Partial Resolution." *Psychological Review 105*(3), July 1998: 602–605.

Heneman, Herbert G. (1974). "Comparisons of Self- and Superior Ratings of Managerial Performance." *Journal of Applied Psychology, 59*(5): 638–642. https://doi.org/10.1037/h0037341

Job, R., and F. Soames. (1988). "Effective and Ineffective Use of Fear in Health Promotion Campaigns." *American Journal of Public Health 78*(2), 1988: 163–167. doi:10.2105/ajph.78.2.163

Kahneman, Daniel, Jack Knetsch, and Richard Thaler. (1991). "Anomalies: The Endowment Effect, Loss Aversion, and Status Quo Bias." *Journal of Economic Perspectives 5*(1): 193–206.

Kahneman, Daniel, and Amos Tversky. (1979). "Prospect Theory: An Analysis of Decision Under Risk." *Econometrica 47*(2): 263–291.

Karrass, Chester L. (1992). *The Negotiating Game: How to Get What You Want* (Rev. ed.). New York: HarperBusiness.

Leshner, Glenn, Paul Bolls, and Kevin Wise. (2011). "Motivated Processing of Fear Appeal and Disgust Images in Televised Anti-Tobacco Ads." *Journal of Media Psychology: Theories, Methods, and Applications 23*(2): 77–89.

Lytle, Anne L., Jeanne Brett, and Debra Shapiro. (1999). "The Strategic Use of Interests, Rights, and Power to Resolve Disputes." *Negotiation Journal 15*: 31–52.

Magee, Joe C., Adam D. Galinsky, and Deborah H. Gruenfeld. (2007). "Power, Propensity to Negotiate, and Moving First in Competitive Interactions." *Personality and Social Psychology Bulletin 33*(2): 200–212. https://doi.org/10.1177/0146167206294413

Ross, Michael, and Fiore Sicoly. (1979). "Egocentric Biases in Availability and Attribution." *Journal of Personality and Social Psychology 37*(3): 322–336.

Schweinsberg, Martin, Gillian Ku, Cynthia S. Wang, and Madan M. Pillutla. (2012). "Starting High and Ending with Nothing: The Role of Anchors and Power in Negotiations." *Journal of Experimental Social Psychology 48*(1): 226–231. https://doi.org/10.1016/j.jesp.2011.07.005

Thorndyke, Perry. W. (1977). "Cognitive Structures in Comprehension and Memory of Narrative Discourse." *Cognitive Psychology, 9*(1): 77–110. https://doi.org/10.1016/0010-0285(77)90005-6

Tsaousides, Theo. "7 Things You Need to Know About Fear." (2015). *Smashing the Brainblocks* blog, *Psychology Today*. www.psychologytoday.com/us/blog/smashing-the-brainblocks/201511/7-things-you-need-know-about-fear

Tversky, Amos, and Daniel Kahneman. (1973). "Availability: A Heuristic for Judging Frequency and Probability." *Cognitive Psychology 5*: 207–232.

Tversky, Amos, and Daniel Kahneman. (1974). "Judgment Under Uncertainty: Heuristics and Biases." *Science 185*(4157): 1124–1131.

Tversky, Amos, and Daniel Kahneman. (1981). "The Framing of Decisions and the Psychology of Choice." *Science 211*(4481): 453–458.

Ury, William L., Jeanne Brett, and Stephen Goldberg. (1988). *Getting Disputes Resolved: Designing Systems to Cut the Costs of Conflict*. San Francisco: Jossey-Bass.

Chapter 7

Ames, Daniel. R., and Mason, Malia. F. (2015). "Tandem Anchoring: Informational and Politeness Effects of Range Offers in Social Exchange." *Journal of Personality and Social Psychology, 108*(2): 254–274. https://doi.org/10.1037/pspi0000016

Brehm, Jack W. (1956). "Postdecision Changes in the Desirability of Alternatives." *The Journal of Abnormal and Social Psychology 52*(3): 384. https://doi.org/10.1037/h0041006

Brown, Nicola, Daniel Read, and Barbara Summers. (2003). "The Lure of Choice." *Journal of Behavioral Decision Making 16*(4): 297–308. doi:10.1002/bdm.447

Franconeri, Steven, Andrew Hollingworth, and Daniel J. Simons. (2005). "Do New Objects Capture Attention?" *Psychological Science 16*(4): 275–281.

Galinsky, Adam. D., Gillian Ku, and Thomas Mussweiler. (2009). "To Start Low or to Start High? The Case of Auctions Versus Negotiations." *Current Directions in Psychological Science, 18*(6): 357–361. https://doi.org/10.1111/j.1467-8721.2009.01667.x

Gilbert, Daniel T., and Jane E. J. Ebert. (2002). "Decisions and Revisions: The Affective Forecasting of Changeable Outcomes." *Journal of Personality and Social Psychology, 82*(4): 503–514. https://doi.org/10.1037/0022-3514.82.4.503

Jones, Edward E., and Richard. E. Nisbett. (1971). *The Actor and the Observer: Divergent Perceptions of the Causes of Behavior.* In E. E. Jones, D. E. Kanouse, H. H. Kelley, R. E. Nisbett, S. Valins, and B. Weiner (Eds.), *Attribution: Perceiving the Causes of Behavior* (pp. 79–94). Mahway, NJ: Lawrence Erlbaum.

Leonardelli, Geoffrey, Jun Gu, Geordie McRuer, Victoria Medvec, and Adam D. Galinsky. (2019). "Multiple Equivalent Simultaneous Offers (MESOs) Reduce the Negotiator Dilemma: How a Choice of First Offers Increases Economic and Relational Outcomes." *Organizational Behavior and Human Decision Processes 152*, May 2019: 64–83.

Miller, George A. (1956). "The Magical Number Seven, Plus or Minus Two: Some Limits on Our Capacity for Processing Information." *Psychological Review 63*: 81–97.

Sinaceur, Marwan, William Maddux, Dmitri Vasiljevic, Ricardo Perez Nückel, and Adam D. Galinsky. (2013). "Good Things Come to Those Who Wait: Late First Offers Facilitate Creative Agreements in Negotiation." *Personality and Social Psychology Bulletin, 39*(6): 814–825. https://doi.org/10.1177/0146167213483319

Theeuwes, J., A. F. Kramer, S. Hahn, and D. E. Irwin. (1998). "Our Eyes Do Not Always Go Where We Want Them to Go: Capture of the Eyes by New Objects." *Psychological Science 9*(5): 379–385. doi:10.1111/1467-9280.00071

Tversky, Amos, and Daniel Kahneman. (1974). "Judgment Under Uncertainty: Heuristics and Biases." *Science, 185*(4157), 1124–1131. https://doi.org/10.1126/science.185.4157.1124

Whyte, Glen, and James K. Sebenius. (1997). "The Effect of Multiple Anchors on Anchoring in Individual and Group Judgment." *Organizational Behavior and Human Decision Processes, 69*(1): 74–85. https://doi.org/10.1006/obhd.1996.2674

Chapter 8

Baltes, Boris, Marcus Dickson, Michael Sherman, and Cara Bauer. (2002). "Computer-Mediated Communication and Group Decision Making: A Meta-Analysis." *Organizational Behavior and Human Decision Processes* 87(1): 156–179.

Colvin, Geoff. (2020). "The Hidden—But Very Real—Cost of Working from Home." *Fortune*, Aug. 10, 2020. fortune.com/2020/08/10/remote-work-from-home-cost-zoom-innovation-google-goldman-sachs/

Gilovich, Thomas, Kenneth Savitsky, and Victoria Medvec. (1998). The Illusion of Transparency: Biased Assessments of Others' Ability to Read One's Emotional States." *Journal of Personality and Social Psychology* 75(2): 332–346.

Kiesler, S., and L. Sproull. (1992). "Group Decision Making and Communication Technology." *Organizational Behavior and Human Decision Processes,* 52(1): 96–123.

Purdy, Jill, Pete Nye, and P. V. (Sundar)Balakrishnan. (2000). "The Impact of Communication Media on Negotiation Outcomes." *International Journal of Conflict Management* 11(2): 162–187.

Schaerer, Michael, Mary Kern, Gail Berger, and Victoria Medvec. (2018). "The Illusion of Transparency in Performance Appraisals: When and Why Accuracy Motivation Explains Unintentional Feedback Inflation." *Organizational Behavior and Human Decision Processes* 144: 171–186.

Straus, Susan G., and Joseph E. McGrath. (1994). "Does the Medium Matter? The Interaction of Task Type and Technology on Group Performance and Member Reactions." *Journal of Applied Psychology* 79(1): 87–97.

Swaab, Roderick, and Adam D. Galinsky. (2007). "How to Negotiate When You're (Literally) Far Apart." *Negotiation* 10(2): 7–9.

Swaab, Roderick, Mary Kern, Daniel Diermeier, and Victoria Medvec. (2009). "Who Says What to Whom? The Impact of Communication Setting and Channel on Exclusion from Multiparty Negotiation Agreements." *Social Cognition* 27(3), June 2009: 385–401.

Chapter 9

Babcock, Linda, and George Loewenstein. (1997). "Explaining Bargaining Impasse: The Role of Self-Serving Biases." *Journal of Economic Perspectives* 11(1): 109–126.

Bunkley, Nick. (2009). "With Low Prices, Hyundai Builds Market Share." *The New York Times,* Sept. 21, 2009. www.nytimes.com/2009/09/22/business/global/22hyundai.html

Carnevale, Peter, Kathleen O'Connor, and Christopher McCuscker. (1993). "Time Pressure in Negotiation and Mediation." In A. J. Maule & O. Svenson (Eds.), *Time Pressure and Stress in Human Judgment and Decision Making* (pp. 117–127). New York: Springer.

Galinsky, Adam D., Vanessa Seiden, Peter Kim, and Victoria Medvec. (2002). "The Dissatisfaction of Having Your First Offer Accepted: The Role of Counterfactual Thinking in Negotiations." *Personality and Social Psychology Bulletin 28*(2), Feb. 2002: 271–283.

Galinsky, Adam D., Thomas Mussweiler, and Victoria Medvec. (2002). "Disconnecting Outcomes and Evaluations: The Role of Negotiator Focus." *Journal of Personality and Social Psychology 83*(5), March 22, 2002: 1131–1140.

Hughes, Jonathan, and Danny Ertel. (2020). "What's Your Negotiation Strategy?" *Harvard Business Review,* July, 2020. hbr.org/2020/07/whats-your-negotiation-strategy

Kahneman, Daniel, Jack Knetsch, and Richard Thaler. (1991). "Anomalies: The Endowment Effect, Loss Aversion, and Status Quo Bias." *Journal of Economic Perspectives 5*(1): 193–206.

Malito, Alessandra. (2019). "More Americans Are Leaving Their Money in 401(k) Plans After Retirement—Should You?" *MarketWatch*, Oct. 31, 2019. www.marketwatch.com/story/more-americans-are-leaving-their-money-in-401k-plans-after-retirement-should-you-2019-10-31

Narayanan, Jayanth, Ivy Buche, Lindsay McTeague, Amit Joshi, and Maude Lavanchy. (2018). "The Art and Science of Negotiation." *IMD*, International Institute for Management Development, Feb. 2018. www.imd.org/research-knowledge/articles/negotiation-skills-to-achieve-positive-outcomes/

Pruitt, Dean G. (1981). *Negotiation Behavior*. Cambridge, MA: Academic Press.

Raiffa, Howard. (1982). *The Art and Science of Negotiation*. Cambridge, MA: Belknap Press.

Valdes-Dapena, Peter. (2009). "Laid off? Hyundai Will Take Your Car Back." *CNN*, Jan. 5, 2009, money.cnn.com/2009/01/05/autos/hyundai_assurance/index.htm

Acknowledgments

My clients and MBA students have been asking me to write a book for years. Some clients even introduced me to book editors and agents and actively encouraged me to put down in writing what I covered in the customized sessions that I was conducting for them. I was initially worried that if I described the strategies in writing, clients would no longer need me to conduct training for them. I loved working with them and did not want to lose this, so I delayed putting pen to paper.

As my consulting practice exploded with new clients and my kids were growing, I felt like I did not have the time to write the book because I was so busy being a mom, a room parent, a professor, the cofounder of the Kellogg Center for Executive Women, a consultant, a CEO, and an adviser to companies around the globe. When I turned 50, I decided the time had come to write the book that I had thought about for so long. However, speaking, which is a very natural skill to me, seemed so much easier than writing.

I might never have started this book without the incredible support of a few people at that time. Dr. Sara Soderstrom, a former PhD student who is now a tenured professor at the University of Michigan, helped me to see that I could translate the many stories I would share in sessions into lessons that others could learn from if I wrote them down. This was a critical starting point.

Jenna Baskin, the first managing director for Medvec & Associates, literally wrote down every word I said in hundreds of client sessions. Without this initial transcription, I am not sure that I would have ever started writing. Jenna left Medvec & Associates to return to Australia and become the CEO of a very successful company there. Even from Australia, she monitored the Google Doc to track my writing progress. She motivated me in incredible ways throughout this project, and her many transcripts from my sessions were invaluable.

Every busy person knows that they need a deadline to turn intention into action, and Mike Campbell, the acquisitions editor at John Wiley & Sons, was instrumental in this translation. His confidence in the project gave me the self-assurance to keep writing. Mike also gave me access to a wonderful editor, Gary Schwartz, who read every chapter and provided valuable feedback.

I did not realize, though, that writing is only the first part of producing a book. There is so much else that needs to be done, such as generating all of the tables and figures, doing research, finding citations, tracking key words, and creating an index and bibliography. My team from Medvec & Associates played such a vital role in this. I want to thank Rachel Stern, Marshall Makk, and Charles Stater for their many contributions to this project.

I also want to convey special thanks to Barbara Abelson and Dr. Gail Berger, who read every single word and edited every chapter. Barbara did this before I submitted the first version to Wiley, and Gail did this as we finalized the chapters. They were my thought partners in the best way to convey critical messages and tell my stories. They both ensured that you could hear my voice through the pages. Their support was essential to this project, and while there might have been a book without them, it would have been a very poor book with a lot of inappropriate semicolons.

Additionally, I want to thank my many clients who trusted me to provide advice on their critical negotiations. It is my privilege to teach their people and coach their teams. I love seeing their incredible success in their negotiations and hope that others will learn from their stories.

I definitely have to thank the scholars who taught me the principles I teach to others. Dr. Eugenia Gerdes, my psychology professor and adviser at Bucknell, first provoked my interest in psychology and research. She built confidence in a young woman from a small town in Ohio and encouraged me to combine my interests in psychology and business.

Dr. Tom Gilovich, my adviser at Cornell, started me on my academic trajectory, imparted immense wisdom, and trained me in how to conduct research, communicate the results to readers in vivid and memorable ways, and convey compelling lessons from the research in a classroom. Tom and I conducted many research projects together that formed the foundation of my academic career, and we had the privilege of working with many incredible co-authors, including Dr. Daniel Kahneman, the recipient of the 2002 Nobel Prize in Economics. Tom is a remarkable teacher, researcher, and scholar, and I would not be a professor or an adviser today without Tom's guidance.

My first foray into negotiations came when I was the teaching assistant for an amazing negotiations course cotaught by Dr. Kathleen McGinn (née Valley) and Dr. Richard Thaler at Cornell. Kathleen

McGinn went on to become a distinguished professor at Harvard, and Richard Thaler moved to the University of Chicago and was later awarded the 2017 Nobel Prize in Economics, but the class they taught together at the Johnson School sparked my initial interest in negotiation and changed my life. Kathleen and Dick both inspired me and supported me in my pursuit of this topic, and I am forever indebted to them for the impact they had on my career.

I left Cornell to come to the Kellogg School at Northwestern University to be able to work with legends in the field of negotiations such as Dr. Max Bazerman (who later moved to Harvard) and Dr. Maggie Neale (who later moved to Stanford). Maggie and Max guided me as a young professor at Kellogg along with Dr. David Messick, Dr. Jeanne Brett, Dr. Leigh Thompson, Dr. Keith Murnighan, and the inimitable Dean Donald Jacobs. These academic leaders had an enormous impact on my thinking, my teaching, my confidence, and my ambition.

I also want to thank my posse of girlfriends. I have an amazing set of incredibly successful women who surround me and motivate me every day. They know who they are and that their encouragement has been key to me.

But most of all, I must thank my family. My mom is my rock of solid support, my biggest cheerleader, and, as Bette Midler sings, the "wind beneath my wings." She always encourages me to soar. My mom and dad made tremendous sacrifices to send me to Bucknell and launch my career.

I also want to thank my husband, Paul, and my sons, Barrett and Tyler, for their incredible patience as I wrote the book, for reading chapters, providing feedback, being the source of many stories, and generating new ideas for topics that I should include. I love the three of you so much and really appreciate all your support.

—Dr. Victoria H. Medvec

About the Author

Dr. **Victoria Husted Medvec** is a leading global expert in negotiation strategy, corporate governance, and decision making. She is sought after by CEOs, senior leaders, and boards of directors to advise on critical strategic decisions and transactions.

For the last two decades, as CEO of the consulting firm Medvec & Associates, Dr. Medvec has advised on mergers and acquisitions, significant customer contracts, regulatory filings, and partnership agreements. Her clients include hundreds of leading global corporations including one-third of the Fortune 100, such as Google, IBM, McKesson, Cisco, and McDonald's, as well as smaller, fast-growing organizations. She has worked across a variety of industries, ranging from technology, professional services, energy, financial services, and real estate to food and beverage, pharmaceutical, and biotech.

Dr. Medvec partners with CEOs and other senior leaders for extended periods of time to drive results with a focus on long-term strategy, particularly around sustained revenue growth and customer engagement. Her work has enabled companies to differentiate their offerings and products, deftly navigate their competitive landscapes, create dramatic revenue growth, and most importantly, change their market position.

Since 1995, Dr. Medvec has also served on the faculty at the Kellogg School of Management at Northwestern University, where she is the Adeline Barry Davee Professor of Management and Organizations. Her research has been published in top academic journals, as well as highlighted in numerous popular media outlets, including *The Wall Street Journal*, *The New York Times*, *The Washington Post*, and the *Today* show.

Dr. Medvec is also the cofounder and executive director of Kellogg's Center for Executive Women. In this role, she pursues her passion for advancing women into senior roles in companies and onto boards of directors. She created the Women Director Development Program, and over the past 15 years she has helped to prepare more than 800 senior executive women for roles on boards. Dr. Medvec speaks across the country on topics relating to women in leadership, corporate governance, and board decision making.

Dr. Medvec has served on public and private company boards for more than a decade. She is also a Ringleader in Ringleader Ventures, a unique venture fund that drives innovation and solutions by matching start-up technologies with corporate needs.

Dr. Medvec lives in Jackson Hole, Wyoming, and Lake Forest, Illinois, with her husband and two sons.

Index